"Beyond the Suffering is ren hopeful. W. E. B. DuBois sa ...ans had a great gift to give if it would only be received: the gift of double vision; the insight of a people who were simultaneously at home and forced to live as aliens. That gift, baptized in the Spirit, is on display here. It will illumine, trouble, and heal."

John Ortberg, pastor and author

"Drawing on the riches of the African American tradition, this book sheds new light on spiritual formation and Christian nurture. A splendid contribution and a great gift!"

Timothy George, Dean, Beeson Divinity School, Samford University; executive editor, *Christianity Today*

"Even though some ask, 'Why, God, is this happening to me?', the good news found in black folk religion is that 'trouble don't last always.' It is through suffering that healing, character, and spiritual formation take place. The plight and predicament of African American people are a testimony to the church universal. The voices of unlettered black folk teach us how, despite storm clouds hovering in the midnight hour, joy does, indeed, come in the morning. Kellemen and Edwards warm the soul with this scholarly reflection of the mind. Beyond suffering lies the power of new life and new beginnings."

Dwight N. Hopkins, author, *Being Human:
Race, Culture, and Religion*

"The amazing grace in the lives of blacks in America gives hope to us all of God's redemptive desire to touch our souls. This book underscores such a legacy."

David Anderson, pastor, Bridgeway Community Church; author, *Multicultural Ministry: Finding Your Church's Unique Rhythm*

"This is a deeply moving and helpful book. Kellemen and Edwards clearly describe the legacy of African American soul care and spiritual direction that comes to us beyond the suffering and also because of the suffering African Americans have experienced. I highly recommend *Beyond the Suffering* as crucial reading for everyone involved in soul care, spiritual direction, and counseling."

Rev. Dr. Siang-Yang Tan, PhD, professor of psychology, Fuller Theological Seminary; senior pastor, First Evangelical Church Glendale, Southern California

"This book addresses the spiritual chauvinism of contemporary ministry. That is, we prefer the latest trends and fads of the present and ignore the wisdom of our African American parents. In *Beyond the Suffering: Embracing the Legacy of African American Soul Care and Spiritual Direction*, Kellemen and Edwards join a growing movement today in denominations and theological seminaries that mine the practices of the past in order to discern the wisdom of our ancestors that informs us today.

This work shows how doctrines like grace and sin were used pastorally by both lay and clergy to foster soul care, spiritual direction, and pastoral care. The book will be helpful for those who want to understand how the practical theological wisdom of the past is essential to minister today."

Edward P. Wimberly, vice president for academic services/provost,
Interdenominational Theological Center

"*Beyond the Suffering* tells the story of people who faced the challenges of depression, pain, loss, relational trauma, and despair of epic proportions—without professional therapists, mega-church ministries, or antidepressants. The authors use the actual testimonies of these individuals to describe how they found courage and comfort in God and in each other. Their ability to develop a healing community, against all odds, is greatly informative to our efforts today. This is a unique *must-read*, not just on the elements of multicultural ministry, but on the very core elements of ministry to all people in pain."

Michael R. Lyles, MD

"This book rips the truth about soul care from the hands of the elite and hands it to those who lived and taught it in the crucible of suffering. The gospel's ability to transcend race, abuse, and evil of every kind is powerfully presented. It shook me up."

Bill Hull, author, *Choose the Life:
Exploring a Faith That Embraces Discipleship*

"What can be said of *Beyond the Suffering*? It captured my heart! The cultural heritage picks up where remembering our "Roots" ended and brings into full bloom the fruit of cultivating our legacy. The abundance of grace exhibited by the authors as they present what has been a very sensitive dialogue provides a compelling read of life's encounters with a divine God and the reality of the rough places we have trod. Every person from the pulpit to the pew that ministers to and interacts with those in the African-American community will benefit from embracing the Lord's presence in this redemptive, restorative work that outlines healing for the nations. Thoroughly researched to include the various voices of humanity from biblical scholars to slave narratives, the text provides refuge and solace in the sanctuary of Christ. Each chapter closes with an opportunity for us to learn together as it helps us move from a context of slavery to dealing with everyday issues that are universal. *Beyond the Suffering* is a delicate balance of comfort and confrontation from two true spiritual friends. You are invited to drink deeply from the traditions and timeless wisdom that have been forged through years. This text will encourage you to take pride in who you are and all that you have potential to and are destined to become. Read, write, rejoice, and celebrate. The Lord has seen, he has heard, he knows, and he has come down to help you move beyond the suffering."

> **Dr. Sabrina D. Black**, president, National Biblical
> Counselors Association; chairperson, Black African
> American Christian Counselors; clinical director, Abundant
> Life Counseling Center; coauthor, *HELP! For Your Leadership*
> and *Counseling in African American Communities*

"*Beyond the Suffering* reaches into the past to bring spiritual-caregivers eye-opening insights and proven methods for helping those who are suffering. It gives lay and professional counselors the courage to share the challenging truths of God's Word to those who are facing life's deepest challenges."

> **Sam Hodges**, senior producer, the Church Initiative

"I was hesitant when I picked up this manuscript since so much written about racism today ends up being racist. This book is delightfully different! A colleague with whom I shared it commented, 'It is historical, factual, emotional, spiritual, scriptural, and thought provoking.' The authors have succeeded in touching the heart through situational narrative. By telling the story they engage the reader in the historical reality without pointing fingers. Truly a must-read!"

> **Howard A. Eyrich**, ThM, DMin, president emeritus, Birmingham Theological Seminary; director, Briarwood Counseling Ministries, Briarwood
> Presbyterian Church, Birmingham, Alabama

BEYOND THE SUFFERING

Embracing the Legacy of African American
Soul Care and **Spiritual Direction**

Dr. Robert W. Kellemen

and Karole A. Edwards

BakerBooks
Grand Rapids, Michigan

© 2007 by Dr. Robert W. Kellemen and Karole A. Edwards

Published by Baker Books
a division of Baker Publishing Group
P.O. Box 6287, Grand Rapids, MI 49516-6287
www.bakerpublishinggroup.com

Printed in the United States of America

Library of Congress Cataloging-in-Publication Data
Kellemen, Robert W.
    Beyond the suffering : embracing the legacy of African American soul
care and spiritual direction / Robert W. Kellemen with Karole A. Edwards.
        p.   cm.
    Includes bibliographical references.
    ISBN 10: 0-8010-6806-1 (pbk.)
    ISBN 978-0-8010-6806-5 (pbk.)
    1. African Americans—Religion. I. Edwards, Karole A., 1964– II. Title.
BR563.N4K45 2007
277.3′0808996073—dc22   2007014305

Unless otherwise indicated, Scripture is taken from the HOLY BIBLE, NEW INTERNATIONAL VERSION®. NIV®. Copyright © 1973, 1978, 1984 by International Bible Society. Used by permission of Zondervan. All rights reserved.

Scripture marked KJV is taken from the King James Version of the Bible.

Scripture marked Message is taken from *The Message* by Eugene H. Peterson, copyright © 1993, 1994, 1995, 2000, 2001, 2002. Used by permission of NavPress Publishing Group. All rights reserved.

"Minstrel Man," from *The Collected Poems of Langston Hughes* by Langston Hughes, edited by Arnold Rampersad with David Roessel, Associate Editor, copyright © 1994 by The Estate of Langston Hughes. Used by permission of Alfred A. Knopf, a division of Random House, Inc.

Contents

Foreword

Anumber of historians have asked the question, "What can we learn from the African American experience in America?" I believe this is a critical question because one of my long-standing convictions has been that one of the most representative pictures of New Testament Christianity since the early church is the African church in America during its slavery experience.

Coauthors Bob Kellemen and Karole Edwards have provided the Christian community creatively written documentation of the powerful lessons the contemporary church can learn from the African American church during slavery and from the lives of people birthed from the womb of that era. They artfully equip us to see in a new light the past family album of a people as they uncover the buried treasure hidden to most who don't know the history of this special group of God's family members.

Most students of history focus on the pain of the African American experience in America. There was a lot of pain! And we should not minimize that pain.

However, as the title suggests, *Beyond the Suffering* goes further. It shows us how the pain experienced by people from the African American culture can be redeemed to give life to people from *any* race or culture that values truth born out of biblically informed experience.

The captivating true stories and firsthand narratives have a therapeutic and healing quality for the reader and those they serve. After you read *Beyond the Suffering*, you will have a deeper understanding of how God forged character in people through their suffering, and you will be able to apply many valuable insights to your personal life and future ministry.

Beyond the Suffering also models how two people from different races (Bob and Karole), committed to understanding and validating the significance of past human experience through the lens of Scripture, can enrich our ministry to others. Without a doubt, this book makes a vital contribution to pastors, counselors, and laypeople serving those from the African American tradition. But its greatest contribution will be helping the church of Jesus Christ redeem priceless lessons from a painful past so that we can bring healing to people from *all* races.

Dr. Anthony T. Evans

Acknowledgments

Writing *Beyond the Suffering* has been a truly collaborative experience. Our co-laboring team of "feedback friends" has faithfully prayed for us and skillfully offered us their multicultural wisdom. Two in particular spent enormous amounts of time sharing their insights—thank you, Wendy Fotopolous and Marian Martin.

First and above all, I (Karole) thank God, the Maker and Ruler of all creation, for being who he is. I thank him for giving life and breath to all; for scripting the days and times; for saving and changing lives through the revelation of himself and his glory (that is, Jesus); for unraveling hearts and continuously turning them toward home; and for being all and being greater than all. I thank him for creating and unfolding his perfect plan. He has established and orchestrated a confluence of events, and he graciously wields undeserving humans as instruments in them.

I also thank him for those sojourners and wanderers who have traveled before us, sojourners who in days past walked the rough and rugged roads lying before them, relying on faith and prayer to reach a "better resurrection." He gave each one the privilege of becoming a member of his universal body to fulfill a unique purpose and prepare a way for those to come. For them, I am grateful.

11

And finally, I thank him for those he has given in this day who offer encouragement and support. This includes my family members and friends, each of whom has been a unique gift and a special blessing not only during the development of this book but also in life. I pray that he continues to make himself known through them.

I (Bob) could not have even attempted this project without the encouragement of my family. My wife, Shirley, has beautifully sustained, healed, reconciled, and guided my faith in ways beyond description and in times beyond numbering. Shirley, no one I have ever met dispenses grace like you. Thank you for living out your faith with compassion and sensitivity.

My son, Josh, has demonstrated wisdom from God far beyond his years. Josh, your hunger for truth inspires me. Thank you for living out your faith with insight and courage.

My daughter, Marie, has enveloped my life with the joy of Jesus. Marie, your commitment to Christ amazes me. Thank you for living out your faith with tenderness and selflessness.

I also thank the multicultural student body at Capital Bible Seminary. Your witness of harmonious relationships with one another and humble learning from one another is what prompted my research and writing.

I can't wait to get to heaven to thank the great cloud of African American witnesses whose lives we write about. Honestly, I'm not so sure that we've "written" this book so much as we've "edited" it. We have simply sought to be faithful recorders and retellers of the stories of those who have gone before us, of those who have moved beyond the suffering.

Most importantly, I thank the Lord of the journey. In my weakness, you have shown yourself not only strong but also rest-giving. I can't wait for the day when I fall before you in worship, leap onto your lap for an eternal embrace, and jump into your arms for a longed-for, undeserved, but grace-given high five.

Introduction

So Great a Cloud of Witnesses:
The Stories That Really Matter

*Does I 'member much 'bout slavery times? Well, there is no
way for me to disremember unless I die. I got 'membrance like
they don't have nowadays. That 'cause things is going round
and round too fast without no setting and talking things over.*

quoted in B. A. Botkin, *Lay My Burden Down*[1]

*The suffering witness of slave Christians constitutes a major
spiritual legacy not only for their descendents but for the nation as a whole, for any who would take the time to heed the
testimony of their words and of their lives.*

Albert Raboteau[2]

As we've penned *Beyond the Suffering*, two images have
guided our storytelling: *a treasure map* and *a family
album*. Lace up your hiking boots as you join us on a hunt for

buried treasure. Then, returning home, slide on your slippers, grab your favorite beverage, and peer over our shoulders as we share some family photos.

Together our two pictures illustrate that *Beyond the Suffering* is a gift *from* African Americans and a gift *to* African Americans. This book is for everyone fascinated by stories that portray victory snatched from the jaws of defeat. It's for everyone who longs to know how Christ transforms victims into victors. It's for everyone who wants to help suffering and struggling people discover healing for their hurts and grace for their disgrace.

A Treasure Map: A Gift *from* African Americans

Our first guiding image consists of a treasure map showing the way to buried riches. Combined, we possess nearly a half century of experience as treasure hunters. For me (Karole), the journey began as I delved deeper into historical African American studies and essays and discovered a cavern of invaluable truth. As the depth of my search increased, the fruit from the effort became more and more abundant. The richness of the studies revealed the brilliantly woven story that God has written and revealed through the historical story line of the African and then the African American community. It is a story of *his* grace and power.

It is said that the doctrine of grace both humbles people without degrading them and exalts people without inflating them. My research on the African American community's history and experience has been both humbling and exalting for me. In short, it was a gift of God's grace. And as I was being changed by the story unfolding before me, I wondered how others might also be changed by seeing *his story* unfolding through *our history*.

For me (Bob), the journey began in 1981 when I was a seminary student witnessing rival factions debating which current model of biblical counseling could claim the mantle of accuracy and relevancy. During the ongoing and often heated discussions, I kept thinking, "Surely the church has *always* been about the business of helping hurting and hardened people, hasn't it?"

Few in the current debate seemed to be looking beyond the current options. I started looking *beyond*. I started looking *before*. I committed myself to a lifelong search for the ancient paths and stumbled upon the buried treasure of historical soul care (sustaining and healing) and spiritual direction (reconciling and guiding). (In chapter 1 we explain these terms and how they relate to our lives and ministries.)

When God joined us as a coauthoring team, we laser-focused our search. We sought to unearth the buried treasure of wisdom about soul care and spiritual direction contained in the story of African American Christianity. The African American church has always helped hurting and hardened people through the personal and corporate ministries of sustaining, healing, reconciling, and guiding. *Beyond the Suffering* uncovers the great spiritual riches of this African American Christian tradition.

Beyond the Suffering uses this four-dimensional model (sustaining, healing, reconciling, and guiding) as a grid to map the marvels of historical African American ministry. This traditional and widely recognized pattern enables us to distill practical principles for lay spiritual friendship, pastoral care, and professional Christian counseling.

We desire to inspire today's generation with the voices of past African American Christians speaking through the pages of *Beyond the Suffering*. By listening to these historical narratives, we will learn to speak to today's world with relevance—sharing Christ's changeless truth for our changing times.[3] *Beyond the Suffering* aims to assist African American *and* non-African American laypeople, pastors, and Christian counselors to become more spiritually aware and skillful by deriving modern implications from these recovered resources.

Further, it purposes to equip all believers for more effective cross-cultural ministry.

A Family Album: A Gift *to* African Americans

Henry H. Mitchell devoted decades of his life to teaching African American church history. At the conclusion of one such class, a student remarked, "You teach Black Church history like it's your own family album." As an African American teaching predominantly to African Americans, Professor Mitchell replied, "You're absolutely right, and that's how every one of *you* should view it. It's not abstract data required to pass a course. It's the spiritual history of *our* family."[4]

By developing pictures of African American soul care and spiritual direction, *Beyond the Suffering* tells the untold story of African American mutual ministry. Here we'll discover family pictures found in African American slave narratives, autobiographies, biographies, interviews, testimonies, speeches, slave spirituals, gospel hymns, sermons, poems, books, and letters of spiritual counsel. *Beyond the Suffering* offers the African American story told by African Americans for all Americans—for all people.

G. K. Chesterton explains the need for such a book when he observes that history is democracy extended through time. History gives "votes to the most obscure of all classes, our ancestors. It is the *democracy of the dead*." It refuses to submit to "those who merely happen to be walking about."[5] For far too long, we have silenced the voices of past African American Christians.

Beyond the Suffering ends the silence by giving voice and vote to our African American forebears in the faith. It listens to their voices communicating the unique shapes and textures of their practice of spiritual care.

Thus our aim here is to contribute to contemporary soul care and spiritual direction as seen through the eyes, experienced in the souls, and told from the lips of past African American believers. *Beyond the Suffering* develops a contemporary model of personal ministry that is distinctively grounded both in the Word of God and in the legacy of African American believers.

One Plan, One Plea, and One Proviso

In telling the story of African American sustaining, healing, reconciling, and guiding, we will trace our heavenly Father's affectionately sovereign hands powerfully at work in African American history *from enslavement to emancipation*. Steering the historical narrative through many dangers, toils, and snares, his grace has created beauty from ashes.

Our Plan: Tracing His Hands

Our narrative begins where the horrible journey began for the free Africans—being stolen from their people, their purpose, and their property to become property. The story then travels with the slaves in the communal experience of the trans-Atlantic passage and the "bitter waters" of the slave holds in the belly of the slave ships. It continues with the slave auction laments of separated family members and the hardships of daily slave life.

These experiences lay the foundation for a biblical "sufferology"—an African American theology of suffering. We hear the consolation of their slave conversion narratives, showing how God cut loose their tongues and freed their spirits to soar beyond the limits imposed by society.

We next move to the slave plantation and the "Invisible Institution"—the secret and prohibited church gatherings. Here the hush arbors, ring shouts, testifying, exhorting, preaching, and slave spirituals all offer personal applications and ministry insights.

17

We then trace the initial development of the independent African American churches in the North and South. Sermons, speeches, autobiographies, and letters of spiritual counsel express the depth of individual and corporate mutual ministry. Here we highlight representative "founding fathers" and "sisters of the Spirit," telling the story of their courageous and creative soul care and spiritual direction.

Throughout each chapter, we will weave together individual stories and highlight common themes. You will enjoy the voices of male and female, enslaved and free, pastor and layperson, Northerner and Southerner.

Our Plea: Joining Our Hands

Given our focus, we cannot escape graphic images that could lead African Americans to groan all over again and cause non-African Americans to struggle with "ancestral guilt" anew. Please believe us when we stress that *nothing* could be further from our intent.

We're convinced that God's grace has brought us—all of us—safe this far, and that his grace will bring us—all of us—home. By Christ's grace, we can trade our sorrows; we can trade our shame; we can lay them down for the joy of the Lord.

Thus our title: *Beyond the Suffering.* Yes, there has been suffering. Yes, there has been sinning. Grace moves us *beyond* both.

Prolonged groaning and guilt could be ingredients in a recipe for disharmony. Again, nothing could be further from our intent.

We're convinced that through Christ's grace we are constantly changed by the One who remains ever the same. Where disharmony abounds, shalom super-abounds. What if we *all* moved *beyond* the suffering *together*? What if a non-African American saw a groaning African American brother or sister and came alongside to offer sustaining and healing

18

soul care? What if an African American saw a guilt-wrenched non-African American brother or sister and came alongside to offer reconciling and guiding spiritual direction?

Call us naive, but we have witnessed it happen, by God's grace, numerous times in our lives as we've journeyed together on this treasure hunt to develop pictures for our family album. Call us excited! We are filled with grace-laced anticipation as we pray for you as we all journey together *Beyond the Suffering*.

Our Proviso: Worshiping His Nail-Scarred Hands

Free and enslaved African Americans needed spiritual sustenance as a weapon against the damaging impact of living in a land without sanctuary. Some sought relief by relying on lingering spiritual traditions from their original culture or by following non-Christian religious practices. Others physically resisted the abuses of their captors. Still others pursued physical freedom by escaping to free Northern states and Canada. However, many in the community of Africans in America sought hope from above. Many recognized and accepted the promise of freedom found through the future hope and present help that Christ offers.

Thus we are not naively supposing or ahistorically proposing that all African Americans converted to Christianity. Instead we are focusing our historical research and limiting our soul care and spiritual direction implications to self-proclaimed African American adherents of Christianity. Some came to know Christ early, on their mother's lap or their father's knee. Others wrote decades later, looking back on their lives through the new lenses of Christian faith, even if earlier in their lives they were not yet drawn into Christ's circle.

Thus all the African Americans whom we highlight in *Beyond the Suffering* professed faith in Christ and evidenced a worshipful trust in his nail-scarred hands. Their communal interpretations and applications of biblical truth provided the soul care and spiritual direction foundation on which they survived and thrived in the New World. Centuries later, surrounded by so great a cloud of witnesses, we build on the foundation that they laid.

1

An Unbroken Circle

Ask for the Ancient Paths

*La, me, child! I never thought any body would care enough
for me to tell of my trials and sorrows in this world! None but
Jesus knows what I have passed through.*

Octavia Albert, *The House of Bondage*[1]

*Ahistorical people are at great risk. They tend to fill the void
of intergenerational connections with noise and activity.*

Barbara Holmes, *Joy Unspeakable*[2]

Living in a generation without answers, facing abuse from
every direction with pending destruction crouching
around the corner, Israel desperately needed to heed God's
counsel: "Stand at the crossroads and look; *ask for the ancient
paths*, ask where the good way is, and walk in it, and you will
find rest for your souls" (Jer. 6:16, emphasis added).

God pictures his people as lost travelers on a life-and-death journey. Confronting a fork in the road, they must stop to ask directions because the ancient markers are overgrown and need to be searched out again.

But whom should they consult? Their fellow travelers find themselves just as blinded by their corrupt culture. Heeding the words of Moses, they are to "remember the days of old; consider the generations long past. Ask your father and he will tell you, your elders, and they will explain to you" (Deut. 32:7).

If they are humble enough to seek wisdom from the former generations and discover what their ancestors learned, then they will find rest for their souls—soul care and spiritual direction. Unfortunately, in their arrogance they say, "We will not walk in it" (Jer. 6:16).

A Forgotten Art: Reclaiming Our Historical Mantle of Mutual Ministry

Are we so different? In swiftly changing times, as we desperately search every which way for spiritual solutions, we seem to lack respect for the traditional, time-tested ways in which God's people have dealt with personal problems. We prefer the latest trends and newest fads.[3]

All the while we could be drinking deeply from the rivers of historic Christianity. Specifically, we could be feasting from the root system of African American Christianity. Given the anchorless times that African Americans endured, given the endless abuses that they survived and despite which they thrived, who has history better equipped to direct us to the ancient paths of soul rest?

The history of African American soul care and spiritual direction provides a spiritual root system deep enough to withstand high winds and parching drought so that our souls can be nourished and our spiritual lives can flourish.[4] By following in

African Americans' footsteps, we can reclaim the ancient gifts of soul care and spiritual direction, restore the forgotten arts of sustaining, healing, reconciling, and guiding, and experience a reformation in how we minister to one another.

Beyond the Suffering joins a rising chorus summoning Christians back to their roots. The singers in this chorus suggest that we probe historical models of spiritual care for their implications for ministry today. They recommend that we examine how Christians dealt with spiritual and emotional issues *before* the advent of modern secular psychology.

Too often we conceptualize personal ministry models without the aid of the historical voices of the church. According to Thomas Oden, some Christians are only willing to listen to their own voice or the voice of contemporaries in the dialogue. "Christians have usually been losers when they have neglected the consensual writers of their own history and tradition."[5]

Wayne Oates notes that Christians "tend to start over from scratch every three or four generations." Therefore, we do not adequately consolidate the communal wisdom of the centuries because of our "antipathy for tradition." As a result, we "have accrued less capital" in the form of proverbs, manuals of mutual ministry, and a theology of body life.[6]

William Clebsch and Charles Jaekle present a convincing explanation for our lack of contact with the history of Christian mutual care: "Faced with an urgency for some system by which to conceptualize the human condition and to deal with the modern grandeurs and terrors of the human spirit, theoreticians of the cure of souls have too readily adopted the leading academic psychologies. Having no pastoral theology to inform our psychology or even to identify the cure of souls as a mode of human helping, we have allowed psychoanalytic thought, for example, to dominate the vocabulary of the spirit."[7]

Today's crying needs drown out yesterday's relevant answers. Why? We lack a sufficient awareness of the victorious ways in which people have faced life issues in bygone centuries.

The Democracy of the Dead: Listening to Inspiring Voices from the Past

God never gives great events without great historians. The great historians of African American Christian history are the African Americans who experienced that history. They are best equipped to accurately depict their religious life and spiritual character.

What they have to say is of value to all people. Speaking about African American religion in the South, Paul Jersild explains, "As a European American contributing to this work, I believe the most significant point I can make is to stress the challenge as well as the opportunity for whites not only to learn about but also to experience something of the depths of African American religious life, shaped as it has been by the oppressive history of slavery and discrimination. While African American readers will certainly profit from a careful consideration of this volume, its contents pose a particular invitation to European Americans to apprehend the identity and promise of the black community on a profound level."[8]

What Jersild notes about the *broad* history of African American religion, we say about the *specific* history of African American soul care and spiritual direction. African Americans have much to teach everyone about mutual ministry.

For us to learn from their history, we need to see their stories *through their eyes* and hear their stories *from their lips*. A slave known to us only as Morte states it poetically: "Go in peace, fearing no man, for lo! I have cut loose your stammering tongue and unstopped your deaf ears. A witness shalt thou be, and thou shalt speak to multitudes, and they shall hear."[9]

In 1855 John Little, a fugitive slave who had escaped to Canada, uttered his perceptive commentary about conveying the realities existing under slavery: "'Tisn't he who has stood and looked on, that can tell you what slavery is—'tis he who has endured."[10]

24

A former slave named Mr. Reed concurs. "If you want Negro history, you will have to get it from somebody who wore the shoe, and by and by from one to the other, you will get a book."[11] *Beyond the Suffering* listens to the cut-loose tongues of African Americans and walks in shoes that fit their feet.

Unfortunately, this is not how the story has usually been told. History has typically consisted of tales told by the victors.[12] Speaking specifically of slavery, historian Charles Nichols notes, "Nearly everyone concerned with American slavery has had his say, but in our time we have forgotten the testimony of its victims."[13]

This has long been the legitimate complaint of free and enslaved African Americans. In the opening editorial statement of *Freedom's Journal*, the editor wrote on March 16, 1827, "We wish to plead our own cause. Too long have others spoken for us."[14]

The victims of oppression have suffered again when their stories have been told by their oppressors.[15] Everyone suffers when this occurs, for we all lose the rare privilege of hearing the ringing voices of wisdom that can only be forged through the crucible of suffering.

William McClain describes what we *all* gain when we listen to African American voices: "The Black religious tradition in America, while unique to Black Americans, can contribute much and has made a vast difference in the Christian church in this nation. For it has been Black people's understanding of God in the context of their own experience, i.e., Black experience, in which they have groped for meaning, relevance, worth, assurance, reconciliation, and their proper response to the God revealed in nature and in Jesus Christ."[16] Our challenge is to derive a universally applicable contemporary model of soul care and spiritual direction grounded in the historical experience of African American Christians—as *they* have told it.

25

Reading God's Treasure Map

Together we've chosen the path less traveled—the path of ancient wisdom. Continuing our journey, we stumble upon a treasure map directing us to the riches of biblical insights for living found in messages from African American Christian forebears.

Arriving at our destination, we find a treasure beyond measure. We find so much truth for life that we're overwhelmed. How do we sort it all out, decode it, translate it? How do we integrate the changing with the changeless and balance the demands of today with the treasures of yesterday?

Somehow we must enter into durable fellowship with those who have gone before us. From our personal comradeship with them, we need to formulate an approach to spiritual care that is vital for our time *and* firmly grounded in the best traditions of the past.[17] We require a model, a map, or a grid that can alert us to currently forgotten but time-tested modes for meeting people's spiritual needs.

Various means are available for tapping into the riches of past African American personal ministry resources. As we noted in the introduction, we've chosen to use the traditional model of soul care (sustaining and healing) and spiritual direction (reconciling and guiding) to guide us as we probe into the past beliefs and practices of our ancestors in the faith.

Our use of this model is not an attempt to cloak the complexity of mutual ministry. Nor is it an effort to force African American spiritual care into shoes that do *not* fit its feet. We highly esteem the uniqueness of the African American practice of soul care and spiritual direction.

In this regard, it is important that we recognize three distinctive ways in which African Americans have provided soul care and spiritual direction. First, "pastoral care" has not been the exclusive domain of the pastor. Certainly, African American pastoral leaders have offered skillful sustaining, healing, reconciling, and guiding. However, as Edward Wimberly notes in his groundbreaking book *Pastoral Care in the Black Church,* "Pastoral care is a communal concept. It exists wherever persons minister to one another in the name of God."[18] Therefore, as you read, expect to find numerous examples of mutual care provided by laypeople and pastors alike.

Second, African American sustaining, healing, reconciling, and guiding have not been exclusively individual endeavors. In our "psychologized" society, often when we think of care we think of counseling, and when we think of counseling we think of one individual helping another individual. Though this one-to-one care certainly took place repeatedly in African American church history, you should also expect to read numerous moving examples of family, group, and communal soul care and spiritual direction.

Third, much African American sustaining, healing, reconciling, and guiding took place from the pulpit during preaching and in the congregation during worship. Sometimes we tend to dichotomize between the "pulpit ministry of the Word" and the "personal ministry of the Word." No such separation occurred in African American ministry. African American Christians used preaching, singing, baptizing, and dozens of other means to offer one another spiritual care.

Mapping Soul Care and Spiritual Direction

Spiritual care is an extremely complex activity that took place in countless ways over hundreds of years in African American Christianity. Therefore, we need to carefully define our terms—sustaining, healing, reconciling, and guiding—so they can help us explore what African American Christians have done to provide spiritual care.

Once we understand these specific definitions, we can use them to ask concrete questions when reading sermons, letters of spiritual counsel, slave narratives, slave spirituals, and other historical documents. This aids us in uncovering the richness and diversity of African American Christian care as it has been exercised in the past. It also helps us to draw out relevant applications for our current practice of Christian care-giving.

Plotting the Map of Soul Care and Spiritual Direction: The Twin Themes

Experts examining the history of spiritual care have consistently identified the twin historical themes of soul care and spiritual direction. John McNeil's *A History of the Cure of Souls* traces the art of soul care throughout history and various cultures. He says, "Lying deep in the experience and culture of the early Christian communities are the closely related practices of mutual edification and fraternal correction." Speaking of the apostle Paul, McNeil notes, "In such passages we cannot fail to see the Apostle's design to create an atmosphere in which the intimate exchange of spiritual help, the mutual guidance of souls, would be a normal feature of Christian behavior."[19]

Throughout his historical survey, McNeil explains that mutual edification involves *soul care* through the provision of sustaining (consolation, support, and comfort) and healing (encouragement and enlightenment). Fraternal correction includes *spiritual direction* through the provision of reconciling (discipline, confession, and forgiveness) and guiding (direction and counsel).

In *Clinical Theology*, Frank Lake clarifies that historically soul care deals with *suffering* while spiritual direction deals with *sin*. He summarizes his breakdown when he notes that "pastoral care is defective unless it can deal *thoroughly* with these evils we have suffered as well as with the sins we have committed."[20] Throughout church history, biblical care-givers have dealt with both suffering *and* sin, deprivation *and* depravity, hurting hearts *and* hard hearts, comforting *and* confronting, soul care *and* spiritual direction.[21]

28

Plotting the Map of Sustaining, Healing, Reconciling, and Guiding: The Four Tasks

Clebsch and Jaekle offer the classic description of traditional spiritual care. The care of souls has historically involved "helping acts, done by *representative Christian persons, directed toward the healing, sustaining, guiding, and reconciling* of *troubled persons* whose troubles arise *in the context of ultimate meanings and concerns."*[22]

Kenneth Leech observes that Clebsch and Jaekle's definition has become the standard definition for pastoral care and spiritual counseling, noting that the Association for Pastoral Care and Counseling adopted the definition into their constitution.[23] Thomas Oden suggests that the four tasks of sustaining, healing, reconciling, and guiding "try to absorb and work seriously with a wide variety of confessional and denominational viewpoints on ministry." They try to "reasonably bring all these voices into a centric, historically sensitive integration, with special attention to historical consensus."[24]

The framework of the two themes and four tasks provides a perspective—a historical way of viewing and thinking about spiritual friendship, pastoral care, and professional Christian counseling. It is the map that we will use to systematically organize what African American Christians have done to provide Christian care.

Combining the two themes and the four tasks creates the following profile of historical spiritual care:

Soul care: comfort for suffering
    sustaining
    healing
Spiritual direction: confrontation for sinning
    reconciling
    guiding

The chart below expands this outline. The rest of this chapter provides examples of these terms from the African American experience and explains how we will use them throughout

Soul Care and Spiritual Direction
Sustaining, Healing, Reconciling, and Guiding

Soul Care: The Evils We Have Suffered

"God Is Good Even When Life Is Bad"

*Soul care givers compassionately identify with people in pain
and redirect them to Christ and the Body of Christ
to sustain and heal their faith so they experience
communion with Christ and conformity to Christ
as they love God (exalt God by enjoying and trusting him) and love others.*

Sustaining: *"It's Normal to Hurt"*
Sense Your Spiritual Friend's Earthly Story of Despair
Empathize with and Embrace Your Spiritual Friend
Healing: *"It's Possible to Hope"*
Stretch Your Spiritual Friend to God's Eternal Story of Hope
Encourage Your Spiritual Friend to Embrace God

Spiritual Direction: The Sins We Have Committed

"God Is Gracious Even When I Am Sinful"

*Spiritual directors understand spiritual dynamics
and discern root causes of spiritual conflicts,
providing loving wisdom that reconciles and guides people
so they experience communion with Christ and conformity to Christ
as they love God (exalt God by enjoying and trusting him) and love others.*

Reconciling: *"It's Horrible to Sin, but Wonderful to Be Forgiven"*
Strip Your Spiritual Friend's Enslaving Story of Death
Expose Your Spiritual Friend's Sin and Reveal God's Grace
Guiding: *"It's Supernatural to Mature"*
Strengthen Your Spiritual Friend with Christ's Empowering Story of Life
Equip and Empower Your Spiritual Friend to Love

Robert Kellemen, *Spiritual Friends*[25]

Beyond the Suffering to distill personal applications and ministry implications.

Roadmap Marker Number One: Soul Care through Sustaining—*"It's Normal to Hurt"*

As an African American author, interviewer, and pastor's wife, Octavia Albert offered her Louisiana home as a gathering place for ex-slaves. For her book *The House of Bondage*, she interviewed numerous ex-slaves, in particular spending extensive time with Charlotte Brooks, known as "Aunt Charlotte." Speaking *of* Aunt Charlotte, Albert conveys her empathy: "Poor Charlotte Brooks! I can never forget how her eyes were filled with tears when she would speak of all her children: 'Gone, and no one to care for me!'"[26]

Speaking *to* Aunt Charlotte, Albert enters her agony: "Aunt Charlotte, my heart throbs with sympathy, and my eyes are filled with tears, whenever I hear you tell of the trials of yourself and others. I've read and heard very often of the hard punishments of the slaves in the South; but the half was never told."[27] Imagine Aunt Charlotte thinking that no one would ever want to listen to her, thinking no one would ever care—then having this college-educated pastor's wife recording her words and weeping with her!

Octavia Albert embodies historic sustaining. For over two thousand years, Christian sustaining has emphasized consolation and *compassionate commiseration*, believing that *shared sorrow is endurable sorrow*. Its practitioners have offered *empathy* in the original sense of the word: feeling deeply the feelings of another. Historic sustainers have joined others in their pain by communicating that *"It's normal to hurt."* When the fallen world fell on their spiritual friends, they connected with them by acknowledging that *"Life is bad."* When their friends felt the sentence of death and despaired even of life, like the apostle Paul in 2 Corinthians 1:8–9, they *climbed in the casket* with them, identifying with their feelings of despair.

They have also provided *comfort* in the original sense of the word, offering "co-fortitude" by coming alongside to lend support and to instill courage in a hurting heart. Their ministry drew a line in the sand of the soul, finding a stopping place against full retreat by rejecting denial and surrender, replacing them with candor and the will to survive. They purposed to help hurting people endure and transcend irretrievable loss. Finding people facing such loss, they offered wise pilotage for souls in danger of floundering in external distress (known as level one suffering) and inner doubt (known as level two suffering).

Level one suffering involves what happens *to* us. It is the painful external "stuff" of life to which we respond internally. Level two suffering involves what happens *in* us. It relates to how we face what we are facing. It is the suffering of the mind that gives rise to fear and doubt as we reflect on external suffering.

Given this understanding of historic sustaining, as we engage directly the accounts of African American mutual ministry, we can ask specific questions. We can use specific compass points on our map of sustaining soul care to plot the nature of their care-giving. When ministering to hurting people, how did African American Christians

communicate compassionate commiseration,

employ the principle that shared sorrow is endurable sorrow,

practice empathy by feeling deeply the feelings of others,

join others in pain by communicating that "*It's normal to hurt,*"

connect with others by acknowledging that "*Life is bad,*"

climb in the casket to identify with feelings of despair,

provide comfort by coming alongside to lend support and
to instill courage,

help others endure and transcend irretrievable loss,

offer wise pilotage for souls in danger of floundering,

draw a line in the sand of the soul, finding a stopping place
against full retreat, and

enhearten others to find strength to face and survive life's
difficulties?

In all of these probes, we're zealous to uncover the unique
ways in which African American Christians practiced the
historical soul care art of sustaining. We will celebrate their
distinctive contributions as a gift *to* African Americans. And
we will apply their distinctive contributions to our lives and
ministries as a gift *from* African Americans.

Roadmap Marker Number Two: Soul Care through Healing—*"It's Possible to Hope"*

Absalom Jones was born in slavery on November 6, 1746,
in Sussex, Delaware. At age sixteen he moved to Philadelphia,
and by age thirty-eight he was able to purchase his freedom.
Along with Richard Allen, he became a lay preacher for the
African American members of St. George's Methodist Episcopal Church. By 1794 he was ordained a deacon in the African
Episcopal Church, and in 1804 he was ordained a priest.

On January 1, 1808, in Philadelphia's St. Thomas's African Episcopal Church, Jones preached a sermon entitled "A
Thanksgiving Sermon on Account of the Abolition of the
African Slave Trade." The sermon parallels American slavery,
the bondage of the Jews in Egypt, and God's personal and
powerful exodus rescue of his people.

Jones begins his message by reading Exodus 3:7–8: "And
the LORD said, I have surely seen the affliction of my people
which are in Egypt, and have heard their cry by reason of

their taskmasters; for I know their sorrows; and I am come down to deliver them out of the hand of the Egyptians" (KJV). Commenting on this passage, Jones first highlights God's sustaining care for his people.

He then begins to explain God's healing involvement in their plight: "In this situation, they were not forgotten by the God of their fathers, and the Father of the human race. Though, for wise reason, he delayed to appear in their behalf for several hundred years, yet he was not indifferent to their sufferings. Our text tells us that he saw their afflictions, and heard their cry: his eye and his ear were constantly open to their complaint: every tear they shed was preserved, and every groan they uttered was recorded, in order to testify, at a future day, against the authors of their oppressions."[28]

Do you detect Jones's underlying message? God's delay in rescuing the Israelites *and* his delay in rescuing African Americans are part of his wise and caring plan, no matter how inscrutable that plan may appear to human eyes.

Next, with stirring imagery, Jones describes the personal nature of God's healing presence. "But our text goes further: it describes the judge of the world to be so much moved, with what he saw and what he heard, that he rises from his throne—not to issue a command to the armies of angels that surround him to fly to the relief of his suffering children—but to come down from heaven in his own person, in order to deliver them out of the hands of the Egyptians. Glory to God for this precious record of his power and goodness."[29]

Jones personifies historic healing. For over two thousand years, Christian healing has underscored the encouragement that comes through enlightened eyes that see God at work behind life's miseries and mysteries. Its practitioners have understood that "when life stinks, our perspective shrinks." Therefore, they have diligently listened for God's eternal story of deliverance. They have asked, in the midst of messes, "What is God up to in this?" They have worked with suffering people to co-create faith stories and Exodus narratives so that people can rejoice in the truth that "*It's possible to hope.*"

When all seemed dark and hopeless, they communicated that "*God is good. He's good all the time!*" Healing soul physicians enabled their spiritual friends to say with the apostle Paul, "But this happened that we might not rely on ourselves but on God, who raises the dead" (2 Cor. 1:9). They *celebrated the resurrection* and raised the roof because of the empty tomb.

They have also emphasized faith eyes or spiritual eyes by using scriptural truths to enlighten people to enter new dimensions of spiritual insight and to empower them to cross the threshold toward new levels of spiritual maturity. If sustaining brought *surviving*, then healing produced *thriving*. Even when situations could not change, attitudes and character could. Historic healers followed a biblical sufferology (theology of suffering) that taught that crisis provided a door of opportunity which could produce forward gain from victim to victor. Through creative suffering, they placed themselves and their spiritual friends on God's anvil to be master-crafted according to his perfect will.

With this understanding of historic healing, we can ask precise questions as we sift through firsthand accounts of African American ministry. When ministering to hurting people, how did African American Christians

encourage and enlighten people to see God at work behind the scenes,

co-create new faith stories and Exodus narratives,

help people to experience the truth that "*It's possible to hope,*"

communicate that "*God is good,*"

celebrate the resurrection and the empty tomb,

enable people to enter deeper dimensions of spiritual insight,

empower people to cross the threshold toward new levels
of spiritual maturity,
help people to thrive in parched conditions,
develop and share a biblical sufferology,
equip people to move from victims to victors, and
practice the art of creative suffering?

Through such probing questions, we'll learn together
the essence of healing as historically practiced by African
American believers. As we learn, we'll grow in our abilities
as physicians of the soul who bring Christ's healing touch
to hurting human hearts.

Roadmap Marker Number Three: Spiritual Direction through Reconciling—*"It's Horrible to Sin, but Wonderful to Be Forgiven"*

From 1927 to 1929, Andrew Polk Watson interviewed
an unnamed formerly enslaved male born in 1845 in South
Carolina. His remarkable conversion narrative bears all the
hallmarks of historic reconciling. "All of my family were
God-fearing, and I came up in an atmosphere charged with
faith, hope, and the Holy Spirit. Outwardly we sung; in-
wardly we prayed."[30] Prior to his own reconciliation with
God, he was enticed by their Christian walk. "I heard and
remember the joy and happiness that filled the older people's
hearts, I believe all the more that the seed was planted in
my heart."[31]

Though his family members' faith sunk deep into his soul, he
had never personally entered into a relationship with God through
Christ. Years later, as an adult, he experienced conversion.

The darkest hour of the night is just before the break of
day. The darkest hours of my life as a slave came just before
freedom, and in the same way, in my trials with sin, when

36

everything seemed lost I was delivered. No sooner had I surrendered and cried out, "Lord, have mercy!" than the work
was done. It seemed as if a great burden were lifted from
me, and my soul took a leap and left the old body. A great
light came from above, and a voice cried, "Lo, I am the way.
Trust and believe." My soul took the air, and having wings
like a bird I flew away into a world of light with thousands
of other images like myself; all the time a voice was crying,
"Peace! Peace! Peace! Free! Free! Free!"[32]

This anonymous convert exemplifies historic reconciling.
For over two thousand years, Christian reconciling has focused on guilt *and* grace, sin *and* forgiveness, repentance *and*
mercy, shame *and* shalom. Its practitioners have understood
that reconciliation with God requires a personal awareness of
the truth that "*It's horrible to sin, but wonderful to be forgiven.*"
Therefore, they practiced the art of loading the conscience
with guilt and lightening the conscience with grace. They
helped people to see that "*God is gracious even when they
were sinful.*" Historic reconcilers were *dispensers of grace.*

In their understanding of human nature, they emphasized
God's original *creation* of humanity in his image, humanity's *fall* into sin, and believers' *redemption* through Christ's
grace. They also underlined a threefold need for reconciliation—with God (due to alienation), with others (due to
separation), and with self (due to dis-integration). Thus they
focused on restoring people to a right relationship with God,
others, and self through confrontation, repentance, confession, and forgiveness.

Using this model of historic reconciling, we can map what
African Americans did when providing reconciling spiritual
direction. We can ask, when ministering to hardened people,
how did African American Christians

maintain an integrated focus on guilt *and* grace, sin *and*
forgiveness,

37

help people to personalize the complementary truths that *"It's horrible to sin, but wonderful to be forgiven,"*

enlighten people to the truth that *"God is gracious even when we are sinful,"*

load the conscience with guilt,

lighten the conscience with grace,

dispense grace to each other,

teach about creation, fall, and redemption,

restore people through reconciliation and restoration with God, others, and self,

confront sin, and

grant forgiveness?

Probing questions like these cause us to probe our own hearts. Are we in right relationship with God, others, and ourselves? Are we practicing the soul physician art of reconciliation from a biblical perspective in a biblical way?

Roadmap Marker Number Four: Spiritual Direction through Guiding—*"It's Supernatural to Mature"*

Peter Randolph was born a slave and owned, with eighty-one others, by Carter Edloe of Prince George County, Virginia. Freed in 1844, when Edloe died, Randolph and sixty-six others moved to Boston, where he was licensed as a Baptist preacher at Twelfth Baptist Church. In 1893 Randolph penned his concise but informative autobiography, *From Slave Cabin to Pulpit*. In it he writes about the guiding wisdom that he needed in facing bewildering moral issues.

"One of the most perplexing difficulties I met with at the beginning of my religious work in the South was the 'Marriage Question.'"[33] Husbands and wives were sold and separated, and then forced to marry someone else. With emancipation, hundreds returned home to find their former spouse remarried. Additionally, the state now required an official legal marriage ceremony for African American couples. Randolph wrote, "The perplexing part was, as I have intimated, to determine which were the right ones to marry. This state of things existed not only in Virginia, but all through the South. There was great need of competent pastors to meet this, and other phases of religious work."[34]

Randolph typifies historic guiding. For over two thousand years, Christian guiding has concentrated on the wisdom necessary to apply God's Word in complex situations in order to promote spiritually mature lifestyles. Its practitioners have understood the prerequisite for wise choices—a redeemed, maturing, God-dependent heart and mind. Rather than presenting self-sufficient sources for wisdom for living, they taught that "*It's supernatural to mature.*" They did so by *stirring up the gift of God* that already resided within the new creation God had redeemed. They taught about the new nature (sainthood) and the new nurture (sonship).

Building on these foundations, practitioners of guiding performed *devil craft*—shared discovery of biblical principles for spiritual victory over Satan during times of spiritual warfare. They also engaged in the mutual exploration of scriptural principles to help perplexed people to make confident choices in matters of the soul. Together, guide and disciple discovered practical, proverbial wisdom that equipped the disciple to love God and others in increasingly mature ways.

Following this paradigm of guiding, we can detect characteristic methods used by African American mentors as they guided others. We can ask, when ministering to perplexed people, how did African American Christians

convey the God-dependent attitude that "*It's supernatural to mature,*"

stir up the gift of God within redeemed people,

teach biblical principles of the new nature and new nurture,

jointly discern the biblical wisdom principles necessary to
help perplexed people find scriptural guidance,

practice *devil craft* by discovering biblical principles for
spiritual victory over Satan,

help others to find practical, proverbial wisdom, and

equip disciples to love God and others more maturely?

Our purpose is to use these probes to identify the noteworthy methods that African American predecessors in the
faith used to guide people. Through better understanding
of their special style of historic guiding, we can appreciate
their creativity and emulate their ingenuity.

Following the North Star

When enslaved African Americans fled to the North pur-
suing freedom, they had no physical compass save the North
Star. Missouri slave William Wells Brown depicts how vital
the North Star was during his flight with his mother to
freedom: "We remained in the woods during the day, and as
soon as darkness overshadowed the earth, we started again
on our gloomy way, having no guide but the North Star.
We continued to travel by night, and secrete ourselves in
woods by day; and every night, before emerging from our
hiding-place, we would anxiously look for our friend and
leader,—the North Star."[35]

While Brown and his mother followed the physical North
Star, converted African Americans followed the spiritual
North Star. When they found freedom from the slavery of
sin, they received spiritual, internal, eternal direction from
their Friend, Leader, and Savior. Morte, whom we met earlier,
expresses his absolute dependence on divine guidance from
the moment of his conversion: "I again prayed, and there
came a soft voice saying, 'My little one, I have loved you
with an everlasting love. You are this day made alive and

freed from hell. You are a chosen vessel unto the Lord. Be upright before me, and I will guide you unto all truth. My grace is sufficient for you. Go, and I am with you.'"[36]

Fortunately for us, through their narratives, songs, sermons, and interviews, we can all benefit from their spiritual legacy of following God's guidance. We do so by following their North Star, by reading their spiritual compass. Instead of N-S-E-W, their soul care and spiritual direction compass points read S-H-R-G: Sustaining, Healing, Reconciling, and Guiding. Throughout *Beyond the Suffering*, they will gift us with their wisdom—wisdom for ministry today to God's glory forever.

Learning Together from Our Great Cloud of Witnesses

1. Why do you think that our society prefers the latest trends and newest fads over the time-tested wisdom of our Christian predecessors?
2. What negative results occur when we ignore the wisdom of those who have gone before us?
3. Are you at all surprised by our assertion that past African American Christians have a tremendous contribution to make to current Christian ministry? If so, why? If not, what wonderful contributions can you identify that past African American believers have made toward the way that you practice ministry?
4. Concerning soul care and spiritual direction, along with sustaining, healing, reconciling, and guiding:
   a. Have you ever heard these terms before? If so, where? Have you implemented them in your ministry? How so?
   b. Do you have a "model" that you follow as you seek to help suffering people and as you minister to people overcome by besetting sins? Where did you learn it? How effective do you find it?

    c. To what extent are you open to learning a new model of mutual ministry?

5. Of sustaining, healing, reconciling, and guiding:
    a. Which one do you think you most naturally tend toward or lean toward?
    b. Which one do you most desire to further learn about and develop?

6. On a scale of one to ten, with one being "like unwrapping my third wedding gift toaster" and ten being "like a kid unwrapping his or her longed-for gift on Christmas morning," how excited are you about receiving ministry gifts from these past African American believers?

7. How could the message of *Beyond the Suffering* improve your ability to minister cross-culturally?

8. Dream with us a bit. How might God use the message of *Beyond the Suffering* to improve cross-cultural relationships:
    a. In your life?
    b. In your church?
    c. Nationally and internationally?

2

Out of Africa

From Victim to Victor

Because my mouth is wide with laughter and my throat is
   deep with song,
You do not think I suffer after I have held my pain so long?
Because my mouth is wide with laughter, you do not hear my
   inner cry?
Because my feet are gay with dancing, you do not know I die?

   Langston Hughes, "Minstrel Man"[1]

The Christianity of American slaves was born in suffering, the
suffering of capture, middle passage, and enslavement for life.

   Albert Raboteau, "The Legacy of a Suffering Church"[2]

Free-born Africans were ripped away from spouses, parents, children, village, and culture by capture. Stripped of everything, they were transformed overnight from farmers, merchants, scholars, artisans, or warriors into possessions. Without family, without status, they were treated as merchandise, as things—a mere extension of their captors' will.[3]

To comprehend something of the victimization and dehumanization of African enslavement, we must understand the uniqueness of its exercise by Europeans and Americans. Though slavery had been practiced throughout much of human history, normally it was not racially based (i.e., based on skin color and ethnicity). In fact, slaves were often treated with great status. The enslavement of Africans that emerged in Europe and the Americas was far different. Here arose a fully developed theory that viewed nonwhites as nonhuman chattel and inferior property.[4]

James Bradley portrays the dehumanization of capture in all its horror in a letter that he wrote in 1834 while a student at Lane Seminary in Cincinnati. "I think I was between two and three years old when the *soul-destroyers* tore me from my mother's arms, somewhere in Africa, far back from the sea. They carried me a long distance to a ship; all the way I looked back and cried."[5]

Alexander Falconbridge served as a white surgeon aboard several slave ships. Disgusted by what he observed, he wrote "to lay before the public" the honorable character of the Africans despite their despicable treatment. "From these instances I think it may be clearly deduced that the unhappy Africans are not bereft of the finer feelings, but have a strong attachment to their native country, together with a just sense of the value of liberty."[6] Falconbridge so bonded with those enslaved that he later served as the governor of a British colony for freed slaves in Sierra Leone.

In his riveting account of the hardships endured by enslaved Africans on the slave ships, he details the degrading examination that captured Africans suffered. They were minutely inspected like animals, and if they had bad eyes or teeth or any other defect they were rejected, beaten severely, often put to death, sometimes instantly beheaded.[7] Those "fortunate" enough to be healthy immediately "experience an earnest of those dreadful sufferings which they are doomed in the future to undergo."[8]

Without a doubt, free-born Africans were victims of an inhumane institution. Yet they were also victors wrestling to maintain their humanity and personhood. But how? In the midst of soul destroyers, where did they find soul deliverance? Their "capture narratives" tell their tale and provide our answer.

Born Free

"I . . . acknowledge the mercies of Providence in every occurrence of my life."[9] These words from the pen of the Christian Olaudah Equiano might seem trite until we realize that they introduce the narrative of his harrowing kidnapping and enslavement.

Equiano was born free in 1745 in the kingdom of Benin on the coast of Africa, then known as Guinea. He was the youngest of seven children; his loving parents gave him the name Olaudah, signifying *favored one*. Indeed, he lived a favored life in his idyllic upbringing in a simple and quiet village where his father served as the "chief man" who decided disputes and punished crimes and where his mother adored him dearly.

Bathed in Tears: Weeping with Those Who Weep

When Equiano was ten, it all came crashing down. "One day, when all our people were gone out to their works as usual, and only I and my dear sister were left to mind the house, two men and a woman got over our walls, and in a moment seized us both; and, without giving us time to cry out, or make resistance, they stopped our mouths, tied our hands, and ran off with us into the nearest wood: and continued to carry us as far as they could, till night came on, when we reached a small house, where the robbers halted for refreshment, and spent the night."[10]

His kidnappers then unbound Equiano and his sister. Overpowered by fatigue and grief, they had just one source of relief. "The only comfort we had was in being in one another's arms all that night, and bathing each other with our tears."[11]

Equiano and his sister model a foundational principle of sustaining empathy: weeping with those who weep. Far too often we rush in with words, and far too often those words are words of rescue. *Our hurting friends need our silence, not our speeches.* The shed tear and the silent voice provide great enrichment for our spiritual friends.

Equiano and his sister were soon deprived of even the comfort of weeping together. "The next day proved a day of greater sorrow than I had yet experienced; for my sister and I were then separated, while we lay clasped in each other's arms; it was in vain that we besought them not to part us: she was torn from me, and immediately carried away, while I was left in a state of distraction not to be described. I cried and grieved continually; and for several days did not eat any thing but what they forced into my mouth."[12]

Over the ensuing months, Equiano frequently changed masters. Weighed down by grief and a ravenous desire to return to his family, he decided to seize the first opportunity to escape. However, during a failed attempt he realized that the expanse that separated him from his home was too great and too dangerous. "I . . . laid myself down in the ashes, with an anxious wish for death to relieve me from all my pains."[13]

Death refused to visit. Instead, Equiano was sold repeatedly, each time "carried to the left of the sun's rising, through many dreary wastes and dismal woods, amidst the hideous roarings of wild beasts."[14] Being "left of the sun's rising" paints a poetic picture of hopelessness—reflecting an absence of the hope that people have when they are "right of the rising sun" and thus anticipating that the sun will soon approach to dispel their darkness.

Equiano had been traveling in this manner for a considerable time when one evening, to his great surprise, traders brought his dear sister to the house where he was staying. "As soon as she saw me she gave a loud shriek, and ran into my arms. I was quite overpowered; neither of us could speak, but, for a considerable time, clung to each other in mutual embraces, unable to do any thing but weep."[15]

For a time, the joy of their reunion distracted them from their misfortunes. But this, too, passed. "For scarcely had the fatal morning appeared, when she was again torn from me for ever! I was now more miserable, if possible, than before. The small relief which her presence gave me from pain was gone, and the wretchedness of my situation redoubled my anxiety after her fate, and my apprehensions lest her sufferings should be greater than mine, when I could not be with her to alleviate them."[16]

Even in his agony, Equiano offers words of insight into ministry. Note that it was "her presence" that gave him relief from his pain, and that he longed to "be with her to alleviate" her suffering. In your own ministry, before all else fails, implement what never fails—*personal presence.*

Encountering Every Misery for You: Jesus with Skin On

Equiano's empathy for his sister was Herculean. "Yes, thou dear partner of all my childish sports! thou sharer of my joys and sorrows! happy should I have ever esteemed myself to encounter every misery for you, and to procure your freedom by the sacrifice of my own!"[17]

What a model of incarnational suffering. In his letter of spiritual consolation to his long-lost sister, Equiano does more than say, "I understand your feelings." He does more than say, "I feel what you feel." He says, "I am willing to *take on* your pain—to encounter your every misery *for you.*"

Equiano is reminiscent of the apostle Paul, who, in Romans 9:2–3, shares his great empathy and unceasing anguish for his Jewish brethren—feeling their feelings. In this passage Paul wishes himself accursed and cut off from Christ for the sake of his brothers—enduring their misery for them.

Like Paul and Equiano, we are to be "Jesus with skin on." As Jesus pitched his tent among us, took on flesh, assumed the very nature of a servant, was made in human likeness, and became sin for us, so we must intimately engage our spiritual friends. Aloof, detached, arm's-length ministry is neither biblical nor historical.

Hope Deferred Makes the Heart Sick: Candor

Eventually Equiano was sold to a wealthy widow with a son his age. After two months he began to settle in, hoping that he had found a form of stability with his new family. However, his hope vanished when he was stolen again. He rehearses his immeasurable despondency, grasping for words to communicate what exceeds human language: "Thus, at the very moment I dreamed of the greatest happiness, I found myself most miserable: and seemed as if fortune wished to give me this taste of joy only to render the reverse more poignant. The change I now experienced was as painful as it was sudden and unexpected. It was a change indeed from a state of bliss to a scene which is inexpressible by me . . . and wherein such instances of hardship and fatigue continually occurred as I can never reflect on but with horror."[18]

Have you been there? At the moment of your greatest happiness, life intrudes. Misery waltzes in. The poison of misfortune spoils your banquet of joy. If so, then what? Pretend? Ignore? Seek a diversion?

Equiano chooses candor. He chooses journaling. Both are wise choices. Hope deferred makes the heart sick, and heart sickness requires the biblical medicine of candor both with God and with self. Very often, such candor is most effective when pen hits paper and we write with honesty about the instances of hardship and fatigue that we experience.

It was during these evil circumstances and many more to come that Equiano acknowledged his heavenly Father's good heart and Christ's merciful providence *in every occurrence of his life*. He was not alone. The oft invisible hand of God softly yet firmly left his compassionate fingerprints on the trusting hearts of millions of enslaved Africans, including a boy named Quobna Cugoano.

The Ear of Jehovah: *Groaning to God*

Cugoano was born on the coast of present-day Ghana, in the Fante village of Agimaque. In 1770, at the age of thirteen, he was playing with other children, enjoying peace and tranquility and the amusement of catching wild birds, "when several great ruffians came upon us suddenly."[19]

Led away at gunpoint, they eventually came to a town where Cugoano saw several white people, "which made me afraid that they would eat me, according to our notion as children in the inland parts of the country."[20] He was conducted away to the ship after a three-day imprisonment in the barracoon—a euphemistic term for concentration camps where the kidnapped Africans were held without respect to gender, family, or tribal affiliation, until slavers came to buy their cargo. "It was a most horrible scene; there was nothing to be heard but the rattling of chains, smacking of whips, and the groans and cries of our fellowmen."[21]

Cugoano's experience was anything but rare. Torment saturated the months-long experience from capture to importation. The process was physically and psychologically bewildering.[22]

After briefly describing the external debasement of his situation, Cugoano highlights his internal anguish. "I was thus lost to my dear indulgent parents and relations, and they to me. All my help was cries and tears, and these could not avail; nor suffered long, till one succeeding woe, and dread, swelled up another."[23]

He was not isolated in his agony. "The cries of some, and the sight of their misery, may be seen and heard afar; but the deep sounding groans of thousands, and the great sadness of their misery and woe, under the heavy load of oppressions and calamities inflicted upon them, are such as can only be distinctly known to the ear of Jehovah Sabaoth."[24]

How did he, how did they, how do we maintain our souls when treated soullessly? Like Cugoano, we entrust ourselves to Jehovah Sabaoth: the Lord Almighty, the Lord of Hosts who rules over his universe with affectionate sovereignty. Like Hagar, the slave forced to bear her master's child (Gen. 16:1–4), we commune with the God who hears our misery (Gen. 16:11). We pray to "the God who sees me" (Gen. 16:13).

We minister healing soul care to our spiritual friends suffering under unspiritual treatment by encouraging them to groan to God. We encourage such groaning by helping them cling to biblical images of God, the warrior God who spoke the universe into existence and still speaks powerfully today, the God with ears cupped to hear their cries, the God with eyes like the Hubble telescope to see their misery.

The Bitter Waters

Millions of free Africans like Equiano and Cugoano experienced the same progression from freedom, to capture, to barracoon, to inhumane inspection, and then to the holds of the slave ships. Historians have variously labeled their months-long crossing of the Atlantic as "the trans-Atlantic passage," "the Middle Passage," "the slave holds," "the bitter waters," and "rupture."

Barbara Holmes, in *Joy Unspeakable*, explains the terminology while introducing the tragedy. "Although the event is often referred to as the Middle Passage, this label fails to depict the stark realities of a slave ship. Captured Africans were spooned together lying on their sides in ships that pitched with every wave. Together they wept and moaned in a forced community that cut across tribal and cultural lines."[25]

Anthony Pinn describes the bitter waters as the appalling transition from personhood to property. The Africans left Africa connected to family, community, and continent; they were reborn as chattel. They moved from capture to *rupture*, a ritual passage of rebirth from one reality to another.[26] Dying to what was and what could have been, they were born into what never should have been.

The nightmarish voyage of the *Venus* offers sobering evidence of the perils of the bitter waters. French slave traders packed 450 souls into the slave holds in April 1729. Only 320 Africans survived the Middle Passage and disembarkment. According to officials, these survivors were so disease-ridden that more than two-thirds of those sold at auction died soon thereafter.[27] Thus, for 77 percent of the enslaved Africans, the Middle Passage of the *Venus* was their final passage from life to death.

For those who did survive, their human drama of inhumane treatment unfolded in the holds of the slave ships. Like Cugoano, Equiano first feared that he would be eaten when he was forced aboard. Those fears soon gave way to dread and despair. "I was not long suffered to indulge my grief; I was soon put down under the decks, and there I received such a salutation in my nostrils as I had never experienced in my life; so that with the loathsomeness of the stench, and crying together, I became so sick and low that I was not able to eat, nor had I the least desire to taste any thing. I now wished for the last friend, Death, to relieve me."[28]

Again, death did not befriend him. Instead, all night long he was visited by the shrieks of the women, the bitter cries of the men, and the groans of the dying, rendering the whole scene an inconceivable horror.[29]

Equiano's experience was all too common. Falconbridge describes males chained two-by-two with handcuffs on their wrists and irons riveted to their ankles. Sent below to the slave holds, they were stowed so close as to "admit of no other posture than lying on their sides."[30]

Below deck the air was deathly. Falconbridge wrote, "The fresh air being thus excluded, the Negroes' rooms very soon grow intolerably hot. The confined air, rendered noxious by the effluvia exhaled from their bodies, and by being repeatedly breathed, soon produces fevers and fluxes, which generally carries off great numbers of them." In the morning when the ship physician examined the slaves, he "frequently finds several dead; and among the men, sometimes a dead and living Negro fastened by their irons together."[31]

For the women who did not perish, survival was sometimes worse than death. "The officers are permitted to indulge their passions among them at pleasure, and sometimes are guilty of such brutal excesses, as disgrace human nature."[32]

Father Dionigio Carli de Piacenza notes that even the children were huddled together "like herrings in a barrel."[33] The men were laid atop one another, held in their own sewage, and kept in their blood from the whippings and other brutality that they endured.[34]

In such a hopeless state, those who could not find communal hope or hope in God surrendered all hope. Falconbridge records suicides by men and women by refusing to eat, jumping ship, and hanging.[35] Their depression was so common that traders gave it the label "fix melancholy," "whose sufferers became morose, moody, and unresponsive, staring into space, refusing food, and in extreme cases committing suicide, usually by jumping overboard."[36]

What kept others mentally sane and spiritually healthy when so many were abandoning hope? Looking back years later after their salvation in Christ, Equiano and Cugoano traced their survival to a Spirit-inspired emerging trust in the goodness of God.

Creative Communal Expression of the Inexpressible: The Moan

The air was thick with stench and panic as ships like the *Venus* departed the Slave Coast laden with their human cargo. The gruesomeness of their voyage of terror was akin to something out of a horror movie.

But how could they articulate such suffocating physical suffering and psychological agony? And if articulated, would they be understood, since the slavers pitilessly ignored all tribal associations? Groans that could not be uttered and words that could not be communicated became the primal sustaining language known as the *moan*.[37]

As the ships lurched back and forth with each wave, each soul rocked and swayed with despondency. Out of their despair "the moan became the first vocalization of a new spiritual vocabulary—terrible and wonderful, it was a cry, a critique, a prayer, a hymn, a sermon, all at once."[38]

As such, it was desperately defiant. Seemingly destitute of all power, the sufferers grasped hold of the universe, wordlessly shouting, "This is *not* the way it was meant to be!" The pain of enslavement dared them to succumb—to give up hope by losing their voice. In the moan, they reclaimed their voice, their inner personhood, their God-given right to express themselves.

The poem/hymn "The Negro's Complaint" powerfully expresses the mind-set of the moan:

> Forc'd from home and all its pleasures,
> Afric's coast I left forlorn;
> To increase a stranger's treasures,
> O'er the raging billows borne.
> Men from England bought and sold me,
> Paid my price in paltry gold;
> But though slave they have enroll'd me,
> Minds are never to be sold.[39]

Minds can never be sold. It is as if these captives say, "We face our pain, verbalize our pain, but we are more than our pain! You may enslave our bodies, but our pain, our feelings, our souls, these we claim as everlasting gifts from our eternal God." What the psalms of lamentation were to the Hebrews in their enslavement, the moan was to the Africans—cries to one another and to God that refused to relinquish hope.

The fact that a person was enslaved does not communicate everything about that individual.[40] The slave traders rigorously restricted the lives of the captured Africans, but they never completely defined them. The enslaved Africans experienced their own existence internally and expressed themselves externally.

If they could keep their personhood intact under these unimaginable constraints, what about us? Does anyone control our soul? Can any circumstance define our personhood? We have so much to learn from the resilience of these African brothers and sisters.

From them we learn not only about the force of individual perseverance but also about the strength of communal sustaining. The moaners never moaned alone. Enslaved Africans birthed a form of communal care in the midst of shared misery. During the seafaring journey of the bitter waters, the moan began to knit together a community across family, gender, and tribal lines.

The moan "stitches horror and survival instincts into a creation narrative, a tapestry of historical memory that marks the creation of community. On the slave ships the moan became the language of stolen strangers, the articulation of unspeakable fears, the precursor to joy yet unknown."[41] The shared moan was their creative, communal response during their crucible of crisis.

Beauty from Ashes: The Intention of Jehovah

The moan provided sustaining comfort by wordlessly communicating that *it's normal to hurt* because *life is bad.* Such human comfort, though essential, was not and could not be the final word. Captured and ruptured Africans also needed divine consolation teaching that *it's possible to hope* because *God is good*. So they reminded each other that God weaves good for them even from human evil against them.

Such faith, as Cugoano believed, requires spiritual eyes like those of Joseph (see Gen. 50:20). "I may say with Joseph, as he did with respect to the evil intention of his brethren, when they sold him into Egypt, that whatever evil intentions and bad motives those insidious robbers had in carrying me away from my native country and friends, I trust, was what the Lord intended for my good."[42]

Cugoano makes the sweeping affirmation that even in the face of human evil, God is friendly and benevolent, able and willing to turn into good ends whatever may occur. It is the belief that God squeezes from evil itself a literal blessing.[43]

We can journey with our spiritual friends to the God of Joseph and Cugoano who Master-crafts every event of their lives to reveal his glory and bring them good. We can interact with them as we discover the God who fashions for them a crown of beauty instead of ashes, the oil of gladness instead of mourning, and a garment of praise instead of a spirit of despair (see Isa. 61:3).

Equiano taught his readers a similar lesson when he ended his narrative with these closing words of counsel: "I early accustomed my self to look at the hand of God in the minutest occurrence, and to learn from it a lesson of morality and religion; and in this light every circumstance I have related was to me of importance. After all, what makes any event important, unless by its observation we become better and wiser, and learn 'to do justly, to love mercy, and to walk humbly before God!'"[44]

Like Equiano, we practice spiritual friendship by reminding one another that God uses unjust suffering to make us more just, unloving treatment to make us more loving, and arrogant abusers to make us more humble. Like Equiano, we exercise spiritual discipline by orienting ourselves to detect God's hand in every circumstance—no matter how seemingly minute.

Following the North Star

We follow the North Star guidance of the enslaved Africans' responses to capture and rupture by reminding ourselves and our spiritual friends that *we are never alone*. Most of us would consider ourselves condemned prisoners in solitary confinement if we were stowed in the suffocating hold of a slave ship with little air, no portals, and no access to the outside world. Our African forebears teach us that there are always three open portals providing a way of internal release from captivity.

Portal one is *God*—the God of all portals, the God of all comfort who comforts us in all our tribulations. Kidnapped from their homes and hijacked across the world, enslaved Africans encountered a wilderness experience that raised ultimate questions and brought them to a breaking point. On the brink between sanity and insanity, many encountered God—their good God who hears, sees, and cares. Theirs was a dual journey—away from their human home and to their heavenly home. As they journeyed, the chains still clanked, yet their hearts still hummed, or at least moaned.

Portal two is *people*—when the God of all comfort comforts us, he does so in order that we can comfort one another with the comfort that we receive from him. Individually and corporately, the slaves tapped into the Holy Spirit at every turn. In bound community, they shared with one another the Spirit of God within them, their hope of glory. The collective gathering of the power of his presence in their inner being provided life-sustaining strength in the midst of death-bidding despair. The all-surpassing power of God (see 2 Cor. 4:7–9) shared among these captured souls transformed them into "Jesus with skin on."

Portal three is *self*—not the self of self-sufficiency but the self created in the image of God and infused with the Spirit of God. Ramming into the breakers of life, these enslaved men and women could either break or conclude that there is no need to break. At their breaking point, those slaves who entrusted themselves to God discovered a bottomless resourcefulness that enabled them to transform physical bondage into spiritual freedom.[45] Through God, they absorbed the ache of life without abandoning the ship of hope. Even while stowed like animals below deck, they saw the shining North Star of God with upturned eyes of faith looking out spiritual portals.

Learning Together from Our Great Cloud of Witnesses

1. As a result of reading this chapter, how has your perspective on enslavement changed?
   a. Specifically, what has surprised you?
   b. What will you do with your new awareness?
2. Of all the quotes from and about the enslaved Africans:
   a. Which ones stand out as most important to you? Why?
   b. Which ones most impact you personally? How?
3. How would your soul care ministry change:
   a. If you focused on the power of presence?
   b. If you empathetically bathed others in your tears?
   c. If you applied the truth that your hurting friends need your silence, not your speeches?
4. In your own life and in your ministry to others, how vital is candor—honesty with self and with God about the agonies of life lived in a fallen world?

5. Concerning groaning to God:
   a. In your times of suffering, what images of God fill your mind?
   b. How could you help your spiritual friends to see God as the warrior God speaking powerfully today, the God with ears cupped to hear their cries, and the God with eyes like the Hubble telescope to see their misery?
6. What would our churches be like if they were "moaning communities"—if we suffered together rather than alone?
7. Ponder an area of external suffering—something that you have endured that feels suffocating, like a prison sentence, like something out of a horror movie. Which of the three portals (God, others, self) could you open in order to stop letting your circumstances define you and to find the resiliency not to break when you hit the breakers of life?

3

Watered with Our Tears

Slavery in the Land of Liberty

These God-breathing machines are no more, in the sight of their masters, than the cotton they plant, or the horses they tend.

Harriet Jacobs, *Incidents in the Life of a Slave Girl*[1]

When I was a child, my mother used to tell me to look to Jesus, and that He who protected the widow and fatherless would take care of me also.

Peter Randolph, *From Slave Cabin to Pulpit*[2]

They arrived on two ships, one year apart. The second ship, the *Mayflower*, landed in 1620 with 102 Pilgrims seeking religious liberty. The first ship, a Dutch man-of-war, came ashore in 1619 in Jamestown, Virginia, with twenty enslaved African men and women. Captain Jobe of the Dutch man-of-war offered the seventeen men and three women to Sir

John Rolfe's Jamestown settlement in exchange for food. For the leaders of the Jamestown colony, Africans were mere commodities for European trade and servitude. In the land of the free, American slavery had begun.[3]

What began so unceremoniously at Jamestown continued for over two centuries. Recent studies project that the trans-Atlantic slave trade exported to the Americas eleven million Africans who survived.[4] Treated as cargo during the bitter waters of the Middle Passage, they were herded as cattle and sold as chattel once on the American shore.

Immediately upon arrival, formerly free African men and women confronted the dehumanizing nightmare of being put on the market as property. They were sold in one of two ways. They could be purchased through the slave scramble in a barbaric first-come, first-served, one-price-fits-all scheme or through the slave auction block where they were acquired by the highest bidder.

As if being bartered and bought on arrival was not brutal enough, they lived in constant dread of being procured at any time by anyone and moved anywhere away from everyone they knew and loved. Kentucky slave Henry Bibb provides a portrait of the slave's daily terror: "Every day to us was a day of trouble, and every night brought new and fearful apprehensions that the golden link which binds together husband and wife might be broken by the heartless tyrant before the light of another day. Deep has been the anguish of my soul when looking over my little family during the silent hours of the night, knowing the great danger of our being sold off at auction the next day and parted forever."[5]

In addition to suffering the relational agony of recurring forced separation, African Americans endured the internal agony of personal identity theft. Treated as soulless chattel to be bought and sold, would they lose their souls? Given the identity of "slave," could they achieve internal freedom? Renamed by their masters, could they reclaim their own name, their own personhood?

Their firsthand accounts picture familial bonds shattered and hope battered. They tell of the shouts of the auctioneer mingling with the screams of the children and the wails of the parents.

Yet, when listening carefully, we detect the sounds of hope. While enduring the outrage of being bought and sold and while being enraged over the attempted annihilation of their identity, the enslaved African Americans created a biblical sufferology. Through their theology of suffering, they faced hurt candidly and unearthed hope spiritually. Specifically, they coped with the heartbreak of relational separation through the hope of heavenly reunion, and they tackled the depersonalization of identity thievery with the awareness that they bore the image of God.

Slave Sale by the Slave Scramble: Mingling Suffering and Sorrow through Shared Sorrow

British ship's surgeon Alexander Falconbridge watched in horror as slaves were sold by the slave scramble. Every African man, woman, and child could be purchased for an equal price agreed on beforehand by the captain. At noon the doors opened and the purchasers flew upon the slaves "with all the ferocity of brutes."[6] The enslaved Africans were terrified. "The women, in particular, clang to each other in agonies scarcely to be conceived, shrieking through excess of terror, at the savage manner in which their brutal purchasers rushed upon, and seized them."[7]

Olaudah Equiano's personal account of the slave scramble is eerily similar. "On a signal given, (as the beat of a drum), the buyers rush at once into the yard where the slaves are confined, and make choice of that parcel they like best. The noise and clamour with which this is attended, and the eagerness visible in the countenances of the buyers, serve not a little to increase the apprehension of the terrified Africans, who

61

may well be supposed to consider them as the ministers of that destruction to which they think themselves devoted."[8]

According to Equiano, relatives and friends were separated, never to see each other again. "I remember in the vessel in which I was brought over, in the men's apartment, there were several brothers who, in the sale, were sold in different lots; and it was very moving on this occasion to see and hear their cries at parting."[9]

Years later, Equiano pens words of confrontation to his captors that speak wisdom about the power of shared sorrow. "Must every tender feeling be likewise sacrificed to your avarice? Are the dearest friends and relations, now rendered more dear by their separation from their kindred, still to be parted from each other, and thus prevented from cheering the gloom of slavery with the small comfort of being together, and mingling their sufferings and sorrows?"[10]

Equiano teaches that we cheer gloom through the communal comfort of shared sorrows. His words echo well those of the apostle Paul when he teaches that the God of all comfort comforts us "in all our troubles, so that we can comfort those in any trouble with the comfort we ourselves have received from God" (2 Cor. 1:4).

Slave Sale by the Slave Auction

The horrors of the slave auction began long before the actual sale. In 1890 Stephen Jordon told author Octavia Albert his story of enslavement in Louisiana. Remembering it as if it were yesterday, he depicts the degrading slave pen. "I tell you, people were miserable in that old slave-pen. Every day buyers came and examined such slaves as they desired to buy. They used to make them open their mouths so that they could examine their teeth; and they used to strip them naked, from head to foot, to see whether they were perfectly sound. And this they did to women as well as men."[11]

Jordon also candidly expresses the impact that such viciousness had on his own soul. "I tell you, my dear child, it used to seem to me so brutal to see poor women treated in that way by brutal and heartless men. I declare, child, I can't understand it, although I've been right in it. When they would put them naked that way they used to switch them on the legs to make them jump around so that buyers could see how supple they were."[12]

The shame of the slave pen only heightened the humiliation of the slave auction. Peter Randolph provides one of the most vivid accounts ever written about the ghastliness of the auction block. The auctioneer cries out to the bidders, "Gentlemen, here is a very fine boy for sale. He is worth twelve hundred dollars. His name is Emanuel. He belongs to Deacon William Harrison, who wants to sell him because his overseer don't like him. How much, gentlemen—how much for this boy? He's a fine, hearty nigger. Bid up, bid up, gentlemen; he must be sold."[13]

In response, "Some come up to look at him, pull open his mouth to examine his teeth, and see if they are good. Poor fellow! He is handled and examined like any piece of merchandise; but he must bear it. Neither tongue nor hand, nor any other member, is his own—why should he attempt to use another's property?"[14]

Imagine it. Treated like a piece of furniture to be acquired by the highest bidder. Poked and prodded like a pig to be slaughtered. So inhumanely treated that even your own mouth is not actually your own but owned by another.

For some, it was beyond imagination, beyond enduring, beyond comfort. Harriet Jacobs, enslaved until young adulthood in North Carolina, writes years later of the day that she saw a mother forced to lead her seven children to the auction block. "I met this mother in the street, and her wild, haggard face lives today in my mind. She wrung her hands in anguish, and exclaimed, 'Gone! All gone! Why *don't* God kill me?' I had no words wherewith to comfort her."[15] Though

Jacobs was left speechless, others had words of confrontation for the slavers and words of comfort for the separated.

Biblical Imagery Exposing Human Depravity: Truthful Confrontation

With biting sarcasm and biblical imagery, Randolph confronts the hypocrisy of the slave owner while portraying the desolation of the sold slave. "See the slave-holder, who has just bought the image of God, come to his victim, and take possession of him. Poor Emanuel must go away from his wife, never to see her again. All the ties of love are severed; the declaration of the Almighty, which said, 'What God hath joined together, let not man put asunder,' is unheeded, and he must leave all to follow his Christian master, a member of the Episcopal Church—a partaker, from time to time, of the Lord's Sacrament."[16]

Randolph then boldly and bluntly speaks the truth in love: "Such men mock religion and insult God. Oh, that God would rend the heavens and appear unto these heartless men!"[17]

Randolph powerfully presents the biblical teaching that every human being, regardless of race or color, is an eternally valuable person created in God's image. Even more powerfully, he contrasts God's view of the slave Emanuel with Deacon Harrison's treatment of him.

His words of creative confrontation are reminiscent of Nathan's parable of the rich man who stole the poor man's sheep (see 2 Samuel 12). As Nathan said to David, "You are the man!" (v. 7) who sinfully took the life and stole the wife of Uriah, so Randolph preached to Christian America, "You are the men and women!" who committed the horrible sin of enslaving God's image-bearers and of desecrating God's institution of holy matrimony.

In full spiritual armor (see Eph. 6:10–18) and with a knowledge and possession of God's truth (see 2 Cor. 10:3–5),

Randolph opposes the accusatory lies that ascribed a false identity to slaves. By refusing to cede ownership, definition, and control of the slaves' souls to others, Randolph protects the integrity of their identity in Christ and preserves God's sole (and soul) authority over life. Randolph further manifests Christ's righteousness as he labors for the integrity of slave persecutors by praying for their greater apprehension of God.

My Feelings Entering into Your Soul: Mutual Comfort

Randolph asks his Northern white readers to imagine what it would be like for them to have the mother of their babies ruthlessly snatched from them and their beloved children stolen before their eyes. He then calls for Northern white empathy. "Oh, my readers, I wish you could enter into my feelings, or rather, that my feelings might enter into your souls, on this subject!"[18]

What a powerful description of empathy. It is not simply feeling for another; it is not even entering another's feelings. Instead, true empathy allows another's feelings to enter our soul.

Solomon Northup lived free for thirty-three years in Rhode Island until he was kidnapped and enslaved for a dozen years in Louisiana. When he was first stolen, he spent two weeks in a slave pen, where he met an enslaved woman named Eliza, her daughter Emmy, and her son Randall. His account of her separation from her children offers insight into the agony of deprivation, the need for hearing one another's story, how *not* to empathize, and how to feel another's pain.

Northup tells the story of Eliza's life, as she related it to him, in great detail. After years of enslavement, she was promised her freedom and told that she was traveling to Washington, D.C., to receive her free papers. Instead, she was delivered to a trader named Burch. "The hope of years was blasted in a moment. From the height of most exulting happiness to the utmost depths of wretchedness, she had that day descended. No wonder that she wept, and filled the pen with wailings and expressions of heart-rending woe."[19]

Of their enslavement together, Northup writes, "We were thus learning the history of each other's wretchedness."[20] They participated in "Spiritual Friendship 101" by practicing the arts of story sharing and story learning.

Northup and Eliza were eventually conducted to a slave pen in New Orleans owned by a Mr. Theophilus Freeman. A planter from Baton Rouge purchased Randall. All the time the trade was occurring, Eliza was crying aloud, wringing her hands, and begging that Freeman not buy Randall unless he also bought herself and Emmy. When he answered that he could not afford them all, Eliza burst into paroxysm of grief, weeping plaintively. The bargain was agreed on; Randall had to go alone. "Then Eliza ran to him; embraced him passionately; kissed him again and again; told him to remember her—all the while her tears falling in the boy's face like rain."[21]

In response, "Freeman damned her, calling her a blubbering, bawling wench, and ordered her to go to her place, and behave herself, and be somebody. He swore he wouldn't stand such stuff but a little longer. He would soon give her something to cry about, if she was not mighty careful, and that she might depend upon."[22] His callousness models exactly what *not* to do when responding to another's grief.

Northup, on the other hand, entered Eliza's agony. "It was a mournful scene indeed. I would have cried myself if I had dared."[23]

Groaning to the Father of the Fatherless: Perpetual Lament

In another anguishing scene, Randolph writes about a mother named Jenny facing lifelong separation from her children. "Poor mother! who had toiled day and night to

66

raise her little children, feeling all a mother's affection for them, she must see them no more in this world! She feels like mourning—'like Rachel weeping for her children, and would not be comforted, because they were not.'"[24]

Randolph's images are multiplied over and over and over again. To read the slave narratives is to read repeated accounts of parents separated from children, husbands from wives, and brothers from sisters.

In these gripping narratives, we find constant mourning, groaning, and weeping. In their practice of the biblical art of lament, they clung to biblical imagery. "So she [Jenny] commends them to the care of the God of the widow and the fatherless, by bathing her bosom in tears, and giving them the last affectionate embrace, with the advice to meet in heaven. Oh, the tears of the poor slave that are in bottles, to be poured out upon his blood-stained nation, as soon as the cup of wrath of the almighty Avenger is full, when he shall say, 'I have heard the groanings of my people, and I will deliver them from the oppressor!'"[25]

Enslaved African Americans survived by painting pictures of God onto the palettes of their life portraits. They viewed him as the Father of the fatherless, as the God who collects their tears in his bottle of remembrance, and as God the just Judge avenging their suffering, hearing their cries, and delivering their souls.

For example, while Northup lies in a slave pen with fifty fellow slaves, he prays a prayer of personal lament. "My cup of sorrow was full to overflowing. Then I lifted my hands to God, and in the still watches of the night, surrounded by the sleeping forms of my companions, begged for mercy on the poor, forsaken captive. To the Almighty Father of us all—the freeman and the slave—I poured forth the supplications of a broken spirit, imploring strength from on high to bear up against the burden of my troubles, until the morning light aroused the slumberers, ushering in another day of bondage."[26]

His mouth vocalizing his pain and his eyes watching God, Northup draws a line in the sand of retreat. When everything inside screams, "Surrender hope!" he cries out to God, lamenting the evils he is suffering while pleading for strength to endure. He teaches us that the will to survive is soaked in continual lament.[27]

Fixing Your Eyes on the Hope of the Future: Heavenly Reunion

Randolph explains that given such earthly sorrow, enslaved African Americans ministered to one another by emphasizing heavenly reunion. "In parting with their friends at the auction-block, the poor blacks have the anticipation of meeting them again in the heavenly Canaan, and sing:

'O, fare you well, O, fare you well!
God bless you until we meet again;
Hope to meet you in heaven, to part no more.
Sisters, fare you well; sisters, fare you well;
God Almighty bless you, until we meet again.'"[28]

Jacob Stroyer shares one of the most heart-wrenching instances of instilling heavenly hope. Stroyer, one of fifteen children, was born on a plantation in Columbia, South Carolina, in 1849. After the Civil War he became an African Methodist Episcopal minister, serving in Salem, Massachusetts. In his autobiography *My Life in the South*, Stroyer describes the departure of a group of slaves sold South, knowing that they would never see their relatives again, and the accompanying parting scene. "Those who were going did not expect to see their friends again. While passing along many of the negroes left their masters' fields and joined us. . . . Some were yelling and wringing their hands, while others singing little hymns that they had been accustomed to for the consolation of those that were going away, such as:

When we all meet in heaven,
There is no parting there;
When we all meet in heaven,
There is no parting no more."[29]

An enslaved Virginian named William Grimes summarizes it best: "If it were not for our hopes, our hearts would break."[30] Knowing that they would never see one another again in this world, they set their sights on another world.

Perceiving Life from an Eternal Perspective: Spiritual Eyes

To survive enslavement and to sustain one another, African Americans not only set their sights *on* heaven but also looked *from* heaven. They not only fixed their eyes *on* Jesus, they looked at life *through* Jesus's eyes. Knowing that this world was not their home, they found solace by looking beyond what they could have possibly perceived with the natural eye.

By age fifteen, Equiano had been traded numerous times and faced copious dangers. "In these and many more instances, I thought I could plainly trace the hand of God, without whose permission a sparrow cannot fall."[31] With spiritual eyes and commitment to biblical truth, he traced the invisible hand of God affectionately and sovereignly working in every facet of his life.

He preached what he practiced. One day a Creole slave who had been sold more times than he remembered said very movingly to Equiano, "'Sometimes when a white man take away my fish, I go to my master, and he get me my right; and when my master by strength take away my fishes, what me must do? I can't go to any body to be righted.' Then said the poor man, looking up above, 'I must look up to God Mighty in the top for right.'"[32]

Reflecting on his words, Equiano responds, "This artless tale moved me much, and I could not help feeling the just cause Moses had in redressing his brother against the Egyptian. I exhorted the man to look up still to the God on the top, since there was no redress below."[33] When life rams us to the ground, burying us six feet under, with spiritual eyes we must *look up still to the God on the top*.

The Reverend Thomas H. Jones was born a slave in New Hanover County, North Carolina. At age nine his master sold him to a Mr. Jones, who lived forty-five miles away. As he clung to his mother, begging her to protect him, she wept bitterly, crying out, "I can't save you, Tommy." Snatched away from the presence of his loving parents, for thirteen weary years he yearned for his precious home, returning only to find that everyone was sold away except his mother. Reflecting back twenty-two years later, Jones still perceives God's good hand. "I wish to say here to my dear readers, that my life was a checkered one from boyhood up to forty-three years of age, but I see now the hand of God in it all. Like Joseph, I was sold into bondage; but God has never forsaken me."[34]

What perspective births such faith? We see the seeds of Jones's faith in his account of how he endured the enslavement of his own children. "The great God, who knoweth all the secrets of the heart, and He only, knows the bitter sorrow I now feel when I think of my four dear children who are slaves, torn from me and consigned to hopeless servitude by the iron hand of ruthless wrong. I love those children with all a father's fondness. God gave them to me; but my brother took them from me, in utter scorn of a father's earnest pleadings; and I never shall look upon them again, till I meet them and my oppressors at the final gathering."[35]

Seeing life through God's eyes, Jones understands God. "Will not the great Father and God make them and me reparation in the final award of mercy to the victim, and of justice to the cruel desolator?"[36]

We talk today of human reparations; Reverend Jones clings to divine reparations. He understands that *life is unjust, but God is just*. He applies the words of the apostle Peter, who says to Christians enslaved to harsh masters, "For it is commendable if a man bears up under the pain of unjust suffering *because he is conscious of God*" (1 Peter 2:19 emphasis added). Jones walks in the steps of Jesus, who, "when they hurled their insults at him, he did not retaliate; when he suffered, he made no threats. Instead, *he entrusted himself to him who judges justly*" (1 Peter 2:23 emphasis added).

Created in the Image of God, Treated in the Image of Animals

African American slave narratives began with the traditional first words: *I was born a slave.* Yet even while these slaves were owning the fact that they had been owned, their very writing became their personal Emancipation Proclamation.

Elizabeth Keckley, seamstress and spiritual friend to Mrs. Abraham Lincoln, writes, "I was born a slave—was the child of slave parents—therefore I came upon the earth free in God-like thought, but fettered in action."[37] Even the title she chose for her narrative proclaims her awareness of her dual status: *Behind the Scenes, or Thirty Years a Slave and Four Years in the White House.*

How did Keckley and her compatriots manage to remain free in spirit while shackled in body? How did they manage to maintain their humanity when they were treated as less than human?

Claiming, Naming, and Shaming: Withholding Identity

Slave owners considered their African American slaves chattel, a possession, a thing, a measly extension of the master. In 1854 the *Richmond Examiner* exhorted Southern men to act "as if the canopy of heaven were inscribed with a covenant, in letters of fire, that the Negro is here, and here forever; is our property, and ours forever."[38]

71

They institutionalized their perspective through case law. In *Fairchild v. Bell* (1807), the South Carolina high court declared that "the slave lives for his master's service. His time, his labor, his comforts, are all at the master's disposal." In 1828, in Kentucky, the high court pronounced, "However deeply it may be regretted, and whether it be politic or impolitic, a slave by our code is not treated as a person, but (*negotium*) a thing."[39]

What the law attempted to do by statute, owners endeavored to do by naming. William Grimes was born in 1784 in King George County, Virginia, the son of his white planter father and his slave mother. Grimes describes the naming practice. "I will mention here, that as it may appear strange for me to have so many names, to those not acquainted with the circumstance, that it is a practice among the slave holders, whenever one buys a slave of another, if the name does not suit him, or if he has one of the same name already, he gives him what name he pleases. I, for these reasons, have had three different names."[40]

Reverend Stroyer explains the master's insidious motivation for renaming. To allow the slave to use his own name "would be sharing an honor which was due only to his master, and that would be too much for a negro, said they, who was nothing more than a servant."[41]

Slave owners also withheld identity through shaming their slaves by reclassifying them as subhuman. Mrs. Dora Wilson recalls the time when her mistress's daughter sheared Dora's hair and forced her to wear a red bandanna handkerchief. To this little girl, Dora was nothing more than a pet or a doll.[42]

One unnamed formerly enslaved woman remembers her mistress reclassifying her hair. "Mistress uster ask me what that was I had on my head and I would tell her, 'hair,' and she said, 'No that ain't hair, that's wool.'" Her mistress thus redefined her slave, removing her from the human sphere and moving her into the animal domain.[43]

The most despicable shaming occurred from within the established churches. For instance, the standardized Episcopal catechism, in the characteristic question-and-answer format, sought to teach the slave that blackness equaled sinfulness. "Q. Who was the first negro? A. Cain. Q. How did he become so? A. The Lord set a black mark upon him. Q. Did the Southern slave come from him? A. Yes."[44] This twisted perversion of Scripture sunk like a dagger into the hearts of African American image-bearers.

Reclaimed, Renamed, and Unashamed in Christ: Reclaiming Identity

Robbed of family and status when captured in Africa, enslaved African Americans were also stripped of personhood and significance when bartered in America. Though inhumanely treated, they saw themselves as more than dehumanized victims. They rebelled against the satanically-inspired lies of their earthly masters by submitting to the loving truth of their heavenly Father.

The most effective method of undermining the demons of dehumanization was the slaves' biblical assurance that they were *created in God's image*. Harriet Jacob's vile and predatory master pursued her relentlessly for years. Of him and others like him she explains, "They seem to satisfy their consciences with the doctrine that God created the Africans to be slaves. What a libel upon the heavenly Father who 'made of one blood all nations of men!'"[45]

Her conviction was no mere academic exercise but one she learned from her Christian mother and grandmother. They so fondly shielded her that she never dreamed she was a piece of merchandise, liable to be demanded of and abused by her owner at any moment. When she was six years old, her mother died, and then for the first time she learned, by the talk around her, that she was a slave. Jacobs was deeply affected by her mother's Christian model of bearing Christ's image. "They all spoke kindly of my dead mother, who had been a slave merely in name, but in nature was noble and womanly."[46]

After her father also died, Jacobs and her younger brother, Benjamin, lived with their pious grandmother, who treated them with love and dignity as if they were her own children. "There we always found sweet balsam for our troubles. She was so loving, so sympathizing! She always met us with a smile, and listened with patience to all our sorrows. She spoke so hopefully, that unconsciously the clouds gave place to sunshine."[47]

Her grandmother, also known as Aunt Marty and respected by everyone, was to be sold at a private sale. Aunt Marty saw through her master's hypocrisy; she understood very well that he was ashamed of selling her because everyone knew that he had promised her freedom. When the day came, "She took her place among the chattels, and at the first call sprang upon the auction-block. Many voices called out, 'Shame! Shame! Who is going to sell *you*, Aunt Marty? Don't stand there! That is no place for *you*!'"[48]

Without saying a word, she quietly awaited her fate. Finally, a dear white friend bid on her and immediately set her free. Reflecting on her grandmother's character, Jacobs reports that she looked up to Aunt Marty with a respect bordering on awe because she was such a virtuous woman of high spirits who modeled dignity and integrity.[49]

Jacobs also learned God's truth about her true nature from an unusual source—a Southern pulpit. Speaking about how the slaves responded to their new white preacher's affirming sermons, she notes, "Moreover, it was the first time they had ever been addressed as human beings." Jacobs remembers this preacher's farewell message when he had to leave after the death of his wife. "Your skin is darker than mine; but God judges men by their hearts, not by the color of their skins."[50]

Jacobs witnessed the divine source of the enslaved person's reclaimed sense of self. She watched a young slave girl dying soon after the birth of a child fathered by her master. In her agony, the slave girl cried out, "O Lord, come and take me!"

Her jealous mistress stood by and mocked her like a fiend. "You suffer, do you? I am glad of it. You deserve it all, and more too."

The slave girl's mother said, "The baby is dead, thank God; and I hope my poor child will soon be in heaven, too."

"Heaven!" retorted the mistress. "There is no such place for the like of her and her bastard."

The poor mother turned away sobbing. Her dying daughter called out to her feebly. "Don't grieve so, mother; God knows all about it; and HE will have mercy upon me."[51]

Whatever natural power the master or mistress may have had was puny compared to God's supernatural power. Clearly, the slaves' Christian faith was more powerful than their owners' persecution. Christ inspired more love and awe in the slaves than their masters and mistresses ever could.[52]

At his conversion, William Webb experienced Christ's transforming power. "As soon as I felt in my heart, that God was the Divine Being that I must call on in all my troubles, I heard a voice speak to me, and from that time I lost all fear of men on this earth."[53] Divinely inspired truth from God's Word casts out the illicit, untenable canons of others, bringing Webb, and all of us, to the true and lasting freedom found only in Christ.

As part of the Federal Writers' Project in the 1930s, Marjorie Jones interviewed Fannie Moore, who had been enslaved in South Carolina. One day Fannie's mother, Mammy, was working in the fields and troubled in her heart when she prayed to the Lord and experienced salvation. "Den she start singin' and a-shoutin' and a-whoopin' and a-hollerin'."

Mammy's behavior dismayed her mistress. "What all dat goin' on in de field? You think we send you out there just to whoop and yell?"

Threatened with a whipping from the overseer, "My Mammy just grin all over her black wrinkled face and say: 'I'se saved. De Lord done tell me I'se saved. Now I know de Lord will show me de way, I ain't gwine to grieve no more. No matter how much you all done beat me and my chillen de Lord will show me de way. And some day we never be slaves.'"

Mammy's mistress grabbed the cowhide and slashed Mammy across the back. "But Mammy never yell. She just go back to de field a singin'."[54]

Jacobs, Webb, Mammy, and millions of other African American slaves were raped physically, emotionally, mentally, and spiritually. They were progressively stripped of *all* earthly anchors that could have supplied stability. Their names, homes, families, friends, titles, customs, traditions, routines, language, food, clothing, health, dignity—name it and it was taken forcibly from them. Having been left with nothing but their bodies (which they were forced to share with their captors in many ways) and souls (which belonged to them and God alone) and being surrounded by *nothing* outside of themselves that they could call their own, they had only one direction to turn to find answers—upward. Pressured from the North, South, East, and West, they turned their gaze heavenward for perfect and unfailing sustenance.

Following the North Star

We follow the North Star guidance of the enslaved African Americans' response to the separation and shame of being sold by reminding ourselves and our spiritual friends to whom we truly belong. We label this aspect of African American sufferology *remembering*, slightly tweaking the word as *re-membering*. When we remember whose we are, we experience a *re-membering* as spiritual, social, and self-aware beings. We remember that we have been made *members again* of Christ and Christ's family.

The apostle Paul brilliantly merges remembering and membership. "Remember that at that time you were separate from Christ, excluded from citizenship in Israel and foreigners to the covenants of the promise, without hope and without God in the world. But now in Christ Jesus you who once were far away have been brought near through the blood of Christ. For he himself is our peace, who has made the two one and has destroyed the barrier, the dividing wall of hostility" (Eph. 2:12–14).

In *spiritual re-membering*, we refuse to fear those who can kill the body, instead reverencing the One who has absolute power over and complete love for our soul—Christ—whose image we now bear. Formerly separated from God, through Christ we now experience peace with God.

As we live through him and for him, we experience *social re-membering*. Once excluded from the Father's forever family, we are now eternally one with our brothers and sisters in Christ. We can cling to the hope that though we must part now, one day we will meet again, never again to part.

In *self-aware re-membering*, all the shamed, damaged, disparate, dis-integrated pieces of our shattered and battered souls are healed—brought back to wholeness, integrity, unity, shalom, peace. Through *re-membering*, we rest in our new, *true* identity in Christ.

Learning Together from Our Great Cloud of Witnesses

1. Try to imagine the horrors of the slave auction separation.
   a. What do you think the enslaved African Americans felt?
   b. How would you have ministered comfort to them through mingled sorrow?

2. Who has treated you like Freeman treated Eliza?
   a. Who has told you to "quit your blubbering," or "I'll give you something to cry about!"?
   b. What impact did such insensitivity have on you?
3. How can you practice truthful confrontation through the use of biblical imagery? What injustices do you need to confront today?
4. "The will to survive is soaked in continual lament."
   a. What does that mean to you? How could you practice its meaning in your life?
   b. How could you apply this truth in your ministry to others who are grieving?
5. Life is unjust, but God is just.
   a. In your life, where do you need to *look up still to the God on top*?
   b. How could you help others to *trace the invisible hand of God*?
6. God has fashioned an identity for each of us in Christ (see Ps. 139:15–16; 2 Cor. 5:17–18). When this identity is denied (because we esteem ourselves or others either higher or lower than his Word declares), we deny God's truth.
   a. What does God's Word say about your identity in Christ? Who are you in Christ?
   b. In your life, where has your identity been redefined contrary to God's Word?
   c. Where have you redefined the identity of another contrary to God's Word? Where have you ascribed to another a defining story line that does not match God's Word?
7. What sources seek to rob you of your identity and cause you to forget who you are in Christ?
   a. How can remembering that you bear God's image defeat spiritual identity theft?
   b. In ministry, how can you implement the principles of *remembering* as spiritual, social, and self-aware beings?

4

From Sunup to Sundown

Troubled in the Heart

Heavy were their hearts as they daily traversed the long cot-ton rows. The overseer's whip took no note of aching hearts.

Arna Bontemps, *Five Black Lives*[1]

Northerners know nothing at all about Slavery. They think it perpetual bondage only. They have no conception of the depth of degradation involved in that word, SLAVERY; if they had, they would never cease their efforts until so horrible a system was overthrown.

Harriet Jacobs, *Incidents in the Life of a Slave Girl*[2]

Ushered into the world on May 30, 1803, Lunsford Lane from Raleigh, North Carolina, experienced the barbar-ity of daily slavery as "having the heart wrenched from its socket" and "infinitely worse than the terrors of death." He agonized over the fact that he would never consult his own will but was entirely under the control of another. This thought "preyed upon my heart like a never-dying worm." However, even in his bleak circumstances, he never capitulated. "I saw no prospect that my condition would ever be changed. Yet I used to plan in my mind from day to day, and from night to night, how I might be free."[3]

Lane's detailed descriptions, along with hundreds of other firsthand accounts, contrast sharply with the mythological image of idealized Southern plantations and their jasmine and magnolia tales about happy, well-fed, banjo-plucking blacks. Their determined daily resistance stands at odds with the demeaning representation of the black Sambo—the shuffling man-child, the absolute victim. Enslavement did *not* have to produce slavish personalities.[4]

Just what was daily life like for enslaved African Americans? What was it about life from sunup to sundown and from sundown to sunup that they found so despicable? What shape did their daily resistance take? When mistreated, how did they treat one another?

A Hard Life of Cruel Hardships

The narratives of the ex-slaves reveal that most slaves were poorly fed, clothed, and housed; they were relentlessly overworked; and they endured vicious whippings. The women were regularly abused as sexual objects by whites, and the men were viewed as breeders for another generation of captives.

Nowhere to Lay My Head: Burdens and Deprivation

Records from masters and slaves suggest an average waking time for the slaves of four o'clock in the morning. The best estimates place the slaves' workday between twelve and fifteen hours, often with self-care tacked onto the end of the endless workday.[5]

Reverend Thomas Jones, reflecting on his forty-three years of enslavement, notes that after each day's protracted toil, parents would work in their homes cooking, cleaning, sewing, chopping wood, feeding the stock, and caring for their children, till the middle of the night. They would "then snatch a few hours' sleep, to get strength for the heavy burdens of the next day."[6]

Octavia Albert interviewed numerous ex-slaves including John Goodwin. "Uncle John" remembers his mother being forced to leave her baby all alone in the cradle all day long while she worked the field. He also recalls her difficult double duty. "My mammy had to work hard all day long with all the balance of the men. . . . After working all day in the cotton-field she would come home and work half of the night for herself and children. She used to wash, patch, spin, and cook for the next day to carry out in the field."[7]

Famous ex-slave and abolitionist Frederick Douglass reported that there were no beds given for the slaves, unless one coarse blanket be considered such. Reminiscent of Reverend Jones's account, Douglass observes that the greatest privation was not the want of beds but the want of time to sleep. The day's fieldwork done, families consumed many of their sleeping hours in caring for their own needs until they would drop side by side, "on one common bed—the cold, damp floor,—each covering himself or herself with their miserable blankets; and here they sleep till they are summoned to the field by the driver's horn."[8]

Jones from North Carolina, Goodwin from Louisiana, Douglass from Maryland, and James L. Smith from Virginia share remarkably similar accounts. Smith describes slave clothing being made of tow cloth, with nothing but a shirt furnished for the younger children. They dwelt in one-room log cabins on the bare floor with neither furniture nor bedsteads. Their "beds" were collections of straw and old rags, thrown down in the corners. As he puts it, "all ideas of decency and refinement were, of course, out of the question."[9]

Smith tells of mothers going to the fields early in the morning, leaving their "strangely silent and quiet babies" in the care of women too old to do fieldwork. The field hands, having no time to prepare any food for their morning meals, hastily grasped a piece of hoecake and bacon, or anything that was at hand, while scurrying to the field before dawn.[10]

Reverend Jacob Stroyer adds his insights from his days on a South Carolina plantation. Because masters built cabins to maintain two families, slaves had to cope not only with overcrowding but also with privacy issues. Lacking partitions, each family scrounged for discarded boards, nailing them up and stuffing the cracks with old rags. When unable to secure boards, they hung up old clothes as their only divider.

When the family increased, the children usually slept together, both boys and girls, until they married; then a part of another cabin was assigned to the newlyweds. To the best of their ability, given their circumstances, they maintained all rules of modesty. Whenever possible, the young men slept in the kitchen area and the young women slept with their parents.[11]

No Silver Lining Here, but All Silver in Heaven: Broken Homes and Separation

Pastor James W. C. Pennington of Maryland, writing with a shepherd's heart, bemoans another evil of daily slave life—the want of parental care and attention. His parents were unable to give him any attention during the day, and he often suffered much from hunger. "To estimate the sad state of a slave child, you must look at it as a helpless human being thrown upon the world without the benefit of its natural guardians. It is thrown into the world without a social circle to flee to for hope, shelter, comfort, or instruction."[12]

Douglass did not even remember seeing his mother until age seven. "The domestic hearth, with its holy lessons and precious endearments, is abolished in the case of a slave-mother and her children."[13]

In chapter 3 we witnessed with repulsion the anguish of familial separation through slave sale. Even when slaves were not sold, they were often "leased" to other plantations. On still other occasions, slaves from different plantations met at church services or other events, married, but were still forced to live apart. In these situations they often saw their family members only one day per week at best.

Elizabeth Keckley knew little of her father because he was the slave of another man and was only permitted to visit his family at Christmas and Easter. For a brief time he was "allowed" to be enslaved with them. But the golden dream of family reunion faded all too soon. "The announcement fell upon the little circle in that rude log cabin like a thunderbolt. I can remember the scene as if it were but yesterday;—how my father cried out against the cruel separation; his last kiss; his wild straining of my mother to his bosom; the solemn prayer to Heaven; the tears and sobs—the fearful anguish of broken hearts. The last kiss, the last goodbye; and he, my father, was gone, gone forever."[14]

Keckley's earthly despair was all-encompassing; her longing for heaven all-embracing. "The shadow eclipsed the sunshine, and love brought despair. The parting was eternal. The cloud had no silver lining, but I trust it will be all silver in heaven."[15]

Family Life of Empowering Relationships

As beautiful as the heavenly silver lining is, if that were the slaves' only response to daily hardships, then we might think that they viewed themselves as powerless. Nothing could be further from the truth. They defeated earthly despair not only by longing for their future heavenly home but also by empowering their current earthly homes.

Pulling the Rope in Unison: Family Cohesion

It has become something of a cliché to imagine that black families today find it difficult to experience stability because of a long history of instability caused by slavery and racism. While not at all minimizing the obstacles that enslaved African American families have faced, history paints a truer and more optimistic picture *of their response.* Though everything fought against them, enslaved African Americans battled gallantly to maintain family cohesion—a cohesion that provided a sturdy platform from which to handle life courageously.

Jennie Hill was born and enslaved in 1837 in Missouri. Florence Patton interviewed the ninety-six-year-old Hill in 1933. During her interview, Hill adamantly resisted the notion that enslaved families lacked closeness. "Some people think that the slaves had no feeling—that they bore their children as animals bear their young and that there was no heartbreak when the children were torn from their parents or the mother taken from her brood to toil for a master in another state. But that isn't so. The slaves loved their families even as the Negroes love their own today."[16]

Communicating the message of African American family love was so important to Reverend Jones that he bore witness to it on the very first page of his narrative. "I can testify, from my own painful experience, to the deep and fond affection which the slave cherishes in his heart for his home and its dear ones. We have no other tie to link us to the human family, but our fervent love for those who are *with* us and of us in relations of sympathy and devotedness, in wrongs and wretchedness."[17]

Satan longs to blind African Americans to their legacy of family love. He wants all of us to believe that *hardships make it too hard to love*. Hill's family, Jones's family, and millions more like them belie that lie.

Enslaved African American couples sustained strong marital relationships. Venture Smith was born in Dukandarra, in Guinea, about 1729. Kidnapped at age eight, he was purchased by Robertson Mumford a year later. After living with Mumford for thirteen years, Venture married Meg at age twenty-two. They remained together for over forty-seven years, through many trials and tribulations, until parted by death.

Venture's narrative contains an explanation for their marital faithfulness. On the occasion of their marriage, Venture threw a rope over his cabin and asked his wife to go to the opposite side and pull on the rope hanging there while he remained and pulled on his end. After they both had tugged at it awhile in vain, he called her to his side of the cabin and by their united effort they drew the rope to themselves with ease. He then explained the object lesson to his young bride. "If we pull in life against each other we shall fail, but if we pull together we shall succeed."[18] Premarital couples, newlyweds, and seasoned married spouses would all do well to heed Venture's guiding wisdom.

Leaving a Lasting Legacy: Family Character

History has depicted the African American male and the African American father as beaten down by enslavement and racism and therefore incapable of functioning as a positive role model in society and the home. The slave narratives and interviews tell a very different story.

One ex-enslaved person recalls his enslaved father's character. "I loved my father. He was such a good man. He was a good carpenter and could do anything. My mother just rejoiced in him. . . . I sometimes think I learned more in my early childhood about how to live than I have learned since."[19] All he ever needed to learn, he learned in his enslaved home.

Will Adams's father, a foreman on a Texas plantation, always came home exhausted after a long day's work. However, he never failed to take his son out of bed and play with him for hours.[20]

Martin Jackson, who was enslaved in Texas and interviewed there in the 1930s, at age ninety, remembers his father always counseling him. Over half a century later, Jackson notes that his father's reconciling advice and guiding prescriptions still ring in his ear. Among samples he includes: "No use running from bad to worse, hunting better," "Every man has to serve God under his own vine and fig tree," and "A clear conscience opens bowels, and when you have a guilty soul it ties you up and death will not for long desert you."[21] Clearly these sons honored and respected their godly, wise enslaved fathers.

Ex-slave Charles Davenport, age one hundred when Edith Moore interviewed him, loved and respected his father. He reminisces about how slave mothers and grandmothers sang lullabies about fathers' bravery and responsibility.

> Kink head, wherefore you skeered?
> Old snake crawled off, 'cause he's a-feared.
> Pappy will smite him on de back
> With a great big club—Ker whack! Ker whack![22]

Mothers, too, left a lasting, positive impression on their children. Fannie Moore of South Carolina witnesses to her mother's resilience. "My mammy she work in de field all day and piece and quilt all night. Den she have to spin enough thread to make four cuts for de white folks every night. Why sometime I never go to bed. Have to hold de light for her to see by. . . . I never see how my mammy stand such hard work. She stand up for her chillen though. De old overseer he hate my mammy, 'cause she fought him for beatin' her chillen. Why she get more whippin' for dat dan anythin' else."[23]

Josiah Henson writes of the mother from whom he was separated by sale only to be reunited by repurchase after he had fallen ill. "She was a good mother to us, a woman of deep piety, anxious above all things to touch our hearts with a sense of religion. . . . Now I was once more with my best friend on earth, and under her care."[24]

Lucy Dunn was ninety years old when Mary Hicks interviewed her in Raleigh, North Carolina. She shares the standards and premarital counsel that her mother provided when Lucy fell in love with Jim Dunn.

Because purity was so central to her family, Lucy's mother would not allow Jim to walk Lucy to the gate unless she was sitting there on the porch watching. After a year, without them ever having kissed, Jim finally proposed, asking her mother for Lucy's hand in marriage. Mother told him that she would have to talk to Lucy and let him know. "Well all dat week she talks to me, tellin' me how serious gettin' married is and dat it last a powerful long time. I tells her dat I knows it but dat I am ready to try it and dat I intend to make a go of it, anyhow."[25]

The next Sunday night, Lucy's mother informed Jim that he had her permission to marry her daughter. He was so excited that he picked Lucy right up out of her chair there in the moonlight on the porch and kissed her right before her mother who was crying with joy. The next Sunday they were married in the Baptist church at Neuse. Lucy had a new white dress, though times were hard.

Lucy offers a beautiful testimony concerning their marital relationship. "We lived together fifty-five years and we always loved each other. . . . And though we had our fusses and our troubles we trusted in de Lord and we got through. I loved him durin' life and I love him now, though he's been dead for twelve years."[26]

Her mother's protection of Lucy's purity, her premarital counsel, and her interaction with Lucy's future son-in-law all strikingly display how enslaved African American families were *victors, not victims*. Lucy and Jim's marriage, for richer for poorer, for better for worse, in good times and bad, provides a shining example of marital fidelity.

Amanda Berry Smith was born twenty miles from Baltimore, Maryland, in 1837. In her story of her life as an evangelist, she shares testimonies concerning the spiritual impact that her father, mother, and grandmother had upon her.

Every Sunday morning after breakfast her father would call his thirteen children around him and read the Bible to them. "I never knew him to sit down to a meal, no matter how scant, but what he would ask God's blessing before eating."[27] After their evening meal, often of milk and mush, her mother would have all the children say their prayers. Smith never remembered a time when she went to bed without saying the Lord's Prayer as her mother taught it to her.[28] Her grandmother was a woman of deep piety and great faith. She often heard her mother say that it was due to the prayers and mighty faith of her grandmother that they owed their eventual freedom from slavery. "How I do praise the Lord for a Godly grandmother, as well as mother."[29]

Abusing Body and Soul

The accounts of daily hardships provided thus far pale in comparison to the daily brutality of the whip and the all-too-common sexual abuse and rape. Both events molested not only the body but also the spirit—of the victim and his or her family.

Enduring the Whip: Facing Family Insult

Lucretia Alexander, interviewed at age eighty-nine in Little Rock, Arkansas, during the 1930s, possesses vivid memories of her overseer, Tom Phipps. "Mean! Like meanness! Mean a man as he could be! I've seen him take them down and whip them till the blood run out of them."[30]

Writing decades later, Missouri slave William Wells Brown still agonizes over his mother's whipping. One morning she arrived ten minutes late to work as a field hand. As soon as she reached the spot where they were working, the overseer commenced whipping her. She cried, "Oh! Pray! Oh! Pray!" Brown heard her voice, jumped up from the floor, and went to the door. Though the field was some distance from the cabin, he could hear every crack of the whip and every groan and cry of his poor mother. He remained at the door, not daring to venture any farther. "The cold chills ran over me, and I wept aloud. After given her ten lashes, the sound of the whip ceased, and I returned to my bed, and found no consolation in my tears. It was not yet daylight."[31] What sorrow and helplessness this son must have felt.

Pastor Pennington explains with clarity the family shame commensurate with whippings. When his father spoke up after being told to hush, his master pronounced that he would teach him who was master of his tongue and time, then beat him with twenty lashes. "Let me ask any one of Anglo-Saxon blood and spirit, how would you expect a *son* to feel at such a sight?"[32]

Pennington answers his own question. "This act created an open rupture with our family—each member felt the deep insult that had been inflicted upon our head; the spirit of the whole family was roused; we talked of it in our nightly gatherings, and showed it in our daily melancholy aspect." Detecting their melancholy, their master "commenced a series of tauntings, threatenings, and insinuations, with a view to crush the spirit of the whole family."[33]

Unconquered, it was at this time that Pennington, the future fugitive slave, made his fateful decision. "Although it was sometime after this event before I took the decisive step, yet in my mind and spirit, I never was a *slave* after it."[34]

Virginia and New York slave Austin Steward recounts how he felt observing a white man flogging his sister. Strong and athletic as he was, he could raise no hand in her defense, except at the peril of both their lives. God alone understood the conflict of feelings that he endured; God alone witnessed the tumult of his heart. "God knows that my will was good enough to have wrung his neck; or to have drained from his heartless system its last drop of blood! And yet I was obliged to turn a deaf ear to her cries for assistance, which to this day ring in my ears."[35]

Cracking the Whip: Counseling Courageous Waiting and Worship

As the previous vignettes demonstrate, the slaves did not lack for courage, just lack of opportunity to wisely unleash their courage. When Jacob Stroyer was a young man thinking of running away due to whippings, his parents counseled against any attempt which they thought ill-fated. In particular, Stroyer's wise father advised him to pray much over it and to wait for future freedom. When his father spoke of liberty, his words were of great comfort to Stroyer, and his heart swelled with the hope of a free future.

After a long night of family discussion, they knelt down in family prayer, as was their custom. "Father's prayer seemed more real to me that night than ever before, especially in the words, 'Lord, hasten the time when these children shall be their own free men and women.'"[36] The next morning, his father again charged him to carefully keep his advice.

In a day when ungoverned emotional outbursts dot and blot our society, such wise, prayer-saturated parental counsel is well worth conferring and heeding. Much violence could be abated and relational damage avoided by counsel that is timely—pointing others to a better future that is won by making wise decisions today that delay immediate gratification.

Courageous waiting was not the only creative response to the shame of whippings. Amazingly, slaves turned the crack of the whip into a call to worship!

One unnamed slave remembered, "Suddenly, I am jolted by a loud noise, sharp as a pistol shot. Turning I see that it was the crack of a large whip. Near the doorway and drums, a man is wielding the whip. Unnoticed by me, he has taken it from where it hung on the *poteau mitan*. Now he cracks it repeatedly while moving about near the drums. It dawns on me that this is a slaver's whip."[37] However, it is now a black worship leader who cracks the slaver's whip.

What had previously been an instrument of terror, the slaves boldly converted into an instrument of worship. The whip that had beaten them became the drumbeat of worship.

When the hand of a slave cracked the whip prior to worship, the slave ushered his fellow slaves into the unyielding pain of their daily experience. It opened their hearts to the places within them that were hemorrhaging as a result of the master's hand. In being opened to the deepest seat of their hurt, they were thus opened to the deepest seat of worship within them, the deepest place in which God could demonstrate his greatest healing power.

Barbara Holmes explains the healing power of this "inversion ritual." "The situations meant to divest them of their humanity strengthened communal ties and personal resolve. . . . Even the very tools of torture were divested of their power through inversion and sacred ritual." The sound of the whip is a "reminder that trouble doesn't last always. . . . In the hands of the delivered, the whip is an instrument of remembrance, used ritually now because God has been faithful."[38]

African Americans gave new meaning to an evil practice. They deconstructed its old message—"You are an animal to be thrashed!—and reconstructed a new message—"You are a child of God who worships your faithful God in loving community!"

What tool of abuse can we convert? What dashed dream can we invert?

Nothing that happens *to* us must *define* us. To keep past loss and trauma from defining us, we must *redefine* it. By the very act of creative, courageous redefinition, we reclaim our God-given authority over evil—just as our African American forebears did.

Resisting Rape and Lewd Advances: Longing for Someone to Confide In

The most horrific aspect of slave family life was the rape of black women by their masters and others. Marjorie Jones of Asheville, North Carolina, at age eighty-eight in the 1930s, reflects back on the immoral slave culture of the South. "Plenty of the colored women have children by the white men. She know better than to not do what he say. . . . Then they [masters] take them very same children what have they own blood and makes slaves out of them."[39]

Harriet Jacobs, the victim of constant lewd advances from her master, expresses her despondency because of the birth of a daughter. "When they told me my new-born babe was a girl, my heart was heavier than it had ever been before. Slavery is terrible for men; but it is far more terrible for women" who inevitably must endure licentious assaults on their virtue.[40]

Jacobs describes the onset of such onslaught in her own life. "But I now entered on my fifteenth year—a sad epoch in the life of a slave girl. My master began to whisper foul words in my ear. Young as I was, I could not remain ignorant of their import."[41] She felt that "every where the years bring to all enough of sin and sorrow; but in slavery the very dawn of life is darkened by these shadows."[42]

Her master, Dr. Flint, tried his utmost to corrupt the pure principles that her grandmother had instilled in her. He flooded her young mind with unclean images such as only a vile monster could imagine. She turned from him with disgust and hatred, but he was her master. She was compelled to live under the same roof with him—where she saw a man forty years her senior daily violating the most sacred commandment. He told her that she was his property and that she must be subject to his will in all things. "My soul revolted against the mean tyranny. But where could I turn for protection?"[43]

Jacobs longed for someone to confide in and "would have given the world to have laid my head on my grandmother's faithful bosom, and told her all my troubles." However, Dr. Flint swore that he would kill her if she was not as silent as the grave. Being very young, Jacobs felt "shamefaced about telling her [grandmother] such impure things, especially as I knew her to be very strict on such subjects."[44]

In desperation, and in hopes of causing her master to leave her alone, Jacobs had two children out of wedlock with a free African American. Her shame was profound. "With me the lamp of hope had gone out. The dream of my girlhood was over. I felt lonely and desolate."[45] On the brink of despair, she cries out, "Why does the slave ever love? Why allow the tendrils of the heart to twine around objects which may at any moment be wrenched away by the hand of violence?"[46]

What was she to do? And what are we to do when life kills the dreams we dream; what recourse do we have? We, like Jacobs, can turn to those who love us unconditionally. "Still I was not stripped of all. I still had my good grandmother, and my affectionate brother." Of him she writes, "When he put his arms round my neck, and looked into my eyes, as if to read there the troubles I dared not tell, I felt that I still had something to love."[47]

Her affectionate brother was a skillful spiritual friend. Consider his relational competencies: the appropriate use of physical touch, the meaningful application of eye contact, accurately reading body language, sensing unspoken pain, and communicating unconditional love. And consider the result of his ministry: the rebirth of love.

Confronting Shameful Behavior: It's Horrible to Sin and Wonderful to Forgive

Jacobs's saintly grandmother was also a skillful spiritual friend. Upon finally learning of Dr. Flint's advances, Jacobs's grandmother confronts him, telling him plainly what she thinks of his character. She then forcefully rebukes him: "I tell you what, Dr. Flint, you ain't got many more years to live, and you'd better be saying your prayers. It will take 'em all, and more too, to wash the dirt off your soul." When he responds by asking if she knows to whom she is speaking, she boldly replies, "Yes, I know very well who I am talking to." Flint then backs down, leaving the house in a great rage.[48]

The moment Flint leaves, Jacobs's eyes meet those of her grandmother. The anger is gone, replaced with tenderness. Jacobs expresses amazement that her infidelity did not lessen her grandmother's love for her. "She was always kind, always ready to sympathize with my troubles."[49]

Where Jacobs's brother illustrates expert sustaining, her grandmother exhibits adroit reconciling. She literally takes her life in her hands to stand toe-to-toe with a white master. Even when she rebukes him, she retains concern for him—for his eternal destiny. She also demonstrates the vital ability to shift quickly from righteous anger to tender compassion evidenced by her expression of unconditional love.

Jacobs's grandmother lived a remarkably consistent life as an ambassador of reconciliation. Years later, after Jacobs had escaped North to freedom, she received a letter from her grandmother announcing that Dr. Flint was dead, leaving behind a distressed family. "Poor old man! I hope he made his peace with God."[50]

Jacobs is dumbfounded. Remembering how Flint had defrauded her grandmother of the hard earnings she had loaned, how he had tried to trick her out of the freedom her mistress had promised her, and how he had persecuted her children and grandchildren, she writes, "She was a better Christian than I was, if she could entirely forgive him."[51]

As Christ's ambassador of reconciliation, Jacobs's grandmother teaches that there are no wrongs that grace cannot bury. There are no evils that are so odious that forgiveness cannot cover them.

Following the North Star

On a daily basis, African American slaves suffered vicious victimization. Yet they fought their way to personal and interpersonal victory. How? Their victory over daily abuse was found in Jesus through their daily, even moment-by-moment practice of their Christianity.

Charlotte Brooks explains it this way to Octavia Albert. "I tell you, child, religion is good anywhere—at the plowhandle, at the hoe-handle, anywhere. If you are filled with the love of my Jesus you are happy."[52]

For Brooks, her religion was no "pie in the sky, sweet by and by" pabulum. Listen to the next sentence out of her mouth: "Why, the best times I ever had was when I first got religion, and when old marster would put me in that old jail-house on his plantation all day Sunday."[53] Jailed physically on the Sabbath, spiritually every day was a free Sabbath, a day of jubilee for Brooks.

What mind-set enabled their inner freedom? Brooks and others understood that *trials make us God-dependent*. Speaking to her interviewer Albert—and now to us—she says, "You see, my child, God will take care of his people. He will hear us when we cry. True, we can't get any thing to eat sometimes, but trials make us pray more."[54]

The lack of trials can lead to a slackening of faith. As Brooks shared with Albert, "I sometimes think my people

95

don't pray like they used to in slavery. You know when any child of God gets trouble that's the time to try their faith. Since freedom it seems my people don't trust the Lord as they used to. 'Sin is growing bold, and religion is growing cold.'"[55]

While Brooks provides an African American slave sufferology explaining the source of *personal* victory, James Smith offers an African American slave sufferology explaining the source of *interpersonal* victory. He understands that lack of toil leaves us insensitive, while *trials make us other-sensitive*. "The life that is buoyant with hope, living perpetually in God's sunshine, realizing every thing that is sweet in existence, has little in it that touches the chord of sympathy. . . . Yet there are those in toils and trials that reap an experience that, when made known, unfold a lesson of admonition and comfort to others. . . . Yet, flowing out of this, we see the Guiding Hand preparing us for better things, moulding us for a better life."[56]

God's guiding hand leads us down the trail of trials where we not only see the light at the end of the tunnel but become a light unto the world. As Smith summarizes, "No mystery was ever deeper than that which shrouds the path by which men were led into bondage, and no system was ever more cruel and intolerant than that which inflicted stripes and burdens upon men, without cause, and deprived them of liberty and the right to life. Yet when we look back upon God's dealings with his early people, and see how they wrought in bondage and suffered in their wanderings from it, it reveals His power of bringing good out of evil, light out of darkness, and becomes a school of wisdom to the world."[57]

We follow the North Star guidance of the enslaved African Americans' response to their daily affliction by adhering to their slave sufferology. We walk their trail of trials by trusting Jesus day by day, clinging to the truth that trials make us *God-dependent* and *other-sensitive*.

Learning Together from Our Great Cloud of Witnesses

1. As a result of reading this chapter, how has your perspective on daily enslavement changed?
   a. Specifically, what has surprised you?
   b. What will you do with your new awareness?
2. Try to imagine the horrors of daily slave existence.
   a. What do you think they felt?
   b. How would you have ministered to them?
   c. How would you have confronted their abusers?
3. Whether married or single, how can you apply African American family cohesion to your family and personal relationships?
4. What hardships are you facing that seem to make it too hard to love? How can the witness of the African American slaves empower you to defeat that lie?
5. Whether married or single, how can you apply African American family character to your family and personal relationships?
6. Nothing happens to us that must define us. What loss or trauma could you redefine to reclaim your God-given victory and authority over evil?
7. As you walk the trail of trials in your life and as you journey with others, how can you apply two core themes in African American sufferology:
   a. Trials make us *God-dependent*?
   b. Trials make us *other-sensitive*?

5

Deep Is the Hunger

Emancipation from the Slavery of Sin

*After my conversion I was happy, and I spent a whole week
going over the community, telling everybody what happened to
me. I was the happiest person in the whole world. I have gone
on praising the Lord since that time.*

quoted in Clifton Johnson, *God Struck Me Dead*[1]

*It has always been an extremely strange fact that, both during
the days of slavery and during the first decade after the war,
so few individuals escaped complete demoralization and so
few developed neuroses. It seems to me that we shall find an
explanation in the [conversion] narratives that follow.*

Paul Radin, foreword to *God Struck Me Dead*[2]

On a quiet battlefield night at 10:00 p.m., the orderly
of Brigadier General Charles S. Russell came to Garland H. White's tent, woke him up, and handed him an order.

The bleary-eyed African American chaplain squinted as he read the handwritten missive.

"Rev. Garland H. White, Chaplain of the 28th U.S. Colored Troops: Sir:—You are requested to call upon Samuel Mapps, private in Co. D, 10th U.S.C.T, now under sentence of death, and now confined in the Bull-pen, to prepare him to meet his Savior. By official orders, Gen. C. S. Russell."[3]

Reverend White was an escaped slave now serving as chaplain of a black regiment from Indiana. He was one of only fourteen African American chaplains commissioned in the Union Army. Later he became a Methodist minister—his battlefield ministry providing hands-on training better than any seminary ever could.

Like white soldiers, some of the black troops ran afoul of military law. Private Mapps was convicted of trying to murder his captain. It was Chaplain White's responsibility to tell Mapps of his fate and to prepare him for death—and life after death.

Knowing this, White immediately puts pen to paper. "Gen. C. S. Russell, Commanding this Post: Sir:—I have the honor to acknowledge receipt of your order respecting my visiting Private Samuel Mapps, Co. D., 10th U.S.C.T. In reply, I would say I will comply promptly, and do all in my power to point him to the Lamb of God that taketh away the sins of the world. Yours, G. H. White, Chaplain."[4]

Loading the Conscience with Guilt: *It's Horrible to Sin*

Meeting Mapps at the prison, White inquires, "Well, my friend, how stands your case?" Mapps begins to plead his innocence and enters into a lengthy discussion of his trial. White promptly shifts the focus. "I came to see you, not to discuss a point of law as to the nature of your trial and decision, for that is all useless, my friend, and I must tell you that today, at 12 o'clock you will be executed—yes, you will be shot. Now, let you and myself kneel down and address a throne of grace where you may obtain mercy and help in time of need."[5]

No beating around the bush. No chit-chat. All business. All salvation business.

Mapps complies and prays fervently, after which White reads several passages of Scripture and sings a hymn, "Jesus, Lover of My Soul." Some historians falsely conclude that African Americans generally converted to a generic God. Nothing could be further from the truth in Mapps's case and in the vast majority of conversion narratives. Mapps and millions of others specifically converted to Christ based on a biblical understanding of who he is—Savior—and who they were—sinners.

White was not naive. Realizing that Scripture reading, prayer, and singing were only preparatory to personal response, he then "spent some time in reasoning upon what he thought about religion." To which Mapps candidly replies, "It is very good, and I wish I had it."[6] White next cites in plain terms the case of the dying thief who surrendered his life to Christ while hanging next to him on a cross. This gives Mapps hope. They then pray again, and Mapps seems relieved.

At this moment the wagon with a squad of guards appears before the door. Mapps does not see them; White does. While Mapps continues to pray fervently, an officer enters, announcing that the time has come "to repair to the place of execution."

White writes, "I told him to stand up and walk with me. I took his arm, and went out to the gate where thousands of persons had assembled to see him. He entered the wagon, and sat on his coffin. I then got in with him, took a seat by his side, and commenced talking and praying all the way."[7]

What a picture! We talk about climbing *in* the casket to enter another's agony. Chaplain White sits *on* the casket to share Mapps's dying experience.

Lightening the Conscience with Grace: *It's Wonderful to Be Forgiven*

Positioned in front of the firing squad, White asks Mapps one last time, "Do you feel that Jesus will be with you?"

"Yes," he replies.

"Do you put all your trust in him?"

"I do," is his answer.

"Do you believe that you will be saved?"

"I do; for though they may destroy my body, they cannot hurt my soul."

White then prays this benediction: "Eternal God, the Master of all the living and Judge of all the dead, we commit this our dying comrade into thy hands from whence he came. Now, O my Lord and my God, for thy Son's sake, receive his soul unto thyself in glory. Forgive, him—forgive, O thou Blessed Jesus, for thou didst die for all mankind, and bid them to come unto thee, and partake of everlasting life. Save him, Lord—save him, for none can save but thee, and thee alone. Amen. Good-by, my brother, good-by."[8]

The order is now given: "Ready! Aim! Fire!" All earthly life is extinguished. Eternal life commences.

White brilliantly, lovingly, and scripturally enlightened Mapps to see that *it's horrible to sin but wonderful to be forgiven*. Skillfully he wove together ancient Scripture and pressing need.

Private Mapps's response to Chaplain White's deathbed ministry offers one example of how God reconciled an African American to himself. Through interviews, slave narratives, autobiographies, and letters, we are fortunate to have a multitude of firsthand accounts of personal conversion experiences. These vivid descriptions help us understand the literal turning of heart (*metanoia*—repentance, change of mind), transformation of identity, and reorientation of personhood that occurred at the salvation of African Americans. We have much to learn from them about how to

102

witness to any oppressed and marginalized people, how to explain the need for a Savior, how to encourage repentance, how to offer the grace of forgiveness, and how to explain the changes that occur in one's nurture and nature at salvation.

Identifying with a Suffering Savior

It is important to ponder why African Americans turned to Christianity given the hypocritical religious culture of many of the Christian slave owners. In the midst of suffering through the ordeal of the sin of slavery, how were enslaved people saved by God from the slavery of sin?

Religious Roots: Common Threads in African Religion

Though overgeneralization can lead to oversimplification, to understand African conversions in America, it will be helpful to have some sense of "typical" religion in the Slave Coast of Africa. Religiously and spiritually, Africans were not a *tabula rasa*; they were not a blank slate. It is naive and unnecessary to argue otherwise. As with all uprooted people, African slaves brought their worldviews with them into the diaspora.[9]

Religion permeated every dimension of African life. They carried their spirituality everywhere, refusing to separate the supernatural from the natural, the sacred from the secular, or the spiritual from the profane.[10]

Albert Raboteau, perhaps the premier scholar of slave religion, detects common threads sewn from the disparate mosaic of ancient African worship. They believed in a High God, the Creator, who was somewhat remote and uninvolved, and in lower or lesser gods and ancestor-spirits who were actively and constantly concerned with the daily life of the individual and society.[11]

Dutch traveler William Bosman, describing Slave Coast religion, remarks that the Africans have an "idea of the True God and ascribe to him the Attributes of Almighty and Omnipresent." They believe that he created the universe, and therefore they vastly prefer him before their idol-gods.

"But yet they do not pray to him, or offer any Sacrifices to him; for which they give the following Reasons. God, they say, is too high exalted above us, and too great to condescend so much as to trouble himself or think of Mankind; Wherefore he commits the Government of the World to their Idols; to whom, as the second, third and fourth Persons distant in degree from God, and our appointed lawful Governours, we are obliged to apply ourselves. And in firm Belief of this Opinion they quietly continue."[12] No wonder their hunger was deep when years or decades later they encountered in Jesus Christ the true God who is both near and far, Shepherd and Sovereign, Groom and Creator.

Summarizing his findings, Raboteau concludes, "Widely shared by diverse West African societies were several fundamental beliefs concerning the relationship of the divine to the human; belief in a transcendent, benevolent God, creator and ultimate source of providence; belief in a number of immanent gods, to whom people must sacrifice in order to make life propitious; belief in the power of spirits animating things in nature to affect the welfare of people; belief in priests and others who were expert in practical knowledge of the gods and spirits; belief in spirit possession, in which gods, through their devotees, spoke to men."[13]

Again, is it any wonder, after their years of wandering, that they hungered for the true Mediator between God the Father and his wayward children? In Christ's incarnation, the remote God drew near. In Christ's crucifixion, the holy God was propitiated.

Religious Weeds: Common Threats to African American Acceptance of Christianity

Like any starving person, African Americans searched for sustenance. However, they often initially resisted Christian conversion because of the apparent contradiction between slave owners' professed beliefs and their brutal treatment of their slaves.

Francis Greene interviewed Mrs. Armaci Adams on June 25, 1937. Raised near Norfolk, Virginia, Adams speaks powerfully about the hypocrisy of her Christian master. "Marser daid now an' I ain't plannin' on meetin' him in heaven neither. He were too wicked. Marse was an' ole Methodist preacher an' de last time I seed 'im he was comin' in f'om a revival drunk."[14] Of course, not all white Christians were hypocritical. However, Adams's testimony is consistently repeated in the slave interviews and narratives.

Daniel Alexander Payne explains the inner battle that resulted from such hypocrisy. He was born to free parents in Charleston, South Carolina, in 1811. During his ordination in 1839, he describes the testing of faith caused by Christian duplicity. "The slaves are sensible of the oppression exercised by their masters; and they see these masters on the Lord's day worshiping in His holy Sanctuary. They hear their masters professing Christianity; they see their masters preaching the Gospel; they hear these masters praying in their families, and they know that oppression and slavery are inconsistent with the Christian religion; therefore they scoff at religion itself—mock their masters, and distrust both the goodness and justice of God. Yes, I have known them even to question His existence."[15]

Payne himself, though a minister, struggles to reconcile the ways of Christianity and the ways of Christians. When a new law forces him to stop teaching his fellow African Americans, he writes, "Then I began to question the existence of God, and to say: 'If he does exist, is he just? If so, why does he suffer one race to oppress and enslave another, to rob them by unrighteous enactments of rights, which they hold most dear and sacred?'"[16]

Religious Reconciliation: Common Themes in African American Acceptance of Christ

If spiritually famished African Americans were going to convert to Christianity, then they had to convert on the basis of Christ's life, death, and resurrection as revealed in the Bible, not on the basis of Christianity revealed in the lifestyles of the Christians they knew. Ironically, to find redemption in Christ, African Americans had to redeem Christianity as they saw it practiced. As Howard Thurman wrote, "By some amazing but vastly creative spiritual insight the slave undertook the redemption of a religion that the master had profaned in his midst."[17]

Christ's suffering for humanity's sin was the key that unlocked their hearts and enlightened their eyes. As Dale Andrews put it, "Jesus quickly became the ardent personification of the slaves' own suffering."[18] Their suffering at the hands of Christians caused them to identify with a suffering Savior who suffered at the hands of religious leaders.

At the same time, African American Christians clearly recognized and constantly emphasized the difference between Christ's sinlessness and their personal need for forgiveness from sin. The recurring theme of the conversion narratives was salvation from *sin*, not from suffering. Yes, Christ shared with them the experience of unjust suffering. But more importantly, they shared in Christ's suffering for *their* sins.

Pastor James W. C. Pennington, reflecting on his conversion, seamlessly expresses his understanding of suffering and of sin. Without minimizing for a moment the evils of slavery, he maximizes for all eternity the horrors of his own enslavement to sin and Satan:

I was a lost sinner and a slave to Satan; and soon I saw that I
must make another escape from another tyrant. I did not by
any means forget my fellow-bondmen, of whom I had been
sorrowing so deeply, and travailing in spirit so earnestly; but
I now saw that *while man had been injuring me, I had been
offending God*; and that *unless I ceased to offend him, I could
not expect to have his sympathy in my wrongs*; and moreover,
that I could not be instrumental in eliciting his powerful aid
in behalf of those for whom I mourned so deeply.[19]

Rejecting the "slaveholding gospel" of the institutional
church of that era, enslaved African Americans gave birth
to a regenerated Christianity that reflected fundamental
Christian doctrine while maintaining compatible African
traditions. Their cultural practice of biblical Christianity
provided the new orientation toward life that they needed
given their shattered external circumstances and sinful internal nature. It created the new narrative of *present resilience*
made possible by a Savior who suffered *with* them because
they were sinned against. It also created the new narrative
of *future hope* made possible by a Savior who suffered *for*
them because they were sinners.

Their focus offers an indispensable caution for all soul
physicians. While we are called to sustain and heal people
in their suffering, if we neglect to address their sinning, if
we fail to offer reconciling, then we may enable people to
become *more self-sufficient sinners*. Such one-sided ministry
attempts to empower people to live *this* life more success-
fully while giving them little incentive to turn to Christ's
resurrection power for eternal life later and abundant life
now. We should shudder at the thought.

Hooked in the Heart

How did specific individuals become aware of the horrors of their sin, repent, see the wonders of Christ's forgiv-

ing grace, and believe? One unnamed ex-enslaved person interviewed between 1927 and 1929 by Andrew Watson explains it brilliantly: "Before God can use a man, that man must be hooked in the heart. By this I mean that he has to feel converted. And once God stirs up a man's pure mind and makes him see the folly of his ways, he is wishing for God to take him and use him."[20]

God is the author of conversion, or better, the fisherman of conversion, fishing for men and women. The hook God casts enlightens the eyes, enabling converts to see the foolishness of their sinfulness.

Spiritually Blind: Unaware of My Spiritual Sickness

An African American minister from Tennessee known as Reverend H. offers an unflinching vision of spiritual blindness. "A sinner is dead, but we borned of God are live children. No dead child can understand the works of a live one, because he ain't had his eyes opened. This nobody can do but God. If God don't open your blinded eyes, cut loose your stammering tongue, unstop your deaf ears, and deliver your soul from death and hell, you are dead and can't understand the things we do. You got to be dug up, rooted and grounded, and buried in him."[21] Reverend H. understands that apart from God's spiritual laser surgery, sinners fail to perceive the cancer of sin spreading in their hearts.

Pastor Peter Randolph, looking back on his conversion experience, further enhances our image of spiritual sightlessness. "The eyes of my mind were open, and I saw things as I never did before. With my mind's eye, I could see my Redeemer hanging upon the cross for me. I wanted all the other slaves to see him thus, and feel as happy as I did. I used to talk to others, and tell them of the friend they would have in Jesus, and show them by my experience how I was brought to Christ, and felt his love within my heart—and love it was, in God's adapting himself to my capacity."[22]

In an age when we face the temptation to water down the gospel to make it more palatable to "seekers," we could learn much from Reverend H. and Pastor Randolph. As skillful soul physicians, their diagnosis was insightful and clear. They told themselves and their patients the truth about their spiritual condition. With their diagnosis came their sight-giving prescription. They opened blind eyes to see the Redeemer. Cataracts removed, sinners saw what a friend they had in Jesus. They understood that until we admit that we are sinners, we force away the friend of sinners, for he came to call not the righteous but sinners to repentance, for "It is not the healthy who need a doctor, but the sick" (Luke 5:31).

Spiritually Dead: Unable to Cure My Spiritual Sickness

In African American theology, just how sick are sinners? We're so spiritually sick that we're dead! God draws, enlightens, or hooks the sinner in order to load the conscience with the guilt of sin and with the hopelessness of any human remedy.

In 1750 Pastor George Liele founded what was perhaps the first African Baptist Church. Liele shares how God's Spirit brought him to an awareness of his utter inability to save himself. "I knew no other way at that time to hope for salvation but only in the performance of good works. About two years before the late war, the Rev. Mr. Matthew Moore, one Sabbath afternoon, as I stood with curiosity to hear him, he unfolded all my dark views, opened my best behavior and good works to me, which I thought I was to be saved by, and I was convinced that I was not in the way of heaven, but in the way to hell."[23]

Notice the specific "dark views" that Moore unfolded: "best behavior and good works." The darkest view and the evilest evil is the arrogant belief and self-sufficient confidence that we can save ourselves. African American soteriology (theology of salvation or doctrine of how a person becomes a Christian) clearly echoes the biblical truth that we are impotent to overcome the all-pervasive virus of sin. "For it is by grace you have been saved, through faith—and this not from yourselves, it is the gift of God—not by works, so that no one can boast" (Eph. 2:8–9).

Having been convicted by the Spirit through Moore's message, Liele does what millions of African Americans have done. He spends time "seeking the Lord." "This state I laboured under for the space of five or six months. The more I heard or read, the more I saw that I was condemned as a sinner before God; till at length I was brought to perceive that my life hung by a slender thread, and if it was the will of God to cut me off at that time, I was sure I should be found in hell, as sure as God was in Heaven."[24]

African Americans have not thought of salvation as a quick recitation of the "Sinner's Prayer." For African Americans, for the Puritans, and for much of church history, coming to the point of conversion has included wrestling with self and with God—wrestling to truly surrender to God. Reconciliation with God is not the "works" of praying a prayer; it is the heart surrendered honestly to God after realizing its helplessness apart from Christ.

Andrew Watson interviewed another unnamed African American convert in a vignette entitled "A Preacher from a God-fearing Plantation." This preacher tells of his conversion after seeking and finding the Lord. "I kept praying and seeking . . . I prayed and prayed, and my burden got heavier and heavier. . . . I told him [a friend] that I was sick and that I was not going to eat anymore until I had found God. . . . I realized my helplessness and surrendered. I cried out, 'Lord have mercy!'"[25]

Seeking was neither salvation by works nor lordship salvation. It was simply the acknowledgment that conversion was an internal battle in the heart and that it often took time for the human spirit to yield to God's Spirit. One African American seeker states it succinctly: "Hinder me not, ye must-loved sins, for I must not go with you!"[26] His words are reminiscent of the Puritans' concept of "over-much love"—the worldly idols of the heart that God must dislodge before faith can find a home.

The result of seeking the Lord is "coming through," which Liele's testimony portrays in all its beauty. Seeing his incapacity, perceiving his doom, Liele entrusts himself to Christ by faith for the salvation of his soul. "I saw my condemnation in my own heart, and I found no way wherein I could escape the damnation of hell, only through the merits of my dying Lord and Savior Jesus Christ; which caused me to make intercession with Christ, for the salvation of my poor immortal soul."[27]

Soul physicians of the unsaved soul apply African American "seeking" and "coming through" by helping seekers holistically. Salvation is a clear *rational* conviction, a decided *volitional* choice, and a committed *relational* surrender. The seeker says, "I am a sinner and I cannot save myself. Through the Spirit's enlightenment, I realize and confess my absolute powerlessness against sin (rational conviction). I repent of my sin and turn to God (volitional choice). I surrender my life to Christ as my forgiving Savior. I entrust my soul to God as my holy and loving Father (relational surrender)."

Leaping to My Feet

African American conversion accounts splendidly assimilate the "two sides" of reconciliation. First, God's Spirit hooks in the heart—he loads the conscience with guilt, bringing the sinner to the point of saying, "*It's horrible to sin.*" But the Spirit never leaves us there, as a Pharisee might—"They tie up heavy loads and put them on men's shoulders, but they themselves are not willing to lift a finger to move them" (Matt. 23:4). God's Spirit causes sinners to leap to their feet—he lightens the conscience with grace, bringing the sinner to the place of saying, *"It's wonderful to be forgiven!"*

Jarena Lee's conversion narrative displays the potency of these twin gospel themes. Born on February 11, 1783, in Cape May, New Jersey, Lee grew up with parents ignorant of the gospel. At age twenty-four she was converted under the preaching ministry of a Presbyterian missionary and of Reverend Richard Allen.

The year is 1804, and Lee undergoes deep conviction as she hears the Presbyterian minister preach from the Psalms: "Lord, I am vile, conceived in sin, born unholy and unclean. Sprung from man, whose guilty fall corrupts the race, and taints us all." In response, she writes, "This description of my condition struck me to the heart, and made me feel in some measure, the weight of my sins, and sinful nature. But not knowing how to run immediately to the Lord for help, I was driven of Satan, in the course of a few days, and tempted to destroy myself."[28]

In fact, Lee senses Satan suggesting to her that she drown herself in a brook near her home, in which there was a deep hole where the waters whirled about among the rocks. Resisting this temptation, her mind remains tortured. Continuing to search for peace, she finds only doubt.

Experienced soul physicians recognize her symptoms as the result of preaching guilt without grace. Guilt minus grace always equals Satan's condemning narrative of despair. The apostle Paul prescribes his antidote: "Where sin increased, grace increased all the more" (Rom. 5:20). Competent ambassadors of reconciliation know that *grace is God's prescription for our disgrace*.

Reverend Richard Allen was such a man. Attending an afternoon service at which Allen was preaching, Lee perceives in the center of her heart the sin of malice, *and* she receives the forgiveness of God. "That instant, it appeared to me as if a garment, which had entirely enveloped my whole person, even to my fingers' end, split at the crown of my head, and was stripped away from me, passing like a shadow from my sight—when the glory of God seemed to cover me instead."[29] As he did for Adam and Eve in the Garden, God covers Lee's shameful nakedness with garments purchased in and cleansed by blood.

Immediately she celebrates the wonders of forgiving grace. "That moment, though hundreds were present, I did leap to my feet and declare that God, for Christ's sake, had pardoned the sins of my soul. Great was the ecstasy of my mind, for I felt that not only the sin of *malice*, but all other sins were swept away together."[30]

Lee and a multitude of other African Americans depicted conversion using the biblical metaphor of rebirth. The result of being born again by forgiving grace was twofold: a new *nurture*, having a new relationship to God as beloved sons and daughters, and a new *nature*, having a new identity in Christ as cleansed saints.

Spiritual Aristocracy: Celebrating the New Nurture— Sons and Daughters Reconciled to God

Nancy Ambrose, a former slave and the grandmother of Howard Thurman, helps us understand the life-altering impact that the new nurture had on an enslaved people. Whenever Ambrose perceived that Thurman's sense of self suffered under the blows of a cruel world, she would tell him about the slave preacher from a neighboring plantation who would preach once or twice a year where she was enslaved. The preacher would always bring his message to its climax by dramatizing the crucifixion and resurrection of Christ. When the preacher had finished his sermon, he would pause and stare into each face. Then he would tell them as forcefully as he could: "You—you are not niggers! You—you are not slaves! You are God's children!"[31]

Today we cringe at the language. How do we think the slaves felt? But where sin abounds, grace super-abounds.

Where they were treated like slaves, God calls them children: sons and daughters.

What Ambrose retells is told repeatedly in the conversion narratives. Zilpha Elaw was born in freedom, around 1790, to parents who raised her in the vicinity of Philadelphia. Reflecting theologically and personally on her salvation, she notes, "I enjoyed richly the spirit of adoption: knowing myself to be an adopted child of divine love, I claimed God as my Father, and his Son Jesus as my dear friend, who adhered to me more faithfully in goodness than a brother: and with my blessed Savior, Redeemer, Intercessor, and Patron, I enjoyed a delightsome heavenly communion, such as the world has never conceived of."[32]

Elaw knew how to apply her reconciliation to her daily situation. While she was ministering in Southern slave states, she would often be distressed in her soul by Satan with the fear of being arrested and sold. Filled with terror, she would be tempted to cower in a corner. How did she respond? She reminded herself of who she was to Christ. Inquiring within herself, "from whence cometh all this fear?" she found her faith rallied and her confidence returned. "Get thee behind me Satan, for my Jesus hath made me free." Her fears instantly left her; she vacated her retired corner and came forth a daughter of the King, spiritual aristocracy, to minister in "the presence and power of the Lord."[33]

Elaw served as an artful soul physician of her own soul. She reminds us as doctors of the soul to point disenfranchised people back to the great Soul Physician—their Healer, their Father, their Husband.

Spiritual Nobility: Celebrating the New Nature—Saints Regenerated by God

African American saints also understood their sainthood. Another unnamed former slave interviewed by Watson succinctly captures their understanding. "Ever since the Lord freed my soul I have been a new man. I trust in him to fight my battles, for he is a captain who has never lost a battle or been confounded with cares."[34] This slave, like so many others, quotes from or alludes to numerous biblical passages, not the least of which is Colossians 3:10: "And have put on the new man, which is renewed in knowledge after the image of him that created him" (KJV).

African American believers rediscovered their pristine identity in Christ. They understood, therefore, that it was their spiritual act of worship to be faithful to that renewed and purified new creation in Christ. As they increasingly identified with their new nature in Christ as saints, they ceased to regard themselves as weak and feeble.[35]

Their practice was much better than what frequently occurs today. Far too often we treat Christians as if they are still non-Christians. We counsel them as if they are still old creations in self. We forget that they are no longer sinners in the hands of an angry God but are saints, sons, and daughters in the palms of a loving, all-powerful Father.

The new identity of African American Christians made a difference in how they overcame besetting sins. One former slave talks about her ongoing battle with worldly sins and the victory that she finds after her conversion. "After I passed through this experience I lost all worldly cares. The things I used to enjoy don't interest me now. I am a new creature in Jesus, the workmanship of his hand saved from the foundation of the world, I was a chosen vessel before the wind ever blew or before the sun ever shined."[36] Her identity as a new creation gave her victory over old temptations.

African Americans' new identity in Christ also redefined how they related to others who had sinned against them. Charlie had been enslaved by Mars' Bill, who kept his back constantly sore from whippings. He escaped, joined the "Yanks," and became a Christian. As a freeman, he met Mars' Bill again thirty years later.

As they recognize each other, Bill says, "Charlie, do you remember me lacerating your back?" When Charlie replies, "Yes, Mars'," Bill asks, "Have you forgiven me?"

By now, a large crowd has gathered, for Charlie and Bill are some distance apart and talking loudly. After Charlie shouts that he has indeed forgiven his old, cruel master, Bill is chagrined. "How can you forgive me, Charlie?"

Charlie's answer is instructive. "What is in me, though, is not in you. I used to drive you to church and peep through the door to see you all worship, but you ain't right yet, Marster. I love you as though you never hit me a lick, for the God I serve is a God of love."

Old Mars' Bill then moves toward Charlie, hand held out, tears streaming down his face. "I am sorry for what I did."

Charlie grants forgiveness. "That's all right, Marster. I done left the past behind me."

Charlie then testifies to Christ's redemptive power. "I had felt the power of God and tasted his love, and this had killed all the spirit of hate in my heart years before this happened. Whenever a man has been killed dead and made alive in Christ Jesus, he no longer feels like he did when he was a servant of the devil. Sin kills dead, but the spirit of God makes alive. I didn't know that such a change could be made, for in my younger days I used to be a hellcat."[37]

From hellcat to heaven's saint. From a hateful spirit to Christlike love. That's the power of our new identity in Christ.

Following the North Star

We follow the North Star guidance of converted African Americans by realizing that though many masters may lay claim on us, we are responsible to choose our ultimate master. "For a man is a slave to whatever has mastered him" (2 Peter 2:19). African American slaves understood that suffering can so weary us that we become easy prey to false masters. However, they also understood that we can only serve one master (see Matt. 6:24). Thus, converted African Americans refused to use the sin of slavery as an excuse to remain bound by the chains of sin.

We also learn from our forebears that once we surrender to the Master of the universe, we receive a new mission from our new Master. The conversion experience of a slave named Mary evokes that new mission. Mary reports God saying to her, "My little one, I am God Almighty. I have loved you from the foundation of the world, even with an everlasting love. I have freed your soul from hell, and you are free indeed. You are the light of the world. Go and tell the world what great things God has done for you and lo, I am with you always."[38] Her testimony reflects what we have heard mirrored repeatedly—that at salvation we are given a new nurture and a new nature.

Having confessed the horrors of their sin, African Americans celebrated the wonders of Christ's grace—a grace that not only forgives but also transforms, welcomes, and empowers. Their theology of salvation shows us how to put on our four salvation wedding gowns: Justification clothes us with our new pardon (forgiveness from sin); regeneration clothes us with our new purity (transformed into saints); reconciliation clothes us with our new parentage (welcomed home as God's children); and redemption clothes us with our new power (empowered to be victorious over sin).

Learning Together from Our Great Cloud of Witnesses

1. What can you apply to your ministry from Chaplain White's reconciling ministry to Private Mapps?
2. Hypocritical Christians were a common threat to African American acceptance of Christianity. Of

what hypocritical behaviors, attitudes, and styles of relating do Christians in our day need to repent?

3. African American converts understood that they needed Jesus because they were sinners, not simply because they were sufferers.

a. As we present the gospel today, do we present Jesus primarily as the healer of our hurts or as the Savior of our sins?

b. What can we learn from our African American forebears about biblically presenting Christ's gospel?

4. African American soul physicians taught that sinners were spiritually blind and dead.

a. How can we help seekers become aware of their spiritual sickness?

b. How can we help seekers see that they are unable to cure their spiritual sickness?

5. African American soul physicians understood salvation to be more than a quick praying of a "canned" prayer.

a. What do you think of their view of salvation?

b. Do you agree or disagree that salvation involves a rational conviction, a volitional choice, and a relational surrender? Why or why not?

6. African American soul physicians taught that grace super-abounds over guilt.

a. In our gospel presentations today, do we tend to highlight only guilt, only grace, or a "splendid assimilation" of both? What examples might you cite?

b. What happens in a person's soul if they hear of their guilt but not of Christ's grace?

7. African American converts celebrated the new nurture and the new nature.

a. How aware are *you* of your new relationship to Christ as a son or daughter of the King? How do you apply your spiritual aristocracy to your personal life and relationships?

b. How aware are *you* of your new identity in Christ as a saint cleansed by God? How do you apply your spiritual nobility in order to overcome sin and to forgive others?

6

The Old Ship of Zion

More Than Just Sunday Meetings

*We used to steal off to de woods and have church, like de
Spirit moved us—sing and pray to our own liking and soul
satisfaction—and we sure did have good meetings, honey—
baptize in de river, like God said. . . . We was quiet 'nuf so
de white folks didn't know we was dere, and what a glorious
time we did have in de Lord.*

quoted in James Mellon, *Bullwhip Days*[1]

*The church was a "Noah's Ark" that shielded one's life from
the rain. It was the "old ship of Zion" fully capable of sailing
the seas of life.*

Harold Carter, *The Prayer Tradition of Black People*[2]

When we last visited the "Preacher from a God-fearing
Plantation" in chapter 5, he had just cried out, "Lord
have mercy!" Having confessed his sin, he receives Christ's

grace. "That was the greatest joy of my life. Everything was joy and peace."[3]

But now what?

How did newly converted African American slaves grow in the grace and knowledge of the Lord Jesus Christ? How did they connect to one another in the body of Christ?

Our preacher friend offers us a glimpse. "Meetings back there meant more than they do now. Then everybody's heart was in tune, and when they called on God they made heaven ring. It was more than just Sunday meeting and then no more godliness for a week. They would steal off to the fields and in the thickets and there, with heads together around a kettle to deaden the sound, they called on God out of heavy hearts."[4]

In many creative ways, African Americans gathered for *worship* as prescribed in Hebrews 10:22–23: "Let us draw near to God with a sincere heart in full assurance of faith, having our hearts sprinkled to cleanse us from a guilty conscience and having our bodies washed with pure water. Let us hold unswervingly to the hope we profess, for he who promised is faithful."

African Americans also used many means to assemble for *fellowship* as counseled in Hebrews 10:24–25: "And let us consider how we may spur one another on toward love and good deeds. Let us not give up meeting together, as some are in the habit of doing, but let us encourage one another—and all the more as you see the Day approaching."

Because we all too easily abandon meeting together, we have much to learn from the high priority that African American believers placed on communal worship and fellowship. As Henry Mitchell put it in *Black Church Beginnings*,

> Their needs for guidance and comfort were immense. The awesome importance of this spiritual and emotional support can be seen by the fact that the time to engage in worship was taken from the already too-brief free times away from

field work. Work time already ran from sunup to sundown. Time for worship was taken from the brief period left for the personal needs of sanitation, sleep, food, and child rearing. This spiritual nurture must have been highly treasured indeed to motivate the sacrifice of such limited and precious free time.[5]

Cross-Cultural Ministry

We find evidence from long before multiculturalism became fashionable of mutual worship and fellowship among blacks and whites. Though this was not the norm, we glean cultural competencies from these historical occurrences in which African American believers met their need for spiritual nurture *with* Caucasian believers.

Pulpit Ministry: Expounding the Scriptures Relevantly

In chapter 3 we met Solomon Northup—born free in Rhode Island, then kidnapped and enslaved in Louisiana from age thirty-three to forty-five. Though recognizing the inconsistency of his master, William Ford, a slave-owning Baptist preacher, Northup still notes, "It is but simple justice to him when I say, in my opinion, there never was a more kind, noble, candid, Christian man than William Ford."[6]

Northup details Ford's pastoral ministry to his slaves. "We usually spent our Sabbaths at the opening, on which days our master would gather all his slaves about him, and read and expound the Scriptures. He sought to inculcate in our minds feelings of kindness towards each other, of dependence upon God—setting forth the rewards promised unto those who lead an upright and prayerful life. . . . He spoke of the loving kindness of the Creator, and of the life that is to come."[7]

Pastor Ford related truth to life cross-culturally. Emphasizing the two great commandments, he taught African

American believers how to love one another and how to love God. Ford highlighted the character of God and the hope of heaven. Northup even recounts how Ford's preaching led to the conviction and salvation of another slave, Sam.

Personal Ministry: Encouraging the Saints Relationally

Ford coupled his pulpit ministry with his personal ministry. Speaking of his time with Pastor Ford, Northup notes, "That little paradise in the Great Pine Woods was the oasis in the desert, towards which my heart turned lovingly, during many years of bondage."[8] Perhaps we find it hard to imagine, but even in enslavement, even through ministry offered by a Baptist slave-owner, Northup experienced the ark of safety that is the "old ship of Zion."

What was it about Ford's life and ministry that so affected Northup? During an extended trip by horseback and on foot to the Bayou, Ford "said many kind and cheering things to me on the way."[9] Ford knew how to speak life-giving words (see Prov. 18:21).

He also understood how to connect scriptural narratives to Northup's life narrative. "The goodness of God was manifest, he declared, in my miraculous escape from the swamp. As Daniel came forth unharmed from the den of lions, and as Jonah had been preserved in the whale's belly, even so had I been delivered from evil by the Almighty."[10]

In exemplary fashion, Ford also used probing soul questions and spiritual conversations as he ministered to Northup. "He interrogated me in regard to the various fears and emotions I had experienced during the day and night, and if I had felt, at any time, a desire to pray. I felt forsaken of the whole world, I answered him, and was praying mentally all the while."[11]

Ford then artistically wove together a biblical sufferology that snugly fit Northup's unique situation. "At such times, said he, the heart of man turns instinctively towards his

Maker. In prosperity, and when there is nothing to injure or make him afraid, he remembers Him not, and is ready to defy Him; but place him in the midst of dangers, cut him off from human aid, let the grave open before him—then it is, in the time of his tribulation, that the scoffer and unbelieving man turns to God for help, feeling there is no other hope, or refuge, or safety, save in His protecting arm."[12]

Northup testifies to Ford's relational competence. "So did that benignant man speak to me of this life and of the life hereafter; of the goodness and power of God, and of the vanity of earthly things, as we journeyed along the solitary road towards Bayou Boeuf."[13] According to Northup's assessment, Ford showed that it is impossible to convince someone of God's goodness unless we first reflect God's goodness.

Corporate Worship: Enjoying the Spirit Interracially

James Smith, enslaved in Northern Neck, Virginia, shares a remarkable depiction of worship during an extended revival. Many souls, both whites and blacks, were converted every night. The whites occupied the part next to the altar, while the blacks took the part assigned them next to the door, where they held a protracted meeting among themselves. "Sometimes, while we were praying, the white people would be singing, and when we were singing, they would be praying; each gave full vent to their feelings, yet there was no discord or interruption with the two services."[14]

Though they were imperfectly integrated, clearly the Spirit was shepherding a movement toward mutual acceptance of cultural differences in the name of Christian salvation and growth. Given that in our day Sunday mornings are still the most segregated hours in American life, we would do well to replicate these believers' support for one another's unique worship styles by participating together in cross-cultural church life.

Lest we assume that these few examples were standard, John Brown, born in Talledega County, Alabama, portrays how sporadic such joint worship truly was. "Sunday was a great day around the plantation. The fields was forgotten, the light chores was hurried through, and everybody got ready for the church meeting. It was out of the doors, in the yard fronting the big lot where the Browns all lived. Master John's wife would start the meeting with a prayer and then would come the singing—the old timey songs. But the white folks on the next plantation would lick their slaves for trying to do like we did. No praying there, and no singing."[15]

On one plantation, corporate worship. On the very next, whippings for praying and singing. Such inconsistency, along with twisted sermons, differences in worship styles, and in many cases outright illegality, was what led enslaved African American Christians to birth the "Invisible Institution."

The Invisible Institution

Historians investigating African American religious history have labeled the secretive slave worship services the "Invisible Institution" because much of it was invisible to the eyes of their masters. "In their cabins, woods, thickets, hollows, and brush arbors (shelter of cut branches also called 'hush harbors') throughout the South, slaves held their own religious meetings where they interpreted Christianity according to their experience, applying the stories and symbols of the Bible to make sense out of their lives."[16]

Legal Mandates: Restricting Worship Judicially

Many converted slaves had no choice but to worship stealthily. For instance, in 1800, South Carolina's legislature restricted black religious services. They forbade them "even in company with white persons to meet together and assemble for the purpose of . . . religious worship, either before the rising of the sun or after the going down of the same."[17]

An 1831 Mississippi court ruling outlawed any black from preaching. "It is unlawful for any slave, free Negro, or mulatto to preach the gospel under pain of receiving thirty-nine lashes upon the naked back of the . . . preacher."[18]

Various reasons have been suggested for such laws. Peter Kalm, a Swedish traveler in America from 1748 to 1750, offers his firsthand explanation. He first bemoans the fact that "the masters of these Negroes in most of the English colonies take little care of their spiritual welfare, and let them live on in their Pagan darkness." He next offers their warped reasoning. "There are even some, who would be very ill pleased at, and would by all means hinder their Negroes from being instructed in the doctrines of Christianity; to this they are partly led by the conceit of its being shameful, to have a spiritual brother or sister among so despicable a people; partly by thinking that they should not be able to keep their Negroes so meanly afterwards; and partly through fear of the Negroes growing too proud, on seeing themselves upon a level with their masters in religious matters."[19]

Arthur Greene, enslaved in Petersburg, Virginia, depicts the secret meetings he experienced along with the punishment if caught. "Well—er talkin' 'bout de church in dem days, we po' colored people ain' had none lak you have now. We jes made er bush arbor by cuttin' bushes dat was full of green leaves an' puttin' 'em on top of four poles reachin' from pole to pole. Den sometimes we'd have dem bushes put roun' to kiver de sides an' back from der bottom to der top. All us got together in dis arbor fer de meetin.' Sometimes de paterrollers would ketch 'em den dey whupped all dat had no pass."[20]

Worship and fellowship were so important to believing slaves and so meaningful when they occurred that the slaves could easily forget themselves, putting themselves at risk. "One night dar was er private meetin' gwine on in a cabin.

De slaves was so busy singin' an' prayin,' fergot all 'bout dem old white folks. All of a sudden dar was a knock at de do'. Setch a scatterin' you neber seed."[21]

Pulpit Ministry: Twisting the Scriptures Culturally

As the ex-slaves explain it in their own words, twisted white preaching was another reason for their clandestine meetings. Lucretia Alexander of Little Rock, Arkansas, remembers the sermons the slaves endured. "The preacher came and preached to them in their quarters. He'd just say, 'Serve your masters. Don't steal your master's turkey. Don't steal your master's chickens. Don't steal your master's hogs. Don't steal your master's meat. Do whatsomeever your master tell you to do.' Same old thing all the time."[22]

Alexander further explains that because of such preaching, "My father would have church in dwelling houses and they had to whisper. . . . That would be when they would want a real meetin' with some real preachin'. . . . They used to sing their songs in a whisper and pray in a whisper. There was a prayer-meeting from house to house once or twice—once or twice a week."[23]

Converted slave Frank Roberson paraphrases the style of preaching to which white preachers constantly subjected slaves: "You slaves will go to heaven if you are good, but don't ever think that you will be close to your mistress and master. No! No! There will be a wall between you; but there will be holes in it that will permit you to look out and see your mistress when she passes by. If you want to sit behind this wall, you must do the language of the text 'Obey your masters.'"[24]

Congregational Gatherings: Slipping In and Stealing Away

In order to worship freely, Christian slaves would either slip into a home or steal away to the woods. Sister Robinson of Hampton, Virginia, pictures their effusive joy and their shrewd methods. "Wen dey had these [meetings] the men an' women 'ud come slippin' in fust one den 'nothah until they wuz all in. Then dey'd turn a big pot down at the do' sill so's ta catch the noise wen they shouted an' hallahed. I remembah one 'oman had a big mouf. She uster put huh haid raight in the pot an' jes yell an' hollah an' you couldn't heah huh more'n three foot away."[25]

Numerous depictions of such clandestine worship include illustrations of praying and singing into an iron pot. Historian George Rawick believes that it was less about muffling sound and more about symbolism. It was an image of protection. God, the Potter, miraculously protected those using the pot. Rawick believes it also was a metaphor for the pot that carries life-giving water, and thus it represented God the Thirst Quencher.[26]

Likely, it served multiple functions. The pot was a cunning human mechanism to shelter slaves from oppression. And it was also a potent spiritual portrayal of God, their shelter from the storm.

Cornelius Garner of Norfolk, Virginia, pictures slipping off to the woods, the reason for it, and the nature of slave worship. "De churches whar we went to serve God was 'Pisipal, Catholick, Presberteriens, de same as marster's church only we was off to usselves in a little log cabin way in de woods. De preaching us got 'twon't nothing much. Dat ole white preacher jest was telling us slaves to be good to our marsters. We ain't keer'd a bit 'bout dat stuff he was telling us 'cause we wanted to sing, pray, and serve God in our own way. You see, 'ligion needs a little motion—specially if you gwine feel de Spirret."[27]

One wonders how much of today's segregated worship could be mitigated if we all worked harder to appreciate culturally different ways to experience God. Far too often we pigeonhole certain methods as "rational" and others as "emotional," when in truth God wants us to worship him in spirit and in truth (John 4:24). He commands us to worship him holistically—with all our heart, soul, mind, emotions, and strength (body) (Matt. 22:37).

Experiencing Together the Presence and Power of God

What actually occurred during these covert meetings to make them so fruitful? Pastor Peter Randolph provides the details we seek. "Not being allowed to hold meetings on the plantation, the slaves assemble in the swamps, out of reach of the patrols. They have an understanding among themselves as to the time and place of getting together. This is often done by the first one arriving breaking boughs from the trees, and bending them in the direction of the selected spot."[28]

Imagine the anticipation. On the sly, passing the word: "Psst. We're meeting after sundown tonight. We're going to worship and fellowship!"

Visualize the scene. They're trekking through the woods to the swamplands of Prince George County, Virginia. "Shhh. It's a secret," mother undertones to daughter, with a sly smile and a knowing look. "We're on an adventure, in the grandest adventure of them all," father whispers to son, eyes locking and boldness oozing between them.

For them, worship and fellowship were worth any risk and were approached with tremendous expectancy. Does our commitment to and preparation for gathering together hold a candle to theirs?

Mutual Ministry: First-Century Christianity in Nineteenth-Century America

Once there, then what? Randolph explains, "Arrangements are then made for conducting the exercises. They first ask each other how they feel, the state of their minds, etc. The male members then select a certain space, in separate groups, for

their division of the meeting. Preaching in order by the brethren; then praying and singing all around, until they generally
feel quite happy. The speaker usually commences by calling
himself unworthy, and talks very slowly, until feeling the spirit,
he grows excited, and in a short time, there fall to the ground
twenty or thirty men and women under its influence."[29]

Sound familiar? Their experience sounds like Acts 2:42,
44–47: "They devoted themselves to the apostles' teaching and to the fellowship, to the breaking of bread and to
prayer. . . . All the believers were together and had everything in common. Selling their possessions and goods, they
gave to anyone as he had need. Every day they continued
to meet together in the temple courts. They broke bread in
their homes and ate together with glad and sincere hearts,
praising God and enjoying the favor of all the people."

In Randolph's gathering, they *organized the organism*
("made arrangements for conducting the exercises"). That
is, though valuing spontaneity and the leading of the Spirit,
they also treasured purposeful planning.

They *sustained and healed* ("ask each other how they feel, the
state of their minds"). Given the hardships and hard times, we
might imagine quite the lengthy spiritual conversations—much
different than our typical Sunday morning greetings. We say,
"Hello. How are you?" and without waiting for a response, we
move on to our next target. Imagine, instead, if we *really* asked
how others feel—exploring one another's emotional life—on
Sunday morning, in church! Imagine also if we *truly* probed
one another's state of mind—dealing with each other's thought
life and mental well-being—on Sunday morning, in church!

They *enjoyed small group fellowship* ("then select a certain
space, in separate groups, for their division of the meeting").
So much for the false accusation sometimes lobbed that
small groups are a modern or postmodern invention, bringing secular sociology into the church.

They were *edified by the preached Word* ("preaching in
order by the brethren"). Later we'll see that they would enjoy

testifying by many members, exhorting by some members, and preaching by one primary, called-out leader.

They *engaged in hearing from God and talking to God* ("then praying and singing all around"). They prayed and praised, listened and spoke.

The result? They felt uplifted and experienced the presence and power of God. Together, in the midst of their suffering, they built their ark of safety.

Future Memory: Eternal Christianity in Nineteenth-Century America

But that's not all. Randolph elaborates on the inner condition and the interpersonal consolation as they part. "The slave forgets all his suffering, except to remind others of the trials during the past week, exclaiming, 'Thank God, I shall not live here always!' Then they pass from one to another, shaking hands, bidding each other farewell, promising, should they meet no more on earth, to strive to meet in heaven, where all is joy, happiness and liberty. As they separate, they sing a parting hymn of praise."[30]

What an interesting phrase. How can people simultaneously *forget* their *suffering* and *remind* others of their *trials*? Actually, it's quite brilliant. We can't truly forget the evils we have suffered. Nor should we try. Instead, we should remind ourselves and others of our trials, *but* we must *remember the past while remembering the future*. "Thank God, I shall not live here always!"

What perfect "balance." Don't deny the past. Do dialogue and trialogue (you, your friend, and God in a three-way spiritual conversation) about the past *in light of* the future—eternity, heaven.

Their grip on this world was slack—"Ashes to ashes. Dust to dust. Here today. Gone tomorrow. Like a vapor. Like a fading flower and withering grass."

Their grip on the next world was taut—"Into thy hands I commend my spirit. Even so, come quickly, Lord Jesus. Maranatha."

The result? They are deeply *connected* with *one another*—passing from one another, shaking hands, bidding farewell, promising to meet again someday, somewhere. They are genuinely *content* within their *own souls*—knowing joy, happiness, and liberty, though outwardly experiencing the opposites. They are profoundly *communing* with *Christ*—singing a parting hymn of praise, certainly not for their circumstances, definitely in spite of their situations, but preeminently because of who God is.

How amazing it would be to leave every worship and fellowship service like enslaved African American believers did. If they could, given their lot in life, why can't we?

Everybody Could Be a Somebody

In the Invisible Institution, everybody could be a somebody because they could participate as the Spirit moved them.[31] One ex-slave remembers four main movements in the Invisible Institution's symphony—preaching, praying, singing, and shouting—all of which allowed for Spirit-led participation. "They'd preach and pray and sing—shout too. I heard them git up with a powerful force of the spirit, clappin' they hands and walkin' round the place. They'd shout, 'I got the glory . . . in my soul.' I seen some powerful figurations of the spirit in them day."[32]

Sharing the Word: Mentoring, Testifying, Exhorting, and Preaching

In the Invisible Institution, there were numerous levels of ministry through which believers could share the Word with one another. At a mutual lay level, the slaves shared one-on-

133

one spiritual friendships, exemplified in Randolph's account of asking each other about their feelings and thoughts.

African Americans also provided one-on-one mentoring before, during, and after gatherings. Older males, often called "watchmen," and older females, often called "mothers," "spiritual mothers," or dispensers of "mother wit," were important spiritual guides in the Invisible Institution. Frederick Douglass, for example, frequently sought the counsel of Uncle Charles Lawson, calling him his "spiritual father" and "chief instructor in religious matters."[33]

Jane Lee, or "Aunt Jane," served as Charlotte Brooks's spiritual director. Aunt Jane first served the crucial role of witnessing concerning salvation. Brooks had no one to tell her anything about repentance until Aunt Jane talked to her. "It was dark when I left Aunt Jane; but before I left her house she prayed and sang, and it made me feel glad to hear her pray and sing. It made me think of my old Virginia home and my mother. She sang, 'Guide me, O thou great Jehovah, Pilgrim through this barren land.' . . . I finally got religion, and it was Aunt Jane's praying and singing them old Virginia hymns that helped me so much."[34]

Aunt Jane then discipled Brooks, secretly slipping away at night. "She would hold prayer-meeting in my house whenever she would come to see me. . . . She said people must give their hearts to God, to love him and keep his commandments; and we believed what she said."[35]

So thorough was her discipleship that the disciple (Brooks) became like the discipler (Aunt Jane), emulating her evangelistic model. "I thank the Lord Aunt Jane Lee lived by me. She helped me to make my peace with the Lord. O, the day I was converted! It seemed to me it was a paradise here below! It looked like I wanted nothing any more. Jesus was so sweet to my soul! Aunt Jane used to sing, 'Jesus! the name that charms our fears.' That hymn just suited my case. Sometimes I felt like preaching myself. It seemed I wanted to ask everybody if they loved Jesus when I first got converted."[36]

Parents were primary mentors, especially teaching children how to live in the household of God. One South Carolina African American notes, "My daddy teach we how to sing, teach we how to shout, teach we how to go fast, teach we how to go slow. And then going to meeting, or later going to church, he'll teach we how to behave yourself when we get out to different places before we leave home."[37]

Every believer had the opportunity, as led by the Spirit, to testify. In testifying, men and women told the stories of their encounters with God. In narrative fashion, they articulated common spiritual realities, provided proverbial wisdom for life's journey, shared advice concerning the normal problems of life, offered consolation, and, when necessary, confronted the community.[38]

Conversion and baptism were special times for such testifying, as Isaiah Jeffries's recollection of his mother's witness bears out. "When I got to be a big boy, my Ma got religion at de Camp meeting at El-Bethel. She shouted and sung fer three days, going all over de plantation and de neighboring ones, inviting her friends to see her baptized. . . . She went around to all de people dat she had done wrong and begged dere forgiveness. She sent fer dem dat had wronged her, and told dem dat she was born again and a new woman, and dat she would forgive them."[39]

The slaves called the next "level" of speaking ministry "exhorting." Exhorters ranged from unofficial prayer leaders on the plantation to laypeople licensed to deliver short sermons, often traveling from one plantation to another.

James Smith shares about his exhorting ministry. "Soon after I was converted I commenced holding meetings among the people, and it was not long before my fame began to spread as an exhorter. I was very zealous, so much so that I used to hold meetings all night, especially if there were any concerned about their immortal souls."[40]

All of these ministries develop the premise driving *Beyond the Suffering*: Christ's commission for the church has always emphasized the creation of an atmosphere in which mutual lay spiritual friendship and spiritual mentoring would be common features of our shared life together.

Of course, none of this suggests that it is Christ's plan for his church to be without called-out leaders—pastors, shepherds, soul physicians. The Invisible Institution maintained a remarkable equilibrium between lay and pastoral ministry.

W. E. B. Du Bois submits a compelling portrait of the African American plantation pastor. "He early appeared on the plantation and found his function as the healer of the sick, the interpreter of the Unknown, the comforter of the sorrowing, the supernatural avenger of wrong, and the one who rudely but picturesquely expressed the longing, disappointment, and resentment of a stolen and oppressed people. Thus, as bard, physician, judge, and priest, within the narrow limits allowed by the slave system, rose the Negro preacher, and under him the first Afro-American institution, the Negro church."[41]

Robert Anderson offers his firsthand account of these soul healers. "Our preachers were usually plantation folks just like the rest of us. Some man who had a little education and had been taught something about the Bible would be our preacher."[42]

Their preaching was hope-giving. Charles Davenport remembers one particular sermon. "All us had was church meetin's in arbors out in de woods. De preachers would exhort us dat us was de chillen o' Israel in de wilderness an' de Lord done sent us to take dis land o' milk and honey."[43] Though living in "Egypt," African American Christians clung tenaciously to the hope of exodus.

Some of the slave preachers were illiterate but had managed to memorize large sections of Scripture.[44] A white listener named Luther recounts the spellbinding preaching on Jonah 1:6 of the black Methodist preacher Isaac Cook of South Carolina. "His description of a sinner in the ark of carnal security, afloat on the storm-tossed ocean of life, in

danger of going to the bottom, and yet asleep and uncon-
scious of peril, was to my boyish mind indescribably awful.
I left the place where that sermon was preached under an
irresistible conviction that I had listened to a man of God,
and that the best thing I could do for myself was to take
warning, and seek for refuge in Christ as I had been so faithfully exhorted to do."[45]

These African American shepherds knew their people
well. One white missionary to the slaves observed that when
an African American was "in the pulpit there is a wonderful
sympathy between the speaker and the audience."[46] There
was such an intense relationship between the preacher and
the people that as the preacher fed the people, he fed off
of their responsive engagement. Thus, even while "simply
listening" to the Word, the people were active participants
fulfilling an important role.

In sharing the Word, the Invisible Institution modeled
for us a host of ways to engage every believer. No one came
or left feeling like they were simply a spectator. Everyone
came with anticipation, participated with meaning, and left
encouraged that God had used them to encourage others.

Praising the Lord: Praying, Singing, and Shouting

When sharing the Word, African American believers *heard
from* the Lord *through* one another. In praising the Lord, they
spoke to the Lord *with* one another.

Praying, singing, and shouting were not items on their
to-do list, nor were they lines on an "order of worship" in
a church bulletin. They were opportunities to encounter
God together. As with sharing the Word, praising the Lord
provided the occasion for everyone to participate in the
life of the congregation at a significant level of personal and
communal involvement.[47]

Ex-slave Alice Sewell depicts the Invisible Institution as
seamlessly intertwining praying, singing, communal ministry,

and sustaining empathy. "We used to slip off in de woods in de old slave days on Sunday evening way down in de swamps to sing and pray to our own liking. We prayed for dis day of freedom. We come from four and five miles to pray together to God dat if we don't live to see it, to please let our chillen live to see a better day and be free, so dat they can give honest and fair service to de Lord and all mankind everywhere."[48]

Sewell's vignette contains precise theology—prayer requests were for God's glory ("give honest and fair service to de Lord") and for the good of others ("and all mankind everywhere"). It also speaks of personal commitment—walking five miles for prayer meeting!

The slave spirituals, as we will see in greater detail in the next chapter, were a communal enterprise. Jonas Bost of Newtown, North Carolina, reminisces about one such song. "I remember one old song we used to sing when we meet down in the woods back of the barn. . . .

> Oh, Mother lets go down, lets go down, lets go
>   down, lets go down.
> Oh, Mother lets go down, down in the valley to pray.
> As I went down in the valley to pray,
> Studying about that good ole way,
> Who shall wear that starry crown?
> Good Lord, show me the way."[49]

Most significant is his concluding memory. "Then the other part was just like that except it said 'Father' instead of 'Mother,' and then 'Sister' and then 'Brother.'"[50] They mutually cared for one another as an extended family with concern for every member, whether father, mother, sister, or brother.

The slaves sometimes used the word "shouting" for the excited utterances when deep in worship. At other times it referred to the responses made to the testifier, exhorter, or preacher: "Preach it!" "Come on now, sister!" "Bring it home, brother!" Still other times it was a technical term for the "ring shout."

Barbara Holmes believes that "shout" is a Gullah dialect word of Afro-Arabic origin from *saut*, meaning a fervent dance.[51] That would certainly fit the cultural context of the ring shout or ring dance as it was often practiced in the Invisible Institution.

The ring shout involved a singer who felt moved by the Spirit stepping into the middle of the gathering. The community of worshipers then encircled the singer, chanting, dancing, and clapping. The community provided the bass beat which the singer used to create his or her unique lyrics, appropriate for the specific situation faced by the congregation.[52] The outer circle symbolized the interconnected, communal culture supporting the surrounded singer. Thus, together, they co-created a sustaining, healing narrative.

James Smith vividly pictures the ring shout for us. "The way in which we worshiped is almost indescribable. The singing was accompanied by a certain ecstasy of motion, clapping of hands, tossing of heads, which would continue without cessation about half an hour; one would lead off in a kind of recitative style, others joining in the chorus. The old house partook of the ecstasy; it rang with their jubilant shouts, and shook in all its joints."[53]

The slaves often transformed their sung narrative into a dramatic acted narrative. By combining singing, moving, dancing, and marching, the community became participants in historic deliverance events such as the children of Israel crossing the Red Sea or Joshua's army marching around the walls of Jericho.[54]

With their bodies chained in enslavement, their spirits soared like eagles through the Holy Spirit and through the communal spirit of joint worship. Though not everyone reading these words might feel comfortable worshiping in their style, each of us can ponder how, in the culture of our worship community, we might more effectively participate in shared worship in Spirit and in truth.

Following the North Star

We follow the North Star guidance of African American church life by *combining* worship and fellowship. Too often today we pit against each other loving God and loving others. On the one hand we have the "know God, know your Bible, worship deeply" crusaders. On the other hand we find the "know one another, know mutual ministry, fellowship deeply" champions.

This all seems a tad odd, given Christ's words in Matthew 22:35–40, in which he binds the two greatest commandments into one—love God, and love your neighbor as yourself. "All the Law and the Prophets hang on these two commandments" (Matt. 22:40).

The "church wars" that we tolerate could end if we refused to give credence to this false dichotomy between reaching upward to God and reaching outward to one another. Neither "group" is more spiritual than the other. Our African American forebears demonstrate that true spirituality joins these two beams like a truss.

We also follow the North Star guidance of African American church life by *combining* pastoral ministry and lay ministry. Again, it is unfortunate that today we often pit people against pastors. One group seems to imply that "we don't need trained and ordained ministers; all we need is every member a minister." The other group seems to communicate that "a hospital visit only counts if the pastor does it."

This all seems a little unusual, given Paul's words in Ephesians 4:11–16, in which he connects two great commissions—pastors as equipped equippers, and laypeople as equipped ministers. Christ gave "some to be pastors and teachers, to prepare God's people for works of service, so that the body of Christ may be built up" (Eph. 4:11–12).

The animosity between people and pastors, which we too easily accept, could end if we refused to accept this false division between pastors as "player-coaches" and people as "active participants." Our African American forebears demonstrate that true ministry respects the unique callings and roles of people and pastors.

Additionally, we follow the North Star guidance of African American church life by *combining* the pulpit ministry of the Word and the personal ministry of the Word. In our times, we often pit the pastor's pulpit message against the people's over-the-backyard-fence message. One group tends to communicate, "Nothing but the pulpit!" The other group tends to convey, "Nothing but helping one another!"

This all seems a bit strange given the New Testament church's blended practice of both, seen throughout the book of Acts. "They devoted themselves to the apostles' teaching and to the fellowship" (Acts 2:42).

The antagonism that we allow between pulpit and pew could end if we refused to allow the false distinction between God's Word preached to the crowd by the pastor and God's Word shared in small groups and one-on-one by laypeople. Our African American forebears demonstrate the symmetry that results when we merge pulpit and pew, crowd and small group, the many and the one.

Learning Together from Our Great Cloud of Witnesses

1. "Meetings back there meant more than they do now. Then everybody's heart was in tune, and when they called on God they made heaven ring."
   a. In what ways does your worship experience already mirror theirs?

b. What could make this statement truer in your worship experience today?

2. Pastor William Ford demonstrated cross-cultural competency in his pulpit and personal ministry. What specific aspects of his ministry could you emulate today?

3. James Smith and John Brown pictured harmonious interracial worship.

   a. What needs to happen for this to occur in greater quality and quantity today?

   b. How would God be glorified and the gospel be spread if this did occur more frequently?

4. How could you step out of your comfort zone a bit to appreciate, experience, and enjoy worship in a culturally different way than what you now experience?

5. Concerning worship preparation and sacrifice:

   a. How would you compare your preparations for worship to the preparations made by African American believers in the Invisible Institution?

   b. How would you compare the sacrifices that you make in order to worship with the sacrifices that they made?

6. Reflect back on Randolph's description of Acts 2:42–47 Christianity.

   a. In what ways are you already enjoying Acts 2:42–47 Christianity that beautifully blends worship and fellowship, leaders and laypeople, the pulpit ministry of the Word and the personal ministry of the Word?

   b. How could you experience even more Acts 2:42–47 Christianity?

7. What might it look like in your life to *remember the past* (hurts) *while remembering the future* (hope)?

8. Regarding sharing the Word, what mentoring, testifying, exhorting, or preaching might God be calling

you to? What steps could you take to more boldly and effectively share God's Word?

9. Regarding praising the Lord, within your worship context and cultural setting, what might further enhance your corporate glorification of God?

7

A Sorrowful Joy

Everybody's Heart in Tune

*Through all the sorrow of the Sorrow Songs there breathes
a hope—a faith in the ultimate justice of things. The minor
cadences of despair change often to triumph and calm
confidence.*

W. E. B. Du Bois, *The Souls of Black Folks*[1]

*Joyful sorrow, sorrowful joy, or more accurately, sorrow merg-
ing into joy arose from the suffering of the slaves' lives, a suffering that was touched, however, and so transformed, by the
living presence of God.*

Albert Raboteau "The Legacy of a Suffering Church"[2]

Speaking about reviving the lost heritage of African
American worship and fellowship through the slave
spirituals, Moses Berry recalls his grandmother's admonition:

145

"Dorothy told me to be careful about how much information I shared with the world outside our family. She said, 'If you share something sacred with people who won't respect it, they will try to reduce it to something that they can understand, and miss the sacredness. Therefore,' she said, 'don't let them know about your church music because they'll turn it into dance music or look at it like "folk music," and miss the point that it's the music of suffering people that lifted them from earth to heaven. It's not merely an art form.'"[3]

Along with Dorothy, our hearts grieve deeply when we think that slave spirituals might be trivialized. For many Christians, spirituals are nothing more than a way to sneak the gospel into public high school concerts. Or worse, we view spirituals as quaint relics to drag out of the family attic a few Sundays per year to get our blood pumping with up-tempo music.

Then why risk adding to the caricature by examining them here? Again, Berry's words are instructive. "I have carefully guarded what was handed down to me by my forefathers and mothers, but now we're in such difficult days, that if only one person can be touched by what I've been given, I'll take the risk of having our pearls trampled underfoot."[4]

Having been moved repeatedly by listening to the spirituals *in context*, we feel compelled to share their message here. We invite you to hear with new ears the sorrowful joy expressed by the slave spirituals. Even more, we encourage you to apply the lessons the spirituals teach about mutual ministry in the midst of inhumane suffering.

The Fuel of the Invisible Institution

The fascinating history of the slave spirituals is intertwined with the equally captivating narrative of the Invisible Institution. It was at these secret meetings in the brush arbors and tiny log cabins that the spirituals were not only sung but composed in community.

Too often we see the spirituals simply as words and notes on a printed page. We forget that they emerged as communal songs which were heard, felt, sung, shouted, and often danced with hand-clapping, foot-stamping, head-shaking meaning.[5]

These songs—variously called slave spirituals, Negro spirituals, jubilees, folk songs, shout songs, sorrow songs, slave songs, slave melodies, minstrel songs, and religious songs—are most commonly known as slave spirituals because of the deep religious feelings they express.[6] Singing was integral to reinforcing a sense of community in the Invisible Institution and nourishing soul-healing relationships with God and one another. Says Wyatt Walker, "In the preliterate era of slavery, the fuel of the 'invisible church' was the musical expression constantly fed by the oral tradition."[7]

Gushing Up from the Heart: Improvisational Communal Empathy

To appreciate the meaning, message, and mutual ministry of the slave spirituals, we must understand how and why they were composed. Carey Davenport, a retired black Methodist minister from Texas, had been born enslaved in 1855. He vividly depicts the spontaneous nature of slave spirituals. "Sometimes the culled folks go down in dugouts and hollows and hold they own service and they used to sing songs *what come a-gushing up from the heart.*"[8]

These were not polished, practiced anthems designed to entertain. They were personal, powerful psalms designed to sustain. Barbara Holmes says, "Songs were not carefully composed and copyrighted as they are today; they were 'raised' by anyone who had a song in their hearts."[9]

147

Slave spirituals were shared songs composed on the spot to empathize with and encourage real people in real trouble. Anderson Edwards, a slave preacher, remembers, "We didn't have no song books and the Lord done give us our songs and when we sing them at night it jus' whispering so nobody hear us."[10]

The creation of individual slave spirituals poignantly portrays the giving of soul care at its best. When James McKim asked a slave the origin of a particular spiritual, the slave explained, "I'll tell you; it's dis way. My master call me up and ordered me a short peck of corn and a hundred lash. My friends see it and is sorry for me. When dey come to de praise meeting dat night dey sing about it. Some's very good singers and know how; and dey work it in, work it in, you know; till dey get it right; and dat's de way."[11] Spirituals were born from slaves observing and empathizing with the suffering of their fellow slaves as a way of demonstrating identification and solidarity with the wronged slave.[12]

Creating and singing spirituals in the middle of their predicament became a means for reciprocal bonding. Slaves wove the words into the fabric of their worship and into the tapestry of their everyday life together. Albert Raboteau pictures the resulting communal empathy. "The flexible, improvisational structure of the spirituals gave them the capacity to fit an individual slave's specific experience into the consciousness of the group. One person's sorrow or joy became everyone's through song. Singing the spirituals was therefore both an intensely personal and vividly communal experience in which an individual received consolation for sorrow and gained a heightening of joy because his experience was shared."[13] What a lasting portrait of the truth that *shared sorrow is endurable sorrow.*

In the very structure of the spirituals, we see articulated the idea of communal support. Frequently the spirituals mentioned individual members present, either by name—"Sister Tilda, Brother Tony,"—or by description—"the stranger over there in the corner." This co-creation included everyone in the experience of mutual exhortation and communal support.[14]

Raboteau explains it well. "Drawing from the Bible, Protestant hymns, sermons, and African styles of singing and dancing, the slaves fashioned a religious music which expressed their faith in moving, immediate, colloquial, and, often, magnificently dramatic terms."[15]

The spontaneous creation of the spirituals exemplifies what spiritual directors call "staying in the moment," "being present," and "immediacy." Counseling and spiritual friendships are not so much about skills but about *artful connecting through real and raw relating.* When we see our friend's sorrow, we feel it, experience it, and work at expressing our empathy until we get it right—until our friend experiences us experiencing his or her pain.

Heaven Invading Earth: Integrated Hurting and Hoping

The slave spirituals also illustrate the relational competency of holistically integrating sustaining and healing, hurt and hope, empathy and encouragement, the earthly story and the heavenly story.

Thomas Higginson, a New England abolitionist, commanded the first freed slave regiment to fight against the Confederacy. He recorded the songs sung around the evening campfires by the First South Carolina Volunteers. Writing about their slave spirituals, Higginson highlights their symmetry. "The attitude is always the same. . . . Nothing but patience for this life,—nothing but triumph in the next. Sometimes the present predominates, sometimes the future; but the combination is always implied."[16]

Higginson then illustrates this interplay between patience and triumph. In "This World Almost Done," for instance, we hear patience motivated by future hope:

149

Brudder, keep your lamp trimmin' and a-burnin',
Keep your lamp trimmin' and a-burnin',
Keep your lamp trimmin' and a-burnin',
For dis world most done.
So keep your lamp trimmin' and a-burnin',
Dis world most done.[17]

In "I Want to Go Home," the final reward of patience is proclaimed as plaintively:

Dere's no rain to wet you, O, yes, I want to go
home.
Dere's no sun to burn you, O, yes, I want to go
home;
O, push along, believers, O, yes, I want to go home.
Dere's no hard trials, O, yes, I want to go home.
Dere's no whips-a-crackin', O, yes, I want to go
home.
My brudder on de wayside, O, yes, I want to go
home.
O, push along, my brudder, O, yes, I want to go
home.
Where dere's no stormy weather, O, yes, I want to
go home.
Dere's no tribulation, O, yes, I want to go home.[18]

Notice the frequent, swift movement back and forth between the earthly story of hurt and the heavenly story of hope. We find no linear, quick-fix progress from hurt to hope as if to sing about pain is to eradicate it. Instead, we discover the constant interplay between empathy and encouragement.

This mixing is explained by the African American Christian worldview that the sacred and the secular are inseparable. Heaven invades earth and the boundary, the window or membrane between the two, is thin. Thus to move back and forth, to see heaven storm earth and earth combat heaven, is a normal aspect of how African American sufferology views life. The spirituals reflect this deeper perspective, a deeper philosophy of life than is common in modern Western thought, which has tended to make life too linear and earth and heaven too segregated.

Their holistic view of all reality exposes how we often *wrongly separate hurt and hope.* We avoid the raw honesty of the Old Testament saints and the African American believers when we make life and counseling too linear and when we make earth and heaven too separate. We need to better fuse earth's hurts and heaven's hope.

We also must *reject the false dichotomy between the sacred and the secular.* As Thomas Merton encourages us, "The function of faith is not to reduce mystery to rational clarity, but to integrate the unknown and known together into a living whole, in which we are more and more able to transcend the limitations of our external self."[19]

As lay care-givers, pastors, and professional Christian counselors, we demonstrate this competency when we journey with our spiritual friends, parishioners, and counselees by helping them *see signs of God's goodness even when life is bad.* We join them in their grand adventure, praying, like Elisha, that God will open their eyes to see the world charged with the grandeur of God (see 2 Kings 6:15–17).

Joyful Sorrow: Mingling Suffering and Joy

Enslaved African Americans holistically integrated sustaining and healing because they first holistically experienced sorrow and joy. The following well-known slave spiritual illustrates this truth.

> Nobody knows the trouble I see,
> Nobody knows like Jesus,
> Nobody knows the trouble I see,
> Glory hallelujah![20]

A slave who was initially puzzled by the tone of joyful sadness that echoed and re-echoed in spirituals eloquently explains the paradox: "The old meeting house caught on fire. The spirit was there. Every heart was beating in unison as we turned our minds to God to tell him of our sorrows here below. God saw our need and came to us. I used to wonder what made people shout, but now I don't. There is a joy on the inside, and it wells up so strong that we can't keep still. It is fire in the bones. Any time that fire touches a man, he will jump."[21]

Clearly the message of the spirituals was simultaneously one of personal pain and one of spiritual hope. Ex-slave Henry Lewis remembers a song which starkly contrasts such present pain and future relief:

> My knee-bones achin',
> My body's rackin' with pain,
> I calls myself de child of God,
> Heaven am my aim.[22]

African American Christians understood that life is lived in the minor key. They knew that they could not avoid or evade suffering.

Frederick Douglass recalls that the spirituals reveal "at once the highest joy and the deepest sadness."[23] As the slaves reflected on the human condition, they did not demand answers. However, they did insist on candor about suffering and courageous affirmations of joy. The combination often led to a jarring contrast when they juxtaposed earthly suffering and heavenly hope, as seen in this song:

> Wish I'd died when I was a baby,
> O Lord rock a' jubilee,
> Wish I'd died.[24]

Another eloquent image of life's alteration between ups and downs, sorrow and joy, occurs in one of the lesser-known verses of "Nobody Knows the Trouble I've Had":

One morning I was a-walking down,
Saw some berries a-hanging down,
I pick de berry and I suck de juice,
Just as sweet as de honey in de comb.
Sometimes I'm up, sometimes I'm down,
Sometimes I'm almost on de groun'.[25]

Lucy McKim Garrison wrote a letter published in the November 8, 1862, edition of *Dwight's Journal of Music* that powerfully displays this melding of agony and joy found in the spirituals. "The wild, sad strains tell, as the sufferers themselves never could, of crushed hopes, keen sorrow, and a dull daily misery which covered them as hopelessly as the fog from the rice-swamps. On the other hand, the words breathe a trusting faith in rest in the future—in 'Canaan's fair and happy land,' to which their eyes seem constantly turned."[26]

Today's comforters can imitate the model set by enslaved African Americans who knew how to mingle the many moods of faith, who knew how to sing with "tones loud, long, and deep," and who "breathed the prayer and complaint of souls boiling over with the bitterest anguish."[27] Today's comforters can replicate the soul-stirring honesty of the psalmists of old who knew how to write psalms of complaint and of celebration, of lament and of longing, who knew how to pour out their souls fully to God.

Godforsakenness: Songs of the Soil and the Soul

Slave spirituals about feeling godforsaken further emphasize the impossibility, this side of heaven, of quickly and finally resolving all hurt. When honestly sharing their lamentation over the absence of the felt presence of God, enslaved African Americans followed the psalmists. Most Christians are shocked to learn that the Bible contains more psalms of complaint and lament than psalms of thanksgiving and praise.

153

The writers of the spirituals would not have been surprised. They understood and practiced the historic Christian art of sacred discontent.

Their laments included honest complaints about their external world of "level one suffering"—what was happening *around* and *to* them. Their laments also involved candid complaints about their internal world of "level two suffering"—what was happening *in* them, in their souls and minds, as they reflected on their outer suffering.

William McClain's terminology of "songs of the soil and the soul" best captures our concept of external and internal suffering. "A very real part of the worship of Black people is the songs of Zion. Singing is as close to worship as breathing is to life. These songs of the soul and of the soil have helped to bring a people through the torture chambers of the last three centuries."[28]

As McClain continues, he speaks about the soil of external suffering and the soul of weary hearts. "These spirituals reveal the rich culture and the ineffable beauty and creativity of the Black soul and intimate the uniqueness of the Black religious tradition. These spirituals speak of life and death, suffering and sorrow, love and judgment, grace and hope, justice and mercy. They are the songs of an unhappy people, a people weary at heart, a discontent people, and yet they are the most beautiful expression of human experience and faith this side of the seas."[29]

In fact, it was the soil of suffering souls that birthed the spirituals. "Many of these spirituals were influenced by the surrounding conditions in which the slaves lived. These conditions were negative and degrading, to say the least; yet, miraculously, a body of approximately six thousand independent spirituals exists today—melodies that were, for the most part, handed down from generation to generation. . . . The Negro spirituals, as originated in America, tell of exile and trouble, of strife and hiding; they grope toward some unseen power and sigh for rest in the end."[30]

154

Clearly, the spirituals highlight long-suffering faith in a wearisome world. "These songs of the soul and of the soil have enriched American music and the music of the world. . . . They are the articulate message of an oppressed people. They are the music of a captive people who used this artful expression to embrace the virtues of Christianity: patience, love, freedom, faith, and hope."[31]

Of the six thousand available spirituals, we've chosen to illustrate the soil and soul content of a handful. "Dis Ole World Is Er Mean World" vividly captures the truth that "life is bad":

> Dis ole world is er mean world to try to live in,
> To try ter stay in until you die.
> Without er mother,
> Without er father,
> Without er sister, Lord,
> Ain't got no brother.
> You got ter cry sometimes,
> You got ter pray so hard,
> You got ter mourn so hard.[32]

When the slaves sang that this old world was a mean world to try to live in, they were imparting deep theology, deeply felt. "In this world you will have trouble" (John 16:33).

The spiritual "I'm in Trouble" reflects lamentation over both external suffering and internal suffering—a spiritual of the soil and the soul.

> I'm in trouble, Lord, I'm in trouble,
> I'm in trouble, Lord, Trouble about my grave.
> Sometimes I weep, Sometimes I mourn,
> I'm in trouble about my grave;
> Sometimes I can't do neither one,
> I'm in trouble about my grave.[33]

What depths of despair this spiritual pictures. The singers feel lower than darkness and pain; it is a depiction of the pain of death, which is why they sing, "I'm in trouble about my *grave*." All their resources and hopes are all but gone, and there is *nothing* left to hold on to.

The spiritual "I'm A-Trouble in De Mind" echoes complaint over internal suffering—a spiritual of the soul.

> I am a-trouble in de mind,
> O I am a-trouble in de mind;
> I ask my Lord what shall I do,
> I am a-trouble in de mind.[34]

Enslaved African Americans clearly understood and addressed the inner mental turmoil caused when a good God allows evil and suffering. Recognition and expression of this reality of the trial of faith kept them from wondering if anyone else ever struggled in similar ways.

While we were writing the words of this chapter, a minister called to speak with us because he was horrified by his doubts. "How can I be a Christian and a pastor if I question what God is up to when my life stinks?"

Satan, as he frequently does, was attempting to compound this brother's difficulties by causing him to have doubts because of his doubts! Satan was implying, "No other Christian, and certainly no minister, has ever doubted God. And you call yourself a Christian!"

This brother needed permission to admit his inner mental battles. He needed to know that it's normal to experience "a-trouble in de mind."

Throughout biblical and church history, level two soul suffering has often expressed itself in the haunting refrain of "How long, O Lord?" (see Psalm 13). Enslaved African Americans continued this lament tradition.

> My father, how long,
> My father, how long,
> My father, how long,
> Poor sinner suffer here.

And it won't be long,
Poor sinner suffer here.
We'll soon be free.
De Lord will call us home.
We'll walk de golden streets.
Of de New Jerusalem.[35]

Notice the mixture and blending of endurance and assurance, another historically common practice modeled by believing slaves.

Perhaps no spiritual better encapsulates godforsakenness than "Sometimes I Feel Like a Motherless Chile":

Sometimes I feel like a motherless chile,
Sometimes I feel like a motherless chile,
Sometimes I feel like a motherless chile,
A long ways from home,
A long ways from home.[36]

The haunting repetition, couched in the common earthly slave experience of being children torn from mothers, oozes a depth of pain intimately understood by all those in the slave community. The key was not necessarily that they *were* a motherless child but that they *felt* pain akin to that greatest of deprivations.[37] This connects beautifully with 2 Corinthians 1:3–8, where Paul notes that in *any* trial we can connect with others in their *specific* trials, if we go to the God of *all* comfort in all *our* trials. In the very act of composing a song, of creating a lament, the human spirit joins the flow of God's Spirit to create a channel for communal emotional consolation and spiritual healing.

These soil and soul aspects of the spirituals teach us several core relational competencies. First, they remind us of *the importance of recognizing and empathizing with both levels of suffering.* When life stinks, our perspective shrinks. When our external life is bad (level one or soil suffering), then our internal mental and spiritual life is tempted to despair (level two or soul suffering). Competent counselors and sensitive spiritual friends engage hurting brothers and sisters at both levels.

Second, it is *essential that we grant people the permission to struggle*. We need to admit to others our own battles with doubt. We also need to allow others to express their doubts, disappointments, and discouragement so that the light of the gospel can shine in truth and hope.

Third, we need to *listen for our friends' "language" so that we can communicate in their language*. It's not enough to parrot a model of counseling that says, "Life is bad." Depending on the word choices and culture of our counselee, we could perhaps connect more intimately if we responded, "Sounds like for you life is mean. This old, fallen world is a mean world to try to live in."

Fourth, cross-cultural ministry heightens the need for the ability to *experience the experiences of others*. Identifying with someone with whom we do not share a common cultural background by default can present a great challenge in the area of accurate empathy. In this setting, it is crucial that we lay aside preexisting assumptions. In a sense, we lay aside *self* to be present *with* our spiritual friend and present *to* God—hearing God's voice, listening for God's perspective on our friend's life, and speaking from God's viewpoint to our friend (see John 4:1–30).

We Have Been with Jesus: Personal Trust in a Personal God

In their suffering, the slaves naturally identified with Jesus, their suffering Savior. They depicted him in the spirituals as their ever-present friend and intimate ally.

> He have been wid us, Jesus,
> He still wid us, Jesus,
> He will be wid us, Jesus,
> Be wid us to the end.[38]

158

They embedded the truth of Jesus's personal presence in all that they did. Their belief in Jesus did not consist only in a set of propositions but also in a personal relationship of trust that Jesus was Immanuel—God with them.

The slaves believed that Jesus had entered into their suffering by his suffering. They transcended slavery through belief in a transcendent God who became immanent in the suffering of Christ. That is, the Creator God became their companion. "I Want Jesus to Walk with Me" conveys such personalized faith:

> I want Jesus to walk with me;
> I want Jesus to walk with me;
> All along my pilgrim journey,
> I want Jesus to walk with me.
>
> In my trials, Lord, walk with me;
> In my trials, Lord, walk with me;
> When my heart is almost breaking, Lord,
> I want Jesus to walk with me.
>
> When I'm in trouble, Lord, walk with me;
> When I'm in trouble, Lord, walk with me;
> When my head is bowed in sorrow, Lord,
> I want Jesus to walk with me.[39]

The enslaved believers were able to integrate sorrow and joy only because they were able to integrate Jesus into their daily sorrow and trials, trouble and tribulations.

Just as we experience today, they did not always feel the presence of Christ. In those lonely moments, they longed for "Jesus with skin on"—they longed for a brother or sister to be a spiritual friend pointing them to their ultimate spiritual friend, Jesus.

> Oh that I had a bosom friend,
> To tell my secrets to;

One always to depend upon,
In everything I do!
How I do wander, up and down!
I seem a stranger, quite undone;
None to lend an ear to my complaint,
No one to cheer me, though I faint.[40]

Their longing for connection with Christ reminds us of a central principle of spiritual friendship: We do not point people to ourselves. *We point people to our Savior.* Yes, we do need to be "Jesus with skin on," but because we are finite and fallen, we can't always be there for people, nor are we always there in the right way for people.

These slave spirituals of personal trust in Christ *point us away from solution-focused therapy* with its tendency toward helping people to become more self-sufficient sinners. Offering people earthly solutions without offering them Christ as the final answer is no answer at all.

Trouble Doesn't Last Always: Instilling Lasting Hope

Once connected with Christ, enslaved African Americans faced desperate desolation with profound hope. The slave spirituals teach that life's contradictions are not ultimate, otherwise life would be hopeless and we would be helpless. Slave spirituals teach that there is a better day coming, that God has the power to create beauty from ashes and to transform good out of evil, and that his ultimate purposes are good because *he* is infinitely good.

The slaves yielded to God's sovereign prerogative either to reveal or conceal himself *in this life* because they knew that, though obscured now, his purposes would become clear and his person would be near—in heaven. They shout their heavenly hope of direct access to God in "Soon-a Will Be Done":

160

No more weeping and a-wailing,
No more weeping and a-wailing,
No more weeping and a-wailing,
I'm goin' to live with God.

I want t' meet my Jesus,
I want t' meet my Jesus,
I want t' meet my Jesus,
I'm goin' to live with God.

Soon-a will be done-a with the troubles of the
    world,
Troubles of the world,
The troubles of the world.
Soon-a will be done-a with the troubles of the
    world.
Goin' home to live with God.[41]

Reflecting on this and other spirituals, Howard Thurman explains, "when all hope for release in this world seems unrealistic and groundless, the heart turns to a way of escape beyond the present order."[42]

Enslaved African Americans relied on future hope to endure and transcend every aspect of slavery, from the trans-Atlantic passage to the slave auction and beyond, as illustrated by the following lyrics:

See these poor souls from Africa,
Transported to America;
We are stolen, and sold to Georgia,
Will you go along with me?
We are stolen, and sold to Georgia,
Come sound the jubilee!

See wives and husbands sold apart,
Their children's screams will break my heart;—
There's a better day a coming,
Will you go along with me?

161

There's a better day coming,
Go sound the jubilee![43]

Here we listen to the cry and complaint of African American sufferology along with the comfort and waiting so typical of their future hope.

Thurman beautifully summarizes their faith: "They express the profound conviction that God was not done with them, that God was not done with life. The consciousness that God had not exhausted His resources or better still that the vicissitudes of life could not exhaust God's resources, did not ever leave them. This is the secret of their ascendancy over circumstances and the basis of their assurances concerning life and death. The awareness of the presence of a God who was personal, intimate and active was the central fact of life and around it all the details of life and destiny were integrated."[44]

Theologians label the views expressed in these spirituals "eschatological hope" (from the word *eschaton*, meaning the end times—God's final dealings with humans and his setting things right at his return). The slave communities embraced a theology of the soon-coming Jesus and translated his ultimate return into a sense of his constant presence with them even now.[45] This allowed them to live as if the end times were already at hand. Jesus visited them in their communal singing because he promised that where two or three were gathered in his name, there he was with them (see Matt. 18:20). In other words, they did not have to wait until heaven to enjoy the benefits of their future hope.

We hear their communal hope in the words of the spiritual "Lis'en to de Lam's":

Lis'en to de lam's, all a-cryin',
I wan'ta go to heaven when I die.
Come on sister wid yo' ups an' downs,
De angel's waitin' for to give you a crown.
Come on mourner an' a don't be shame,
Angel's waitin' for you to write-a yo' name.[46]

Notice how the call to the sister and the mourner highlights group sustaining and healing. By joining together in song, they urged one another, even in their ups and downs, to realize that their present sufferings were not worth comparing with their future glory (see Rom. 8:18).

Consider also in this spiritual that their future hope offered them a present identity. Though treated like chattel now, though viewed as subhuman by their white masters, they one day will receive a crown of glory. One day all their shame will be eradicated. One day the names of these crying lambs will be written down in the Lamb's Book of Life!

Life is bad, but God is good is a central lesson taught by these spirituals of heavenly hope. In working with suffering people today, we would be wise to enter deeply the "badness" of their lives while confidently moving with them to see God's active goodness. In particular, we need to help our spiritual friends to see that life's difficulties can never deplete God's ability to dispense grace to help them in their time of need (see Heb. 4:16).

These spirituals remind us that *finding God is more important than finding answers.* They remind us to remind our friends of one of God's main purposes in allowing suffering—in suffering, God is not getting back at us, he is getting us back to himself.

The spirituals show us that *it will be worth it all when we see Jesus.* We can comfort all abuse victims with the message of the spirituals that reflects the message of the Beatitudes: "Blessed are those who are persecuted because of righteousness, for theirs is the kingdom of heaven. Blessed are you when people insult you, persecute you and falsely say all kinds of evil against you because of me. Rejoice and be glad, because great is your reward in heaven, for in the same way they persecuted the prophets who were before you" (Matt. 5:10–12).

163

Grist from the Mill: Composing Narratives of Courage

Listen to what the voices of enslaved African Americans have sung to us so far. Bound together by their common humanity and common suffering, they engaged in real and raw connecting (improvisational communal empathy). They practiced their empathy holistically, neither assuming that hurt would magically vanish nor refusing to address earthly pain with heavenly hope (integrated sustaining and healing). They were able to live out holistic empathy with one another because they had the courage to face life honestly with joyful sorrow (mingling suffering and joy).

Their candor led to crying out to God regarding their sense of being God-forsaken (singing songs of the soil and the soul). Faced with crushing external and internal suffering, they turned to their ultimate spiritual friend, Jesus (personally trusting in their personal God). Even while living face-to-face with God, crushing blow after crushing blow required that they look to the end of their story (instilling heavenly hope).

If their singing voices stopped now, then perhaps the old accusation of "being too heavenly minded to be of any earthly good" might apply. Perhaps the slave spirituals could be perceived to be "too docile"—urging the slave to endure quietly, to survive but not thrive.

Please hear us clearly. Nothing could be further from the truth. Please hear the slave spirituals clearly. The slave spirituals advocated courageous thriving, not docile surviving.

To understand how empowering the spirituals were, we must realize that in African American culture, musicians were healers and healers were musicians. They wove together the practices of making music and restoring health, harmony, and wholeness.[47]

A common theme in historic guiding has been to urge believers to follow the example of other courageous believers. The spirituals followed this model when they exhorted one another to emulate the resilience of those who traveled the road before.

> All dem Mount Zion member,
> Dey have many ups and downs;
> But cross come or no come,
> For to hold out to the end.
> Hold out to the end,
> Hold out to the end,
> It is my 'termination for to hold out to the end.[48]

Such willful determination always to soldier on is the essence of courageous thriving.

The slave spirituals also pointed to the great cloud of witnesses from biblical times, such as in "Little David" and in "Didn't My Lord Deliver Daniel?"

> Little David was a shepherd boy,
> He killed Goliath and shouted for joy.
> Joshua was the son of Nun,
> He never would quit till the work was done.[49]

> Didn't my Lord deliver Daniel, deliver Daniel, deliver Daniel?
> Didn't my Lord deliver Daniel, and why not every man?
> He delivered Daniel from the Lion's den,
> Jonah from the belly of the whale,
> And the Hebrew children from the fiery furnace,
> And why not every man?[50]

By identifying themselves with these biblical heroes, enslaved believers came to see themselves as heroes and heroines in an epic faith struggle. If little David could defeat the giants of his life and lowly Joshua could fight on until the battle was won, then they too could be victorious. If God could deliver Daniel, Jonah, and the Hebrew children, then he could rescue them.

Awaiting such deliverance required long-suffering. "Keep a-Inchin' Along" picturesquely illustrates a healing narrative of perseverance:

> Keep a-inchin' along,
> Keep a-inchin' along,
> Jesus will come by and by.
> Keep a-inchin' along,
> Like a poor inch-worm,
> Jesus will come by and by.[51]

As the slaves sang in the brush arbors, they created an empowering collective experience that enabled them to experience inner freedom and victory long before external emancipation.

These spirituals of perseverance encouraged resilience based on communal support.

> O brothers, don't get weary,
> O brothers, don't get weary,
> O brothers, don't get weary,
> We're waiting for the Lord.
> We'll land on Canaan's shore,
> We'll land on Canaan's shore,
> When we land on Canaan's shore,
> We'll meet forever more.[52]

Notice the continuous emphasis on "brothers" and on "we." Life's battles were meant to be fought never by lone rangers but by a community of elite rangers—a band of brothers and sisters.

As we noted in chapter 1, throughout church history "devil craft" was a core aspect of courageous guiding narratives. Spiritually mature African American believers used devil craft to discern Satan's schemes and provide counter-counsel.

Ole Satan toss a ball at me.
Him tink de ball would hit my soul.
De ball for hell and I for heaven.
What make ole Satan hate me so?
Because he got me once and he let me go.

The Devil am a liar and conjurer too,
If you don't look out he'll conjure you.[53]

When I get dar, Cappen Satan was dar,
Says, young man, young man, dere's no use for
     pray,
For Jesus is dead, and God gone away,
And I made him out a liar, and I went my way.

O, Satan is a mighty busy ole man,
And roll rocks in my way;
But Jesus is my bosom friend.
And roll 'em out of de way.[54]

The writers of these spirituals demonstrated great theological acumen. They highlighted eternal security ("I for
heaven"); the motivation for Satan's rage ("he got me once
and he let me go"); Satan's deception ("the Devil am a liar");
Satan's age-old scheme, begun with Eve, of casting doubts
on God's goodness ("Jesus is dead, and God gone away");
Satan's constant prowling as a roaring lion ("Satan is a mighty
busy ole man"); Christ as the believer's intimate ally ("Jesus
is my bosom friend"); and Christ's power and victory over
Satan ("and roll 'em out of de way").

The songs the enslaved African Americans composed during their brush arbor meetings provided them with scriptural
truth on which to rest their souls. They consistently used
songs to teach character—in particular the character traits
of resilience and persistence.

We follow their soul care and spiritual direction lead when
we *refuse to stop with empathy*. We never want to communicate

pity or the impression that our spiritual friend is "too damaged to ever love" or "has suffered too much to ever find meaning and purpose in life."

The spirituals illustrate several methods that we can emulate for helping others move beyond mere surviving to courageous thriving. We can *point people to examples of others* so that they know that no temptation has seized them except what is common to all humanity (see 1 Cor. 10:13). *Pointing them to examples of biblical characters* instills the confidence that God is faithful and will not let them be tempted beyond their ability to endure but will provide a way of escape and victory (see 1 Cor. 10:13). *Directing them to the body of Christ* for mutual encouragement teaches them the power of spurring one another on (see Heb. 3:12–13; 10:24–25).

The spirituals also emphasize the need for *theologically sound biblical counsel.* In particular, they should motivate us to develop a "Satanology"—a biblical theology of Satan's schemes and how to counter them.

Following the North Star

We follow the North Star guidance of the slave spirituals by keeping God as our North Star no matter how cloudy the sky and stormy the heavens. While bracing ourselves together with suffering brothers and sisters, while embracing honestly the howling storms of life, we refuse to take our eyes off the sun—or off the Son.

We follow the North Star leading of the slave spirituals by communicating that the very nature of God compels him to come to the rescue of the fatherless, the widowed, the lonely, and the solitary. The spirituals were not simply songs but a perspective, a point of view, a philosophy of life, and a theology of God. They offered a worldview that became the bedrock of a spiritual tradition: *God is on the side of the suffering.*[55]

168

The slave spirituals offered a theology of God's relationship to the oppressed: God has set the solitary in families. Psalm 68:4–6 encapsulates the message of the spirituals: "Sing to God, sing praise to his name, extol him who rides on the clouds—his name is the LORD—and rejoice before him. A father to the fatherless, defender of widows, is God in his holy dwelling. God sets the lonely in families, he leads forth the prisoners with singing."

The North Star of the slave spirituals directs us to a God who leads forth prisoners with singing. We never deny the squalor of life in the prison of a fallen world. However, we never allow despair to sink hope. We always remind our spiritual friends that trouble never lasts because God and our relationship to him outlasts and overshadows all.

Learning Together from Our Great Cloud of Witnesses

1. As a result of reading this chapter, how has your perspective on the slave spirituals changed? Specifically, what has surprised you?

2. How would your soul care and spiritual direction ministry change if you shifted from a focus on practicing skills to a focus on "gushing up from the heart" (improvisational empathy, staying in the moment, being present, immediacy)?

3. What does it look like for you to lay aside self to be simultaneously present with your friend and with God, hearing God's voice and reflecting God's words (God's Word)?

4. Concerning the African American practice of integrating hurting *and* hoping:
   a. What happens when a spiritual friend focuses *only* on hurting/sustaining?
   b. What happens when a spiritual friend focuses *only* on hoping/healing?

    c. How could you apply the integration of hurting and hoping to your spiritual friendships?

5. How well are you able to mingle suffering and joy?
    a. Do you face suffering honestly?
    b. Are you able to celebrate God's goodness even while experiencing life's "badness"?

6. Which do you tend to focus on more: songs of the soil (external suffering) or songs of the soul (internal suffering)?
    a. Why do you suppose that is?
    b. How could you better highlight both?

7. In your life, how do you invite Jesus to be your bosom friend? How do you display your personal trust in your personal God even when life seems to be shouting, "God doesn't care!"?

8. In your ministry, how can you practice the art of instilling lasting hope?

9. Concerning composing narratives of courage:
    a. Who do you know who models resilience? How could you emulate that person?
    b. What biblical examples of courageous trust in God strengthen your life?
    c. How are you providing countercounsel (devil craft) to defeat Satan's lying schemes?

8

Sons of Thunder

Founding Fathers

Here lies the dust of a poor hell-deserving sinner, who ven-
tured into eternity trusting wholly on the merits of Christ for
salvation. In the full belief of the great doctrines he preached
while on earth, he invites his children and all who read this,
to trust their eternal interest on the same foundation.
epitaph written for himself by Reverend Lemuel Haynes,
the "Black Puritan"[1]

It is only when we are within the walls of our churches that
we are wholly ourselves, that we keep alive a sense of our per-
sonalities in relation to the total world in which we live. . . .
Our churches are where we dip our tired bodies in cool
springs of hope, where we retain our wholeness and humanity
despite the blows of death from the Bosses of the Buildings.
quoted in Richard Wright, *12 Million Black Voices*[2]

Amerian historians frequently emphasize our "founding fathers." Politically speaking, they highlight white
males like George Washington, John Adams, Thomas Jeffer-

son, Alexander Hamilton, Thomas Paine, and James Madison. Spiritually speaking, they feature white males such as Roger Williams, Cotton Mather, John Winthrop, Jonathan Edwards, and Isaac Backus.

Sadly, historians have often left African American founding fathers missing in action. In particular, the spiritual founding fathers of independent African American church life have been neglected, relegated to the backseat of the historical bus.

In this chapter we seek to recover something of the lost legacy of loving leadership bequeathed to us by African American spiritual forefathers. Of course, one chapter can only offer a taste. But what a taste it is!

As we've listened to the founding fathers of black churches and denominations, our imaginations have been captured by their *humble strength*. Through their humble strength, these spiritual fathers offer unique perspectives concerning how pastors, leaders, and fathers impart soul care and spiritual direction.

In a day when authority tends toward the extremes of dictatorial overpowering or weak abdication, we have much to learn from their Christlike model of *empowering others to serve God through dependence on Christ and the body of Christ*. In a day when African Americans long for godly father figures and at times express a father-hunger,[3] these African American spiritual mentors offer answers that can enlighten and examples that can empower African Americans as well as people of all races.

Examples to the Flock

Throughout church history, developing and displaying the *character* of a soul physician was the absolute prerequisite before focusing on *competence* in soul care and spiritual direction. This has certainly been the case with African

American founding fathers as they strove to practice what they preached. In particular, we learn from them that we sustain, heal, reconcile, and guide as much by our actions (our model) as by our interactions (our message). People listened to their words of counsel because they witnessed them heeding their own counsel.

Walking the Talk: Modeling Christian Manliness

E. Franklin Frazier contends that the historic black church was somewhat passive due to its otherworldly focus.[4] However, firsthand accounts draw a different portrait altogether. Traditionally, manhood has been a central theme in the independent black church.[5] Bishop B. W. Arnett described the organizing conference of the African Methodist Episcopal Church (AMEC) in 1816 as "the Convention of the Friends of Manhood Christianity."[6]

Bishop Daniel Alexander Payne, an early leader in and the official historian of the AMEC, believed that the separation of the AME from the white Methodist Episcopal Church was "beneficial to the man of color" in two ways. "First: it has thrown us upon our own resources and made us tax our own mental powers both for government and support." Second, it gave the black man "an independence of character which he could neither hope for nor attain unto, if he had remained as the ecclesiastical vassal of his white brethren." It produced "independent thought," "independent action," and an "independent hierarchy," and the latter "has made us feel and recognize our individuality and our heaven-created manhood."[7]

Personally, Payne experienced numerous opportunities to live out his Christian manhood. In chapter 5 we shared how devastated Payne was when a new law forced him to stop teaching his fellow African Americans. Wavering on the precipice of doubt, he girds up the loins of his mind with the solemn words, "'With God one day is as a thousand years

173

and a thousand years as one day. Trust in him, and he will bring slavery and all its outrages to an end.' These words from the spirit world acted on my troubled soul like water on a burning fire, and my aching heart was soothed from its burden of woes."[8] Payne engages in a spiritual conversation with himself in which he exhorts himself to see life from God's eternal perspective.

Payne then pens a lengthy poem expressing both his feelings and theological reflections. Of this spiritual exercise he concludes, "The writing of this poem was the safety-valve which let out the superabundant grief that would otherwise have broken my heart and sent me head-long to an untimely grave."[9] Some males decry poetry or journaling as less than masculine. However, Payne, like King David before him, understands the manly value of candid "psalming."

Other males disparage depending on others during times of spiritual despondency. Not Payne. In response to his internal battle with his external situation, he received letters of spiritual consolation from the poetess Miss Mary S. Palmer and her sister Miss Jane Keith Palmer. He reflects in response to these letters, "At a time when my heart seemed ready to burst with grief and my lips ready to deny the existence of God, or to blaspheme his holy name for permitting one race to grind another to powder, such white friends were exceedingly dear and precious to me. I looked on them then, and regard them now, as God's angels sent to strengthen me when the powers of darkness seemed to be let loose against me and against the race which I was so earnestly serving. I can never cease to remember them without emotions of gratitude and love."[10]

Given Payne's circumstances and the culture of the day, we find here triple humility. He models the humility to de-pendently receive help, to gladly receive help from females, and to nonjudgmentally and nondefensively receive help from whites.

174

Throughout his ministry, Payne was a man on a *manly mission*. Soon after his conversion, God called him to a Christ-glorifying, people-serving, and purpose-driven life. "I was in my humble chamber, pouring out my prayers into the listening ears of the Saviour, when I felt as if the hands of a man were pressing my two shoulders and a voice speaking within my soul saying: *'I have set thee apart to educate thyself in order that thou mayest be an educator to thy people.'* The impression was *irresistible* and *divine*; it gave me a new direction to my thoughts and efforts."[11] His life was a manly life of resolute service to others. Leaving the South in 1834, Payne fulfilled his calling by studying at the Lutheran Theological Seminary in Gettysburg and then ministering as a pastor, educator, and influential bishop.

His manliness remained just as strong in the twilight years of his life. When he was in his seventies, Payne refused to stay on a train where he would have been seated in Jim Crow conditions. Standing his ground and confronting the white authorities on the train, he said to them, "Before I'll dishonor my manhood by going into that car, stop your train and put me off."[12]

After Payne left the train, "the guilty conductor looked out and said, 'Old man, you can get on the platform at the back of the car.' I replied only by contemptuous silence." Payne then carried his own luggage, walking a great distance over "a heavy bed of sand" to his next speaking engagement in the deep South.[13] Payne literally walked the talk.

How did such Christian manhood develop? Payne himself credits two men in his life, the one his biological father and the other his spiritual mentor. Payne's father started him on his purposeful life. "I was the child of many prayers. My father dedicated me to the service of God before I was born, declaring that if the Lord would give him a son that son should be consecrated to him, and named after the Prophet Daniel."[14] Imagine the sense of self, the sense of biblical masculinity that Payne's father passed to his son.

He did so not only by naming, but also by modeling. Of his father, Payne testifies, "He was an earnest Christian and a class leader, having two classes under him—what used to be called the Seekers' Class and the Members' Class. He was a faithful observer of family worship; and often his morning prayers and hymns aroused me, breaking my infant sleep and slumbers."[15]

Though blessed by such spiritual fatherly nurture, Payne felt the wound of fatherlessness when his father died when Payne was four. After his mother passed when he was nine, Payne's great-aunt raised him. Seeing his need for a father figure, he joined a church and was "assigned to the class of Mr. Samuel Weston, who from that time became the chief religious guide of my youth."[16]

As valuable as these two male mentors were in Payne's life, he credited another male—the God-man—with being his essential model. "The glorious manhood of Jesus Christ is the only true type of real manhood. . . . Study him, study him as your model; study the perfect model of manhood until he shall be conformed in you."[17] Payne copied the apostle Paul's male mentoring model, "Follow my example, as I follow the example of Christ" (1 Cor. 11:1).

Working the Work: Modeling Ministry Commitment

African American founding fathers also emphasized in their messages and modeled in their ministries a black Protestant work ethic. The oft-imagined but quite mistaken view of African American male slaves as lazy and slothful was crushed by both slave and free African American pastors.

Some slaves in the South were able to establish independent churches during the Revolutionary era. Perhaps the earliest to do so was George Liele. Born in Virginia in 1742, he moved with his master, Henry Sharpe, to Burke County, Georgia, a few years before the Revolutionary War. Liele was converted under the preaching of Baptist Matthew Moore at his master's church. In 1777 Liele founded a black Baptist congregation at Yama Craw, outside Savannah.

Eyewitness accounts applauded his commitment to ministry, even while still a layperson. "He began to discover his love to other negroes, on the same plantation with himself, by reading hymns among them, encouraging them to sing, and sometimes by explaining the most striking parts of them."[18]

Liele's own account equally expresses his passion for serving God and God's people. "Desiring to prove the sense I had of my obligations to God, I endeavoured to instruct the people of my own color in the Word of God: the white brethren seeing my endeavours, and that the word of the Lord seemed to be blessed, gave me a call at a quarterly meeting to preach before the congregation."[19]

Later licensed (by whites) as a minister, Liele served in Yama Craw and in Kingston, Jamaica. As a pastor, he preached twice on Sunday and twice during the week. "I receive nothing for my services; I preach, baptize, administer the Lord's supper, and travel from place to place to publish the gospel, and to settle church affairs, all freely."[20]

Like the apostle Paul, Liele supported himself through his own industry. "My occupation is a farmer, but as the seasons in this part of the country are uncertain, I also keep a team of horses, and wagons for the carrying goods from one place to another; which I attend to myself, with the assistance of my sons; and by this way of life have gained the good will of the public, who recommends me to business, and to some very principal work for government."[21] Like countless other African American founding fathers, Liele's industry became a benchmark urging other African American males toward responsibility and productivity.

Liele's model stuck. One of his converts and disciples, Andrew Bryan, accepted the baton of pastoral leadership at Yama Craw. Like his mentor, Bryan personified sacrificial ministry. White citizens, worried about slave rebellion, had him arrested and whipped twice for holding "illegal" meetings. According to an early Baptist historian, Andrew "told his persecutors that he rejoiced not only to be whipped, but *would freely suffer death for the cause of Jesus Christ.*"[22]

Lemuel Haynes affords yet another exemplar of ministerial modeling. Born in West Hartford, Connecticut, in 1753, of a white mother and a black father, Haynes lived his entire eighty years in Congregationalist New England. He completed his indenture in time to serve in the Continental Army during the Revolutionary War. Privately tutored, Haynes became the first African American to be ordained by any religious denomination. Upon ordination, Haynes then served white congregations for more than thirty years. Among other accomplishments, he achieved notoriety for a sermon entitled "Universal Salvation" that defended orthodox Christianity against the threat of universalism. Middlebury College awarded him the master's degree, *honoris causa*, in 1804, another first for an African American.[23]

At age sixty-five, Haynes left his Rutland, Vermont, parish due to political friction that essentially forced him to choose to resign. His farewell sermon of 1818 emphasized, among other topics, his devotion to the work of the ministry and to the people of his congregation.

Alluding to the words of the apostle Paul, Haynes says, "He that provided the motto of our discourse could say on his farewell, I have coveted no man's silver or gold, or apparel. Yea, ye yourselves know, that these hands have ministered unto my necessity."[24] Like Liele with his black congregation, Haynes felt it was important that his white parishioners recognized his Christlike diligence. Few could legitimately question his work ethic, given that he had preached 5,500 sermons, officiated at over four hundred funerals, and solemnized more than one hundred marriages.

It was also vital to him that they understood his godly motivations. "The flower of my life has been devoted to your service:—while I lament a thousand imperfections which have attended my ministry; yet I am not deceived, it has been my hearty desire to do something for the salvation of your souls."[25]

Haynes acknowledged and wanted his people to realize that the ultimate judge of his motivations was Christ. "I must give an account concerning the motives which influenced me to come among you, and how I have conducted during my thirty years residence in this place: the doctrines I have inculcated: whether I have designedly kept back any thing that might be profitable to you, or have, through fear of man, or any other criminal cause, shunned to declare the whole counsel of God. Also, as to the *manner* of my preaching, whether I have delivered my discourses in a cold, formal manner, and of my external deportment."[26]

Liele, Bryan, Haynes, and thousands of African American pastors like them exemplified in their lives what American Methodist Episcopal Zion (AMEZ) Bishop James Walker Hood taught to pastors under his charge. Born in Southeast Pennsylvania to free parents in 1831, Hood became a leading equipper in the early AMEZ Church. For Hood, the pastor's example was the key to ministry effectiveness. "In all things the minister should be the very best example of good behavior; of untiring and of unselfish devotion to his work."[27]

Empathizing with the Flock

Richard Allen was one of the foremost founding fathers of the African American independent churches. Born in 1760, he was a slave to Benjamin Crew of Philadelphia. Allen came to salvation in Christ around age twenty. He then traveled extensively, preaching the gospel in Delaware and Pennsylvania. In February 1786 he preached at St. George's Methodist Episcopal Church in Philadelphia. He expected to be there one or two weeks, but ministry needs led Allen to a settled place of service in Philadelphia.

Concerned for the well-being of African Americans in this parish, he said, "I established prayer meetings; I raised a society in 1786 of forty-two members. I saw the necessity of erecting a place of worship for the coloured people."[28] However, only three brethren united with him, including the equally important African American founding father Reverend Absalom Jones. Their little band met great opposition, including "very degrading and insulting language to us, to try and prevent us from going on."[29]

Opposition notwithstanding, the Lord blessed their endeavors as they established prayer meetings and meetings of exhortation, with many coming to Christ. Their growing congregation, still without a building, often attended services at St. George's. When the black worshipers became more numerous, the white leaders "moved us from the seats we usually sat on, and placed us around the wall."[30]

It was at this juncture in 1787 that one of the most noteworthy events in African American church history occurred. As the black worshipers took seats that they thought were appropriate, prayer began. "We had not long been upon our knees before I heard considerable scuffling and low talking. I raised my head up and saw one of the trustees, H— M—, having hold of the Rev. Absalom Jones, pulling him up off of his knees, and saying, 'You must get up—you must not kneel here.' Mr. Jones replied, 'Wait until prayer is over.' Mr. H— M— said 'no, you must get up now, or I will call for aid and I force you away.' Mr. Jones said, 'Wait until prayer is over, and I will get up and trouble you no more.'"[31]

By the time the second usher arrived, prayer was over, and "We all went out of the church in a body, and they were no more plagued with us in the church. This raised a great excitement and inquiry among the citizens, in so much that I believe they were ashamed of their conduct."[32]

As a result, they birthed the first independent black church in the North when they rented a storefront and held worship by themselves. Facing excommunication from the "mother church," they remained united and strong. "Here we were pursued with threats of being disowned, and read publicly out of meeting if we did continue to worship in the place we had hired; but we believed the Lord would be our friend. . . . Here was the beginning and rise of the first African church in America."[33]

Nearly twenty years later, in April 1816, when increasing numbers of African Americans could not worship without harassment in the Methodist Church, Allen and others called a conference which established the first African denomination in America. It was resolved "That the people of Philadelphia, Baltimore, etc., etc., should become one body, under the name of the African Methodist Episcopal Church."[34]

Spiritual Consolation: Affectionate Sympathy through Story Sharing

Allen's experience with slavery and prejudice, along with his longing to minister in ways that met the specific needs of his African American brethren, equipped him in unique ways to empathize with his people. In an open letter of spiritual consolation entitled To the People of Colour, Allen models dynamic soul care.

Feeling an engagement of mind for your welfare, I address you with an affectionate sympathy, having been a slave, and as desirous of freedom as any of you; yet the bands of bondage were so strong that no way appeared for my release; yet at times a hope arose in my heart that a way would open for it; and when my mind was mercifully visited with the feeling of the love of God, that he would make way for my enlargement; and then these hopes increased, and a confidence arose as a patient waiting was necessary, I was sometimes favored with it, at other times I was very impatient. Then the prospect of liberty almost vanquished away, and I was in darkness and perplexity.[35]

181

Consider Allen's *holistic empathy*: emotional ("feeling"), rational ("an engagement of mind"), and relational ("an affectionate sympathy"). Notice also how Allen *connects his story to their story* by telling of his level one external suffering ("having been a slave") and his level two internal suffering ("I was very impatient"; "I was in darkness and perplexity"). As a shrewd soul physician, Allen understands how to connect with people through *story sharing*.

He explains exactly why he shares his story. "I mention the experience to you, that your hearts may not sink at the discouraging prospects you may have, and that you may put your trust in God who sees your condition, and as a merciful father pitieth his children, so doth God pity them that love him."[36] Here Allen skillfully intertwines sustaining consolation ("that your hearts may not sink at the discouraging prospects") and healing consolidation ("put your trust in God who sees" and "pitieth"). His focus is on turning their focus back to God.

Allen next shifts to guiding by providing a *current heroic narrative* and a future *freedom narrative*.

> You will have the favor and love of God dwelling in your hearts which you will value more than any thing else, which will be a consolation in the worst condition you can be in and no master can deprive you of it; and as life is short and uncertain, and the chief end of our having a being in this world is to be prepared for a better [*the current heroic narrative*], I wish you to think of this more than any thing else; then you will have a view of that freedom which the sons of God enjoy; and if the troubles of your condition end with your lives, you will be admitted to the freedom which God hath prepared for those of all colors that love him. Here the power of the most cruel master ends, and all sorrow and tears are wiped away [*the future freedom narrative*].[37]

While many historians tend to label African American ministry as either *current social protest* or *future spiritual protection,* Allen, like so many of his ministry compatriots, is able in one paragraph to unite Christlike living now with future living with Christ. He allows no disparity between the two.

Spiritual Connecting: Offering Amazing Tastes of Grace

While Allen exhibits spiritual consolation, Rev. Haynes exemplifies a touching display of spiritual connection between pastor and people. Given that the "CEO model of professional ministry" often creeps into or outright engulfs current pastoral ministry and Christian counseling, all caregivers would do well to imitate Haynes's intimate closeness with his people.

The setting remains his farewell address after thirty years of ministry. As he bids his congregants good-bye, his pain is evident. "I have sometimes thought that, perhaps God designed that I should spend the few of my remaining days among you . . . but the ways of God are mysterious, who often destroys the hope of man. In my solitary reflections, I cast a look towards this house, to bid it a final adieu. . . . Can we suppose that even a Paul was unmoved, when they all wept sore, and fell on his neck, sorrowing most of all that they should see his face no more, Acts 20:37–38."[38]

What surprising openness. Rarely does a modern pastor, leaving because of being forced out, express such vulnerability.

Continuing his moving farewell sermon, Haynes shares, "A thirty-three years ministry had excited such reciprocal endearments, that made the parting like tearing soul and body asunder. . . . My dear brethren and friends, I did not realize my attachment to you before the parting time came. Many disagreeable things have taken place; but still I feel my heart going out toward this people. How many pleasant days have I spent with you in this house? How many hours under your roofs, and delightful visits in your families?"[39]

What surprising kindness. He is candid yet offers no hint of bitterness but amazing tastes of grace. Here is a "father" unafraid of expressing emotions to his "children." No wonder his biographer, Timothy Cooley, writes of Haynes, "He always showed himself a man of a feeling heart, sensibly affected by human suffering."[40] Male leaders of all races can learn much from this spiritual mentor.

Allen, Jones, Haynes, and thousands of African American pastors like them understood what African Americans longed for in their pastor. The words of Rev. Peter Randolph summarize those longings well. Randolph arrived in Richmond, Virginia, twenty-five days after the surrender at Appomattox. Within two weeks the black congregation of Ebenezer Baptist Church invited him to be their first African American pastor.

Randolph understood their needs and desires. "Now they were free and had a voice in selecting their pastor, it is not unreasonable to suppose, that they wanted a pastor who could sympathize with them in their afflictions, and remember the bondman as bound with him. They wanted one who could preach without fear, not only on obedience, but on love, the Fatherhood of God, and the Brotherhood of man, and how Christ came to deliver the captive, and set the bondman free."[41] As exemplified by these narratives, African American shepherds strove to satisfy these longings by relating to their families as caring fathers, not as aloof professionals.

Empowering the Flock

Perhaps the founding fathers' greatest legacy was that they endeavored to leave not a *personal* legacy but a *corporate* one. Ministry was not about themselves but about empowering and equipping the flock to do the work of mutual ministry (see Eph. 4:11–16). Truly they were *fathers*—raising a family of shepherds.

184

Their corporate legacy produced fruit. Because of their examples, African American pastoral care has not simply been about what the pastor does *for* the flock but has involved the mutual ministry *of* the flock for one another. Edward Wimberly writes, "What, then, is this distinct emphasis that makes a black perspective in pastoral care and counseling unique? It is the corporate nature of pastoral care and counseling in the black church. . . . The term *corporate* means that the care of the individual is the function of the whole community, rather than the function of the pastor or any other specially designated person who possesses specialized skills."[42] On the "old ship of Zion," there are no passengers, only crew members.

Entering the Great Family of Holy Freedom: Equipping for Family Life

On April 11, 1862, Congress passed a bill abolishing slavery in the District of Columbia. Rev. Payne, then bishop of the Second Episcopal District of the AMEC, visited President Lincoln to implore him to sign the bill. When Lincoln signed the bill five days later, Payne authored *Welcome to the Ransomed* to equip newly freed African Americans.[43]

Using as his yardstick the apostle Paul's mentoring of Timothy as Timothy pastored the saints at Ephesus, Payne explains the duty of the laity: "But foremost of all the duties which he enjoined upon the Ephesian ministry and laity were those of making 'Supplications, prayers, intercessions, and giving of thanks for all men.'"[44] Having stated the duty and quoted the verse, Payne painstakingly exegetes who to pray to, what to pray for, how to pray, and with what attitude to pray.

Their prayer lives inaugurated, Payne then guides them in the use of their new freedom. "Enter the great family of Holy Freedom; not to *lounge in sinful indulgence*, not to *degrade yourselves by vice*, nor to *corrupt society by licentiousness*,

185

neither to *offend the laws by crime,* but to the *enjoyment of a well regulated liberty.* . . . Welcome to habits of industry and thrift—to duties of religion and piety."[45] As a wise father, Payne teaches his children how to appropriately use their newfound freedom and growing responsibility.

His counsel ranges from the sublime ("We entreat you to never be content until you are emancipated from sin") to the mundane ("Work, work, work!").[46] His advice is practical and culturally sensitive. "Permit us, also, to advise you to seek every opportunity for the cultivation of your minds. . . . *Rest not till you have learned to read the Bible.*"[47]

Payne reserves his most ardent counsel for parents. "But of the children take *special care.* Heaven has entrusted them to you for a *special purpose.* What is that purpose? Not merely to eat and to drink, still less to *gormandize.* Not merely to dress finely in broadcloths, silks, satins, jewelry, nor to dance to the sound of the tambourine and fiddle; but *to learn them how to live and how to die—to train them for great usefulness on earth—to prepare them for greater glory in heaven.*"[48]

Payne exhorts faithful parents to pass the baton of faith to faithful children who would continue the spiritual relay. In this he follows Paul's ministry plan. "And the things you have heard me say in the presence of many witnesses entrust to reliable men who will also be qualified to teach others" (2 Tim. 2:2).

Payne was no pie-in-the-sky pulpit expositor. He understood that what he motivated in the pulpit, he needed to cultivate in the pew *through members mutually equipping one another.* Thus, as part of his leadership, he organized the Mother's Association. "The aim of these was to aid one another in training their children, especially their daughters. . . . Perhaps the greatest curse which slavery inflicted upon us was the *destruction of the home.* No home, no mother; no mother, no home! But what is home without a cultivated intellect, and what the value of such an intellect without a cultivated heart?"[49] Payne envisioned and implemented ministries in his churches through which older women trained younger women, who in turn trained the next generation.

Mutual Aid Societies: Teaching Self-Reliance through Mutual Interdependence

When Reverends Jones and Allen started the Free African Society, it was, according to Charles Wesley, "the first step of the Negro people in the United States toward an organized social life."[50] W. E. B. Du Bois further highlights its historical significance as well as its parental equipping mode: "How great a step this was, we of today scarcely realize; we must remind ourselves that it was the first wavering step of a people toward organized social life. The society was more than a mere club: Jones and Allen were its leaders and recognized chief officers; a certain parental discipline was exercised over its members and mutual financial aid given."[51]

The preamble for the society, written on April 12, 1787, attests to their commitment to follow the biblical pattern of mutual ministry: "Whereas, Absalom Jones and Richard Allen, two men of the African race, who, for their religious life and conversation have obtained a good report among men, these persons, from a love to the people of their complexion whom they beheld with sorrow . . . proposed, after a serious communication of sentiments, that a society should be formed . . . in order to support one another in sickness, and for the benefit of their widows and fatherless children."[52]

Even after planting the African Episcopal Church of St. Thomas, the Free African Society continued as a separate organization for several years. It provided a training ground for the leadership of St. Thomas and other budding African American churches. In fact, Allen's passion was to teach African American Christians self-reliance through mutual interdependence.[53]

The great historian of the African American church, Carter G. Woodson, explains the purpose of this society and others like it. "These societies were organized to meet the crises of life—sickness and death; consequently, they were known as 'sickness and burial' societies."[54] They bore such names as "Love and Charity," "Builders of the Walls of Jerusalem," "Sons and Daughters of Esther," "Brothers and Sisters of Charity," and "Brothers and Sisters of Love." Regardless of the name, the purpose was the same—to *organize the organism* for mutual ministry.

For example, African Americans from John Street Methodist Episcopal Church in New York City took steps toward becoming an independent church, saying they had a "desire for the privilege of holding meetings of their own, where they might have an opportunity to exercise their spiritual gifts among themselves, and thereby be more useful to one another."[55] Under the empowering leadership of founding fathers, African American Christians, with heroism and creativity, crafted connecting communities that not only survived but thrived through mutual care-giving.

Following the North Star

We follow the North Star guidance of African American spiritual founding fathers by *choosing to live for something beyond ourselves.* The (satanic) temptation in life is to build monuments to ourselves. We erect our own "towers of Babel," designed to reach to heaven—so that everyone sees how wonderful *we* are.

Though imperfect, founding fathers like Payne, Liele, Bryan, Haynes, Allen, and Jones each strove *to live for God by living for the next generation.* If we attempted to carve their faces in a modern Mount Rushmore, they would be horrified. Or, if humbly appreciative, each would quickly tell us, "Anything that you may see in me is only because of Christ carved on the tablets of my heart." Furthermore, they would call us to remembrance: "When you see our faces, consider them to be memorial stones." And they would call us to be torch-passers: "Bring your children here. Show them. Empower them. Remind them that in Christ all things are possible!"

To say that they lived for something beyond themselves is quite different from saying that they never thought about themselves. To the contrary, it is obvious that they were consciously aware of the example that they were setting. They understood that they represented Christ, Christians, and *African American Christians*. They took their responsibilities seriously.

Certainly they would have thought, "What would Jesus do?" Additionally, they would have asked, "What would others think of African American Christians based upon my model?" They had an identity in Christ—and it was a *corporate identity*.

Thus, we also follow the North Star guidance of African American spiritual founding fathers by *cultivating our corporate connection*. They did not insist on being in the spotlight, but instead they ushered others into the spotlight. They did not think of the shepherd's staff as something to be greedily grasped; they distributed shepherd's staffs. More than that, they empowered and equipped laypeople for God's calling on their lives as mutual shepherds.

They understood the biblical and historical truth that pastoral care is not what the pastor does but what the people do—what the body of Christ does. They were fathers because they loved to see their kids grow up. They were fathers because they rejoiced in their children's maturity expressed through mutual ministry.

Learning Together from Our Great Cloud of Witnesses

1. You've read about a few of the great spiritual founding fathers of African American church life: Alexander Payne, George Liele, Andrew Bryan, Lemuel Haynes, Richard Allen, and Absalom Jones.

a. What impact could knowledge of African American leaders like these have on Americans? African Americans? African American males?

b. Why do you think that the history of African American leaders like these is so infrequently highlighted? What could be done to reverse this pattern?

2. Concerning modeling Christian manliness:

a. Of the many aspects of Christian manliness modeled by Alexander Payne, which ones stand out to you? Why? How could you apply his model to your life and/or ministry?

b. Payne followed three male models: his father, his mentor, and his Lord. What male models have positively affected your life? How does Christ's perfect model guide you?

3. Concerning modeling ministry commitment:

a. Why do you think that these African American leaders made hard work in the ministry such an important and recurring theme in their lives, messages, and writings?

b. What examples of pastoral ministry commitment have you witnessed? Consider writing a note of appreciation to a hard-working, sacrificial minister who has affected you.

4. Richard Allen modeled spiritual consolation through *story sharing, holistic empathy,* and *providing a current heroic narrative* as well as a *future freedom narrative.* Which of these affectionate sympathy skills would you like to add to your repertoire of spiritual friendship? How will you go about this?

5. Lemuel Haynes modeled spiritual connecting through vulnerability, openness, intimacy, and grace.

a. What godly leaders have modeled these traits for you? How?

b. How could you more effectively model these traits in your life and ministry?

190

6. African American founding fathers empowered the flock by birthing a family of shepherds.
   a. Specifically, what can church leaders today do to equip equippers? What can *you* do?
   b. How can our churches today become "mutual aid societies" of mutual interdependence?

9

Sisters of the Spirit

Mentoring Mothers

*I feel that I cannot present you with a more appropriate keep-
sake . . . than the following contour portrait of my regenerated
constitution—exhibiting, as did the bride of Solomon, comeli-
ness with blackness (Song of Sol. 1:5); and, as did the apostle
Paul, riches with poverty, and power in weakness (2 Cor. 12:9).*
        quoted in William Andrews, *Sisters of the Spirit*[1]

*And she had nothing to fall back on; not maleness, not white-
ness, not ladyhood, not anything. And out of the profound
desolation of her reality she may well have invented herself.*
        Toni Morrison, "What the Black Woman
                Thinks about Women's Lib"[2]

In the South, they faced slavery; in the North, prejudice.
Everywhere they confronted double oppression—they were
black and they were female.

193

Their remarkable stories must be told for the sake of all women, regardless of race. Their independence and strength, boldness and courage, ministry and sacrifice, care and concern, despite overwhelming obstacles, provide extraordinary models for women today.

The historical invisibility of African American Christian women is inexcusable. As the following pages attest, history is replete with countless black female exemplars of soul care and spiritual direction. Their obscurity is due to our willful blindness, not their lack of brilliance. Shining a light on their stories illuminates for all of us the visible, palpable ways in which they sustained, healed, reconciled, and guided not only individuals but an entire nation.[3]

Mother Wit

Feminine African American spiritual directors followed the ancient model that Moses outlines in Deuteronomy 6:6–7: "These commandments that I give you today are to be upon your hearts. Impress them on your children. Talk about them when you sit at home and when you walk along the road, when you lie down and when you get up."

With biological children and with "spiritual" children, with females and with males, older African American women shared their "mother wit"—their proverbial wisdom found in the Scriptures, cultivated in community, and applied to daily life. One former slave from Louisiana offers her picturesque description of mother wit. "I got Mother Wit instead of an education. Lots of colored people in offices and school don't seem to know what Mother Wit is. Well, it's like this: I got a wit to teach me what's wrong. I got a wit to not make me a mischief-maker. I got a wit to keep people's trusts. No one has to tell me not to tell what they say to me in confidence, for I respect what they say, and I never tell. I'm glad I had good raisin'."[4]

The mother wit schoolhouse was life, the textbook was the Bible. The lesson plan highlighted the generational passing of insights for living. The curriculum included reconciling (being taught "what's wrong"), guiding (not being a "mischief-maker"), rapport building ("keep people's trusts"), confidentiality ("I never tell"), respectful listening ("I respect what they say"), and so much more.

Emptying Our Crop: Wisdom from Mother Figures

We first met Amanda Berry Smith in chapter 4 as we listened to how her biological mother and grandmother guided her. Other female relatives and non-relatives were part of her community of counselors.

Smith recounts the agony of her soul due to a loveless marriage with her husband, James. One particular morning her heart was so sore that she felt she "could not bear any more." She prayed, "Lord, is there no way out of this?" As she wept and prayed, "the Lord sent Mother Jones."

In Mother Jones's presence, Smith tries mightily to suppress her tears and her troubles. Seeing through the facade, Mother Jones pointedly inquires, "Well, Smith, how do you do?"

The dam burst. "O, Mother Jones, I am nearly heart-broken; James is so unkind." Smith then shares everything she had tried, in her own effort, to change her husband, and "yet he was unkind."

Mother Jones joins with Smith by sharing her story. "Well, that is just the way Jones used to do me." She then integrates God's story into her story and Smith's story. "But when God sanctified my soul He gave me enduring grace, and that is what you need."

At that moment, the spiritual lightbulb came on. "That is just what I need; I have always been planning to get out of trials, instead of asking God for grace to endure."[5] Through Mother Jones's mother wit, God enlightened Smith to the realization that *finding God is more important than finding relief.*

Earlier in her life, Smith happened upon a book detailing a debate between an infidel and a minister. The infidel's reasoning rang loud in her young mind. "His questions and argument were so pretty and put in such a way that before I knew it I was captured; and by the time I had got through the book I had the whole of the infidel's article stamped on my memory and spirit, and the Christian's argument was lost; I could scarcely remember any of it."

She was terrified to tell anyone. "Oh, if any one should find out that I did not believe in the existence of God. I longed for some one to talk to that I might empty my crop of the load of folly that I had gathered."

In mental and spiritual agony for over a year, she "longed for deliverance, but how to get free. The Lord sent help in this way: My aunt, my mother's half sister . . . whom I loved very much, came to visit father and us children. . . . 'Now,' I thought, 'this will be my chance to unburden my heart.'"

Smith sets the scene before sharing her story and her aunt's explicit counsel. "My aunt was very religiously inclined, naturally. She was much like my mother in spirit. So as we walked along, crossing the long bridge, at that time a mile and a quarter long, we stopped, and were looking off in the water. Aunt said, 'How wonderfully God has created everything, the sky, and the great waters, etc.'

"Then I let out with my biggest gun: I said, 'How do you know there is a God?' and went on with just such an air as a poor, blind, ignorant infidel is capable of putting on."

What does Smith's aunt do? Comfort her? Debate her? Enlighten her? All could have been generically appropriate. However, Smith's aunt knows her niece and what she needs that second.

"My aunt turned and looked at me with a look that went through me like an arrow: then stamping her foot she said: 'Don't you ever speak to me again. Anybody that had as good a Christian mother as you had, and was raised as you have been, to speak so to me. I don't want to talk to you.'"

Would this "shoe fit" in every counseling scenario regarding spiritual doubt? Of course not. Did the shoe fit this foot? Only Smith can tell us.

"And God broke the snare. I felt it. I felt deliverance from that hour. How many times I have thanked God for my aunt's help. If she had argued with me I don't believe I should ever have got out of that snare of the devil."[6]

The "take home" here is not that you should say what Smith's aunt said. The application is to know your spiritual friend, yourself, and the nature of your relationship and thus know how to speak with bold love. Smith's aunt knew that she could speak candidly, and she knew which candid words could smash the devil's trap.

Smith learned her lessons well, developing her own practical mother wit ministry. Speaking of her ministry to those suffering under Satan's tauntings, she explains, "Why does God permit these fierce temptations? It is, I believe, first, to develop the strength and muscle of your own soul and so prepare you for greater service, and second, to bring you into sympathy with others, that are often sorely tempted . . . so that you can help them."

As examples, Smith cites the following situation. "After the dreadful temptation I have spoken of I met two persons that were suffering from the assaults of the old Accuser, as I had."

The first woman, known to us only as "the lady at Sea Cliff," was a schoolteacher and superintendent of a Sabbath school. Satan cast over her soul a heavy black cloud of doubt about her salvation and Christian character.

As she would tell her sad story, "everybody seemed to be in great sympathy with her and tried to help her," and "different ones would try and tell her what to do." That is, they would sustain and guide her generically, without an accurate empathy and lacking a precise understanding of the root of her struggles.

Smith, on the other hand, "saw where she was and knew she was under a temptation of the Devil." How? She listens carefully and prays faithfully. "I heard this young woman's story for three days, so I used to pray for her."

Before Smith, no one had ever intimated that Satan could be the source of this woman's spiritual battle. When Smith does so, the young woman asks her if she ever battled such satanically inspired doubts. "Yes, my child," Smith answers. "I was shut up in prison for three weeks and only just got out the other day."

Enlightened to the truth by someone who correctly understands her and the nature of devil craft, this young woman immediately finds release. "Oh, I see it. Now Satan has been telling me that sanctified people never have a cloud." She then springs to her feet and cries, "I have got the victory, I am saved, I can go home, Jesus has set me free, O, Praise the Lord."

Reflecting on her spiritual conversation, Smith notes, "Then I saw that my experience in the weeks before, had been made a blessing to her, just as Job's experience was intended to be a blessing to men and women through all coming time."[7]

Mother Jones and Smith's aunt passed the baton of mother wit to Smith, who passed it on to many other hurting women. All three of these feminine soul physicians integrated biblical truth filtered through their personal experiences applied distinctively to the unique individuals to whom God called them to minister.

Unbosoming Our Spiritual Conflicts: Equipping Others for Practical Spirituality

In chapter 5 we learned of Zilpha Elaw's early life of freedom in Philadelphia and of her spiritual freedom through conversion at age eighteen. In 1810, at age twenty, she married Joseph Elaw, whose nominal Christianity strained their marriage. Joseph died of consumption in 1823. For the next two years Zilpha Elaw led a school for black children. In 1825 she closed the school to pursue her sense of calling from God—a calling that included a five-year ministry in England.

Throughout her ministry, Elaw emphasized mutual spiritual friendship. She addressed the dedication of her autobiography to "the Saints and faithful Brethren in Christ" in London. Reflecting on their fellowship together, she writes, "If, therefore, there is anything in the soul reviving and thrilling Christian intercourse we have enjoyed together in the Spirit of Christ, and in the holy communion with which we have so frequently met together in the house of God, mingled our ascending petitions at the throne of grace, unbosomed our spiritual conflicts and trials to one another, and listened with devotional interest to the messages of gospel mercy, and the unfolding mysteries of divine grace . . ."[8]

Notice how replete her language is with images of spiritual friendship. Its purpose is to revive the soul; its mode is the practice of awe-inspiring Christian community. Its foundation is the joint worship of Christ; its pattern is mingled fellowship of Christians. Its starting point is sustaining—so beautifully pictured by the phrase "unbosomed our spiritual conflicts and trials to one another." Its high point is healing—so clearly summarized by the concept of grace-based spiritual conversations—"listened with devotional interest to the messages of gospel mercy, and the unfolding mysteries of divine grace."

While encouraging the practice of mutual spiritual friendship, Elaw also practiced mentoring mother wit through spiritual direction. Ministering in Salem, Massachusetts, Elaw "had an extensive circle of young ladies who were constant attendants upon my ministry, and who were in an especial manner my charge in the Lord; these manifested great diligence in their pursuit of the higher attainments of experiential spirituality."[9]

As Jesus with the Twelve and Paul with Timothy, Titus, and Silas, Elaw maintained a community of disciples. Also like Jesus and Paul, Elaw had a discipleship plan or model. Specifically, she focused on the "pursuit of the higher attainments of experiential spirituality." In the context, Elaw explains the vision associated with that statement. The goal of her mentoring spiritual direction was "the love of God being richly shed abroad in their hearts by the Holy Ghost" (communion and connection with Christ) and "the apprehension of, and conformity to, the love of Christ" (conformity to Christ).[10]

Elaw had not only a purpose but a plan. In ancient language we would call it "practicing the presence of Christ." In today's language we would call it "practicing the spiritual disciplines."

In her language, it sounds like this: "Spirituality is such a practical acquaintance with spiritual things, and abiding sense of the existence and agency of spiritual and invisible beings, and converse with them, as gives a complete ascendancy to the moral and mental powers over the animal propensities; but it more especially consists in a discernment of the presence and operations of the Holy Spirit, fellowship with God and his Son Jesus Christ, and the communion of the Holy Spirit, together with an habitual and deep consciousness, and a blooming prospect of the momentous realities of a future life."[11]

This is "classic" spiritual formation—emphasizing a growing attunement to spiritual realities, putting off the old propensities and putting on the new person in Christ, practicing the presence of God, disciplining oneself to receive the graces of God, and focusing on the hope of heaven. Throughout this section of her memoirs, Elaw also describes how she encouraged and equipped her circle of disciples to integrate these virtues into their lives.

In addition to her group mentoring, Elaw shares examples of her individual spiritual direction. Her very pious sister was diagnosed with an incurable disease. Upon learning of this, Elaw travels to see her. Immediately upon her arrival, her sister says to her, "My dear sister, I am going to hell."

Elaw is shocked. "My astonishment was immense at finding her in such an altered condition of mind; for only a forthnight previously she was exulting in the high praises of God."

Elaw, not one to "work alone," assembles a number of her sister's friends, who begin praying that her soul might be "released from the bonds of darkness; but she remained in this horrible state for nearly a week after my arrival."

Elaw struggles as she ministers to her sister. She alternates between being cast down with discouragement because her sister refuses all help and being encouraged with hope when the Spirit whispers to her, "Be of good cheer, thou shalt yet see the glory of God."

Ever resilient, Elaw once again assembles her team of spiritual sisters to pray for her biological sister. While Elaw is praying, her sister exclaims aloud, "Look up, children, the Master is coming!" And, "I again have found Jesus, the chiefest among ten thousand."[12]

As illustrative as the event itself is, Elaw's interpretation of it is perhaps even more instructive. "The antagonizing conflicts of Christian faith, and its triumph through the aids of the Holy Spirit over the powers of darkness, as exemplified on such occasions . . . is the natural cause and effect of exercise of Christian faith, in collision with forces asserted by the gospel to be engaged in hostile action to it."[13]

In a phrase, such deathbed doubts and deathbed rebirths are a result of *spiritual warfare*. In a word, they are due to a *quadralog*. Earlier we learned of *trialogues* in historic soul care and spiritual direction—the threefold conversation between the counselor, the counselee, and the divine Counselor. Elaw understood that every spiritual conversation is a *four-party* call between the counselor, the counselee, the divine Counselor, and Satan—the lying, murdering, condemning counselor of evil. In fact, what makes spiritual direction *spiritual*

201

is this foundational awareness of the invisible spiritual battle occurring during every visible, audible conversation.

Your Maker Is Your Husband: Pointing Others to the Ultimate Spiritual Friend

Julia Foote exemplifies in her life and teaching a common thread among female African American care-givers—that Jesus is the ultimate spiritual friend. These sisters of the Spirit understood that human spiritual friendship never replaces the divine spiritual friend and that the human spiritual director must always direct others to the divine soul physician.

Foote was born in 1823 in Schenectady, New York, the daughter of former slaves who purchased their freedom and espoused a strong Christian belief. From ages ten to twelve, she studied diligently, especially the Bible. At fifteen she moved with her parents to Albany, where she was converted and joined the African Methodist Church.

At nineteen she married George Foote, a sailor, and moved to Boston, where she joined the African Methodist Episcopal Zion Church and began to grow deeply in her faith. Her deepening Christian experience caused a rift between her and George, and he threatened to send her back to her parents. Though they stayed together, they grew more alienated, especially when Foote began to hold evangelistic meetings in her home.

Speaking of why God might allow human suffering and breakdowns in human relationships such as the one between her and her husband, Foote explains, "God permits afflictions and persecutions to come upon his chosen people to answer various ends. Sometimes for the trial of their faith, and the exercise of their patience and resignation to his will, and sometimes to draw them off from all human dependence, and to teach them to trust in Him alone."[14]

For Foote, this was not some theoretical model stuck somewhere up in her head. Bereft of the intimacy she longed for with her human husband, she turned more profoundly and passionately to her heavenly groom.

When her husband left for six months at sea right after yet another argument over her faith, Foote wrote, "While under this apparent cloud, I took the Bible to my closet, asking Divine aid. As I opened the book, my eyes fell on these words: 'For thy Maker is thine husband' (Isa. 54:5). I then read the fifty-fourth chapter of Isaiah over and over again. It seemed to me that I had never seen it before. I went forth glorifying God."[15]

Later, when her husband passed away, she found God to be not only her husband but also her heavenly Father. "While thus laboring far from home, the sad intelligence of my husband's death came to me so suddenly as to almost cause me to sink beneath the blow. But the arm of my dear, loving, heavenly Father sustained me, and I was enabled to say, 'Though he slay me, yet will I trust in him' (Job 13:15)."[16]

Her theological conviction and personal experience of God as husband and Father became the foundation of her ministry to others. Summarizing her purpose and the results of intimate communion with God, Foote explains, "My earnest desire is that many—especially of my own race—may be led to believe and enter into rest; 'For we which have believed do enter into rest' (Heb. 4:3)—sweet soul rest."[17] Foote personally experienced Christ as her ultimate spiritual friend, and she longed for others to enter into intimate intercourse with their ultimate spiritual friend, resulting in soul rest in the soul physician.

Calling Out a People

In September 1832 in Boston, Massachusetts, Maria Stewart did something that no American-born woman of any race before her had undertaken. "She mounted a lecture platform and raised a political argument before a 'promiscuous' audience, that is, one composed of both men and women."[18]

According to her personal testimony, she was a woman of profound Christian faith, moved by the Spirit to "willingly sacrifice my life for the cause of God and my brethren."[19] In the climate of that day, she did indeed take her life in her hands. In her characteristically fiery style, familiar to readers of her articles in *The Liberator*, she argued against the colonization movement to ship African Americans to West Africa. Using biblical imagery, she challenged her racially mixed audience, asking, "Why sit ye here and die?"

She called blacks and whites to action, in particular urging black Americans to demand their God-given rights. "Her message was unsparing and controversial, intended as a goad to her people to organize against the tyranny of slavery in the South and to resist and defy the restrictions of bigotry in the North."[20]

Arousing to Exertion: Biblical Challenge to Personal Growth

To fully comprehend Stewart's staggering accomplishments, we have to backtrack to her less than advantageous upbringing. She describes it:

> I was born in Hartford, Connecticut, in 1803; was left an orphan at five years of age; was bound out in a clergyman's family; had the seeds of piety and virtue early sown in my mind, but was deprived of the advantages of education, though my soul thirsted for knowledge. Left them at fifteen years of age; attended Sabbath schools until I was twenty; in 1826 was married to James W. Stewart; was left a widow in 1829; was, as I humbly hope and trust, brought to the knowledge of the truth, as it is in Jesus, in 1830; in 1831 I made a public profession of my faith in Christ.[21]

Married at twenty-three, widowed at twenty-six, converted at twenty-seven, she challenged a nation at twenty-eight. In the fall of 1831, she entered the offices of William Lloyd Garrison, the editor of the newly established abolitionist newspaper *The Liberator*. Stewart handed Garrison the manuscript of her challenge to African Americans to sue for their rights. Although it was relegated to the paper's "Ladies Department," both ladies and gentlemen received her confrontation.

Stewart entitled her work "Religion and the Pure Principles of Morality: The Sure Foundation on Which We Must Build." She told her readers that she "presented them before you in order to arouse you to exertion, and to enforce upon your minds the great necessity of turning your attention to knowledge and improvement."[22] Here we have a young, female, African American widow writing in a white male abolitionist tabloid as a spiritual director to motivate her people to learning and action.

Stewart adeptly used a bevy of spiritual direction skills to inspire her audience. Notice how in the next portion of her essay she applies the art of *envisioning* to help others see and unearth their buried talents and abilities. "All the nations of the earth are crying out for liberty and equality. Away, away with tyranny and oppression! And shall Afric's sons be silent any longer? Far be it from me to recommend to you either to kill, burn, or destroy. But I would strongly recommend to you to improve your talents; let not one lie buried in the earth. Show forth your powers of mind. Prove to the world that though black your skins as shades of night, your hearts are pure, your souls are white."[23]

Next, Stewart avails herself of the guiding competency of *scriptural exploration*. "Many think, because your skins are tinged with a sable hue, that you are an inferior race of beings; but God does not consider you as such. He hath formed and fashioned you in his own glorious image, and hath bestowed upon you reason and strong powers of intellect. He hath

205

made you to have dominion over the beasts of the field, the fowls of the air, and the fish of the sea (Gen. 1:26). He hath crowned you with glory and honor; hath made you but a little lower than the angels (Ps. 8:5)."[24] Using the biblical truth of the *imago Dei* (image of God), she guides her readers toward the countercultural but scriptural truth that "It is not the color of the skin that makes the man, but it is the principles formed within the soul."[25]

Stewart also mingles reconciling and guiding as she confronts past failures and challenges toward future exploits. "O, ye daughters of Africa, awake! Awake! Arise! No longer sleep nor slumber, but distinguish yourselves. Show forth to the world that ye are endowed with noble and exalted faculties. O, ye daughters of Africa! What have you done to immortalize your names beyond the grave? What examples have ye set before the rising generation? What foundation have ye laid for generations yet unborn?"[26]

She's poking and provoking, prodding and awakening. Responsive hearts would surely experience conviction due to past inaction and stimulation to rekindled action. It is as if Stewart peels open the layers of their hearts, tilts their heads down to look inside, exposes what is not there, envisions what could and should be there, and then makes eye contact to ask, "What legacy are you going to leave?"

Detect in the following vignette the repeatedly interchanging patterns of reconciling (confronting) and guiding (challenging). "O then, do not trifle with God and your own souls any longer [confronting]. Do not presume to offer him the very dregs of your lives [confronting]; but now, whilst you are blooming in health and vigor, consecrate the remnant of your days to him [challenging]. Do you wish to become useful in your day and generation [confronting and challenging]? Do you wish to promote the welfare and happiness of your friends, as far as your circle extends [confronting and challenging]? Have you one desire to become truly great [confronting and challenging]? O then become truly pious and God will endow you with wisdom and knowledge from on high [challenging]."[27]

In perhaps her most frank comments, Stewart challenges black women to not "bury their minds and talents beneath a load of iron pots and kettles." She explains that whites "have practiced nothing but head-work these 200 years, and we have done their drudgery. And is it not high time for us to imitate their examples, and practice head-work too, and keep what we have got, and get what we can?"[28]

How prescient. How far ahead of her time.

And she's just warming up. Stewart also exhorts to a spirit not of aggressive anger, nor of passive resignation, but of assertive courage. "And we have possessed by far too mean and cowardly a disposition, though I highly disapprove of an insolent or impertinent one. Do you ask the disposition I would have you possess? Possess the spirit of independence. The Americans do, and why should not you? Possess the spirit of men, bold and enterprising, fearless and undaunted."[29]

What an inspiring challenge. Stewart is reminding African American women that God endowed them with an equal measure of spiritual power, love, and wisdom. They do *not* have to take a backseat to anyone.

Exhorting to Liberation: Biblical Challenge to Corporate Action

In *Pastoral Care in the Black Church*, Edward Wimberly argues that *liberation* serves as a norm for African American pastoral care. He defines liberation as "the freeing of persons from those internal and external forces that prevent them from moving toward their full potential as self-actualizing, assertive human beings related to God."[30]

In Stewart's comments to this point, we have clearly witnessed liberation from *internal* forces. In the remainder of her letter of spiritual confrontation, we observe liberation from *external* forces. Her words reflect a common theme in African

American spiritual direction. True reconciliation, true liberation, though starting with the individual's relationship to God
through Christ, must continue with *societal* liberation. African
American spiritual direction boldly confronted societal sins,
calling for national repentance and corporate action.

Stewart begins doing so by confronting reality on a national
level—the reality of systemic racism. Surveying the landscape,
she cites case after case of whites nurturing whites. They consecrate their *white* children to God; they wipe the tears from
white orphans; they promote the poorest *whites* to excel. "But
how very few are there among them that bestow one thought
upon the benighted sons and daughters of Africa, who have
enriched the soils of America with their tears and blood: few
to promote their cause, none to encourage their talents."[31]

Stewart then diagnoses the problem: national sin. "Righteousness exalteth a nation, but sin is a reproach to any
people (Prov. 14:34). Why is it, my friends, that our minds
have been blinded by ignorance, to the present moment?"
She next prescribes God's solution: national repentance.
"O, then, let us bow before the Lord our God, with all our
hearts, and humble our very souls in the dust before him;
sprinkling, as it were, ashes upon our heads, and awake to
righteousness and sin not."[32]

In the historic spirit of ancient reconciling, Stewart reminds her readers, blacks and whites, that though it is horrible to sin, it is wonderful to be forgiven because God is
gracious even when we are evil. "The arm of the Lord is not
shortened, that it cannot save; neither is his ear heavy, that it
cannot hear; but it is your iniquities that have separated you
from me, saith the Lord. Return, O ye backsliding children
(Jer. 3:22), and I will return unto you, and ye shall be my
people, and I will be your God."[33]

Here's a woman who practices what she preaches. Here's
a twenty-eight-year-old African American widowed female
using scriptural exploration to call white Americans to repentance and forgiveness.

In case they somehow still missed her message, she concludes with these words: "You may kill, tyrannize, and oppress as much as you choose, until our cry shall come up before the throne of God; for I am firmly persuaded, that he will not suffer you to quell the proud, fearless and undaunted spirits of Africans forever; for in his own time, he is able to plead our cause against you, and to pour out upon you the ten plagues of Egypt."[34]

Stewart places her ultimate trust not in herself, not in black America, not in white America, but in the God who is a liberator. Still, she calls on those who claim to follow him to do what Jesus would do—set the captives free.

Following the North Star

We follow the North Star guidance of African American sisters of the Spirit by *encouraging spiritual sisters with the good news that the Spirit intimately indwells them.* Jarena Lee, whose conversion we witnessed in chapter 5, reminds us of this truth which she experienced.

In the course of six years, five of her family members died, including her husband. "I was now left alone in the world, with two infant children, one of the age of about two years, the other six months, with no other dependence than the promise of Him who hath said—I will be the widow's God, and a father to the fatherless."[35]

As Lee did, we need to help our spiritual friends to see the two primary ways that the indwelling Spirit ministers. First, he uses his other children. Lee recounts, "Accordingly, he raised me up friends, whose liberality comforted and solaced me in my state of widowhood and sorrows. I could sing with the greatest propriety the words of the poet, 'He helps the stranger in distress, the widow and the fatherless, and grants the prisoner sweet release.'"[36]

Such awareness is vital. The temptation when we are hurt by people is to turn *only* to God. This pseudo-spirituality is *not* the way of the Spirit. African American female exemplars like Lee demonstrate that the Spirit uses brothers and sisters of the Spirit to sustain, heal, reconcile, and guide us.

Second, the Spirit does indeed work directly in and on our hurting hearts. Lee understood this truth also. "I can say even now, with the Psalmist, 'Once I was young, but now I am old, yet I have never seen the righteous forsaken, nor his seed begging bread.' I have ever been fed by his bounty, clothed in his mercy, comforted and healed when sick, succored when tempted, and every where upheld by his hand."[37]

This "balancing" awareness is also crucial. The temptation when we are helped by people is to keep turning *only* to people. As we've seen continually in this chapter, these sisters of the Spirit led people to the Spirit for his sustaining, healing, reconciling, and guiding. Our source of spiritual care is not either-or. It is both-and.

We also follow the North Star guidance of African American sisters of the Spirit by *believing that the Spirit actively gifts every redeemed sister*. Harriet Tubman, like so many others, models such giftedness.

When Sarah Bradford authored the second edition of her biography of Tubman, she offered a new subtitle: *The Moses of Her People*. Bradford acknowledges that this "may seem a little ambitious, considering that this Moses was a woman, and that she succeeded in piloting only three or four hundred slaves from the land of bondage to the land of freedom. But I only give her here the name by which she was familiarly known, both at the North and the South, during the terror of the Fugitive Slave Law, and during our last Civil War, in both of which she took so prominent a part."[38]

Since the stories that Bradford collected about Tubman were so amazing, many in her day had a hard time believing that they could be true of a *black woman*. Therefore, Bradford gathered copious testimonies from others to substantiate Tubman's character and ministry.

It is well past time that we demolish such prejudice. It is time that we provide all sisters of the Spirit, regardless of race, with the assurance that they can do great things for God through the Spirit.

The inspiring message of one more historic sister of the Spirit, Florence Spearing Randolph, offers such hope. She said, "History proves that every great man or woman in the world who has climbed the steep stairs of fame, and made a mark in the world was first inspired by hope, 'auspicious hope.' Though many of them were poor, they realized that life was action, life was duty, that God had given existence with full power and opportunity to improve it and be happy; or to despise the gift and be miserable. Life is a mission, or journey, and it is important that we do our utmost to make the journey a successful one."[39]

Learning Together from Our Great Cloud of Witnesses

1. You've read about a few of the great sisters of the Spirit of African American church life: Amanda Berry Smith, Zilpha Elaw, Julia Foote, Maria Stewart, Jarena Lee, and Harriet Tubman.
   a. What impact could knowledge of African American sisters like these have on Americans? African Americans? African American females?
   b. Why do you think that the history of African American females like these is so infrequently highlighted? What could be done to reverse this pattern?
2. Who has offered you mother wit—biblical wisdom filtered through mature life experience and applied to your specific life situation? How? What impact has it had on you?

3. We discovered numerous examples of mother wit in Amanda Berry Smith's life and ministry.
   a. Which ones stand out to you? Why?
   b. How could you apply them to your life and ministry?
4. From Zilpha Elaw, we learned to recognize the *quadralog*: the presence of Satan intruding on every spiritual conversation. How can this awareness affect your spiritual conversations?
5. Julia Foote typified pointing others to Jesus as their ultimate spiritual friend—as their husband and Father.
   a. Why do you think this theme was so common among African American female soul physicians?
   b. How could you apply this theme to your life and ministry?
6. Maria Stewart focused on both personal growth and national repentance.
   a. What did she stir in *your* heart when you read her poking and provoking words of personal growth?
   b. What national sins does our nation need to be liberated from through repentance?

10

This Far by Faith

The Drama of Deliverance

*It looked like the more I prayed the worse off I got. But the
God I serve is a time-God. He don't come before time; he
don't come after time. He comes just on time.*

quoted in Clifton Johnson, *God Struck Me Dead*[1]

*It required no stretch of the imagination to see the trials of the
Israelites as paralleling the trials of the slaves, Pharaoh and
his army as oppressors, and Egyptland as the South.*

Langston Hughes and Arna Bontemps,
The Book of Negro Folklore[2]

Our worldview makes a world of difference in our lives,
especially when our fallen world falls on us. As African
Americans journeyed from enslavement to emancipation,
they faced the same spiritual questions that we all face when
we encounter inexplicable suffering.

213

Nellie, a former slave from Savannah, Georgia, shares her confusion. "It has been a terrible mystery, to know why the good Lord should so long afflict my people, and keep them in bondage,—to be abused, and trampled down, without any rights of their own,—with no ray of light in the future. Some of my folks said there wasn't any God, for if there was He wouldn't let white folks do as they have done for so many years."[3]

It is difficult enough to endure *personal* suffering and ponder God's purposes. The spiritual task grows more challenging when we, like Nellie, open our eyes to a *world* of unjust suffering. Trusting God's plan becomes even more grueling when we see within that world pockets of prejudicial subjugation. Our question moves from "Why me?" to "Why us?" and eventually to "Why God?"

Don't Raise My Hopes: Handling Lost Hope

Somehow African American believers moved *beyond* the suffering. Fittingly, our final chapter shows us how.

Thus far we've traced their tracks from freedom to capture and then to long-awaited emancipation. Sadly, American history teaches us that the freedoms of the Emancipation Proclamation and the Reconstruction era were short-lived.

Hope deferred, then won, only to be lost again, is the greatest snare of all. It is reminiscent of the barren Shunammite woman in 2 Kings 4. After years of childlessness, she is incredulous when Elisha promises her that within a year she will embrace a son. Her deferred hope turns to hope embraced. Regrettably, within a few short years this Shunammite mother again embraces her son—in an embrace of death as he dies in her lap. No wonder she finds Elisha, seizes hold of his feet, and in bitter distress cries out, "Didn't I tell you, '*Don't raise my hopes*'?" (2 Kings 4:28, emphasis added).

This woman's tale resonates with African Americans. They know hope deferred, hope won, then hope lost.

It resonates with all of us. We've all "been there, done that."

How do we handle the vagaries of our ever-changing circumstances? How do we face the tumultuous ups and downs of daily life? How do we trust God's plan when we can't see his hand?

Delivered from Bondage: Leaning on the Lord by Gleaning from His Word

African American exemplars demonstrate how to live by faith in a fallen world. For example, when her mistress questions her about her faith, a slave named Polly explains her hope. "We poor creatures have need to believe in God, for if God Almighty will not be good to us some day, why were we born? When I heard of his delivering his people from bondage I know it means the poor Africans."[4]

Ponder Polly's faith perspective. She moves from "Why me?" "Why us?" and "Why God?" to "*Which God?*" She entrusts her troubled soul to the God of the Bible, who reveals himself to be the Almighty, the good deliverer of the oppressed.

Whether individual narratives, personal letters of spiritual consolation, slave spirituals, gospel songs, public speeches, or pulpit messages, all these writings focus on the narrative of God as *the God of the oppressed*. African American Christians repeatedly turned to scriptural narratives portraying God's character as the Father of the fatherless, whether it was the story of Hagar in the wilderness, the Israelites in Egypt, the children of God in Canaan, or Judah in the Babylonian captivity. "For he will deliver the needy who cry out, the afflicted who have no one to help. He will take pity on the weak and the needy and save the needy from death. He will rescue them from oppression and violence, for precious is their blood in his sight" (Ps. 72:12–14).

The classic African American gospel song "We've Come This Far by Faith" powerfully and poetically articulates the faith of Polly and her spiritual siblings.

> We've come this far by faith leaning on the Lord;
> Trusting in His Holy Word, He's never failed me yet.
> Oh, can't turn around, we've come this far by faith.
> Don't be discouraged with trouble in your life,
> He'll bear your burdens and move all misery and
> strife.
> That's why we've come this far by faith.[5]

Consider the common denominator connecting Polly and this gospel song. Both glean from the Word narrative images of a good God who is touched by the feelings of our infirmities and moved by our misery to move mountains in response to our dependent faith. It's all about narratives—about faith stories. African Americans shared scriptural stories of sustaining, healing, reconciling, and guiding that gave each life value and each day meaning. They co-created both a personal narrative and a national (or corporate, communal, ethnic) narrative that enabled them to survive and thrive by understanding their personal purpose and national calling—*in light of their understanding of the character of God.*

The Tournament of Narratives

The idea of an American "national narrative" drawn from Scripture was not new. When European Christians immigrated to America, they chose a dominant biblical lens through which to view themselves corporately. They were, according to Puritan John Winthrop, "a city upon a hill." As God's new chosen people fleeing the religious tyranny of Europe, if they obeyed God they would "find that the God of Israel is among us, when ten of us shall be able to resist a thousand of our enemies."[6]

From the earliest period of their migration to the New World, European colonists spoke of their journey as the new exodus of a new Israel from bondage in Egypt to the Promised Land of milk and honey.[7] For these early European Americans, America *already was* the Promised Land. White Europeans left Europe in an exodus due to persecution, finding religious and political freedom and likening it to the children of Israel crossing the Red Sea.

This message rings true for their ancestors to this day—they are God's chosen people, and America is an especially God-blessed land. In fact, many would be shocked to realize that anyone has ever seen it any differently.

Bound for the Promised Land: Interpreting the African American Experience

Europeans freely sailed to the "land of the free," but Africans were stolen away from their free lands, stowed in the hideous holds of the slave ships, and brought to the "land of bondage." For Europeans the exodus had *already occurred*; for Africans it was *yet future*. Europeans *lived in* the Promised Land. Africans were *bound for* the Promised Land.

As Raboteau explains, "For African-Americans the journey was reversed: whites might claim that America was a new Israel, but blacks knew that it was Egypt, since they, like the children of Israel of old, still toiled in bondage. Unless America freed God's African children, this nation would suffer the plagues that had afflicted Egypt."[8]

Could two biblically based visions of one nation be any more different? Both shared a common stock of biblical metaphors: Egypt, exodus, the Promised Land. However, each saw the vision through different lenses.

Acknowledging these contrasting visions can increase our cross-cultural connections. For instance, at times European Americans think of African Americans as needing to "assimilate" into American culture. This assumes that American culture *equals* the culture that European Americans single-handedly birthed. As we've seen throughout *Beyond the Suffering,* from 1619 to 1863 and beyond, there has been tremendous interplay between these two "cultures." To suggest that African Americans must assimilate into European American culture negates the equal contributions that African Americans have made in the creation of American culture.

With cross-cultural awareness, we can perceive the issue more accurately. "Minority cultures" are not required to jettison their cultural heritage and be assimilated into one elite, "dominant culture." Instead, all cultural groups (Native Americans, Europeans, Africans, Asians, Hispanics, etc.) can cherish their own culture while at the same time co-creating one new multicultural nation. They jointly weave together a new mosaic, a shared heritage, a collective narrative.

More fully understanding African Americans' vision of themselves in America can also increase our cross-cultural competency. Ministering effectively to African Americans requires an understanding of how African American Christian leaders and laypeople have read and interpreted their American experience. To come to this place of understanding, we need to explore the African American narrative of God's *nature,* the African American *personal* narrative of relationship to God, and the African American *national* narrative of relationship to God.

The God of the Promised Land: Experiencing the God Who Sets the Captives Free

The faith that Polly shared with her mistress and that African Americans sang about in church gatherings combined God's character, their situation, and scriptural themes of liberation. Aunt Jane's counsel to Charlotte Brooks illustrates the intersection of these three components. "Aunt Jane used to tell us, too, that the children of Israel was in Egypt in bondage, and that God delivered them out of Egypt; and she said he would deliver us. We all used to sing a hymn like this: 'My God delivered Daniel, Daniel, Daniel; My God delivered Daniel, And why not deliver me too? He delivered Daniel from the lion's den, Jonah from the belly of the whale, the three Hebrew children from the fiery furnace, And why not deliver me too?'"[9]

For Aunt Jane, the God of Moses, Daniel, Jonah, Shadrach, Meshach, and Abednego is alive and well on planet Earth. His powerful deliverance *then* relates to Aunt Jane and Charlotte *now* because his *character* never changes. He will deliver them from captivity because he is, in his *very nature*, a rescuer. Raboteau noted, "One of the sources that sustained Christian slaves against such temptations to despair was the Bible with its accounts of the mighty deeds of a God who miraculously intervenes in human history to cast down the mighty and to lift up the lowly, a God who saves the oppressed and punishes the oppressor."[10]

Their faith was faith in an *in-the-moment* God—an immanent God who loves to love his children. Ex-slave Simon Brown explains, "The folks would sing and pray and testify and clap their hands, just as if God was right there in the midst of them. He wasn't way off in the sky. He was a-seeing everybody and a-listening to every word and a-promising to let His love come down. . . . Yes, sir, there was no pretending in those prayer meetings. There was a living faith in a just God who would one day answer the cries of His poor black children and deliver them from their enemies."[11]

Their faith was earthy and real. Ex–Virginia slave William Grimes prays to his real God in his real time of need when Grimes's master orders him flogged. "I looked up to heaven and prayed fervently to God to hear my prayer, and grant me relief in this hour of adversity; expecting every moment to be whipped until I could not stand; and *blessed be God* that he turned their hearts before they could arrive at the place of destination: for on arriving there, I was acquitted. God delivered me from the power of the adversary." Grimes assures his readers that he "did not make a feeble attempt to induce my master not to flog me; but put my trust, and offered my prayers to my heavenly Father, who heard and answered them."[12]

These samples teach us a very important truth: *nothing is more important about us than what image of God we hold in our minds*. Some people falsely assume that enslaved and free African Americans were nontheological, that they were all about experience in the heart and not insight in the mind. This simply is untrue. They combined heart and head, experience and theology, faith and fact.

Aunt Lethe Jackson, a household servant for Virginia governor David Campbell, is another splendid example of how a deeply theological image of God sustained African Americans. In a letter to the governor's daughter, Aunt Lethe writes, "When we know that our good Lord is Divine Love & Wisdom in its utmost perfection and that, *that* Love and Wisdom is continually exerted for our welfare how grateful, how active, and how obedient, ought we to be and how confident, in all his mercies."[13]

Their theological understanding of God emphasized his unchanging nature as the I AM of Exodus. While running away from slavery in Kentucky, Henry Bibb feels his heart tremble within him as he ponders the great danger to which he was exposing himself in taking passage on a southern steamboat. "Hence before I took passage, I kneeled down before the Great I Am, and prayed for his aid and protection, which He bountifully bestowed even beyond my expectation; for I felt myself to be unworthy. I then stept boldly on the deck."[14]

The Great I AM can be trusted to set the captives free because it is his enduring, eternal nature. As Bibb explains, "I never omitted to pray for deliverance. I had faith to believe that the Lord could see our wrongs and hear our cries."[15]

Life is a story and God is the main character in that story. For African Americans, the unfolding plot in their story, page after page, has been God the Deliverer's daily deliverance of them. As spiritual friends, they repeatedly turned one another to the faith stories of the Bible so that they could respond to "God's salvation drama as it unfolds and impacts their lives."[16]

God's Chosen People

To move beyond the suffering, believing slaves began with the biblical narrative of who God is. As vital as this was, it could have remained impersonal. As we've seen, it certainly did not. Why? What was the "secret" to the African American ability to relate who God is to their lives?

They clung to biblical narratives of *who they were in relationship to God* and his drama of deliverance. Christian slaves used scriptural imagery to counteract the shaming imagery of enslavement. It is as if they said, "We may be slaves, but so were God's chosen people. In fact, God's people have always been enslaved by God's enemies, and God has always had compassion on his enslaved people. All he asks of his enslaved people is to trust and obey."

Joining God's Larger Story: Transmitting Our Faith Stories

Having a biblical sense of self may seem rudimentary until we recall that African Americans were not perceived or treated as human beings but as chattel. This is why the slave narratives were so monumental. Through the simple act of telling their own life stories, they indicated that blacks, just as much as whites, each had a personal narrative and lived fully human lives with emotions, actions, goals, thoughts, and longings.[17]

Octavia Albert found her motivation for interviewing her fellow African Americans in her conviction that their personal stories were part of God's larger story. Colonel

221

Douglass Wilson was "a colored man of considerable prominence, not only in Louisiana, but in the nation." Albert consistently communicates to him what a rich experience he had before and after the war. She urges him to tell his story because it "would delight almost any one. Don't keep all the good things to yourself; tell us about them sometime."[18]

When Colonel Wilson expresses hesitation about his storytelling because some might think it inappropriate, Albert responds, "'I assure you,' said I, 'you will never hear that from me, because I believe we should not only treasure these things, but should transmit them to our children's children. That's what the Lord commanded Israel to do in reference to their deliverance from Egyptian bondage, and I verily believe that the same is his will concerning us and our bondage and deliverance in this country.'"[19]

Albert is an adroit soul physician. The Scriptures are her soul anatomy textbook. She dispenses ample doses of biblical wisdom as she helps Wilson to see that his storytelling is not self-serving but community-building and God-glorifying. She enlightens Wilson to his role in God's plan: that by his testimony he witnesses to God's exodus-like deliverance of his people.

Insiders in the Drama of Deliverance: Envisioning Our Life Stories

The central biblical motif through which African Americans interpreted their lives and the Scriptures was the exodus/conquest. They were God's chosen people, and he was leading them out of the land of Egypt, across the Red Sea, over the Jordan River, and into the Promised Land of Canaan. Exodus was the archetype drawn from Scripture that became the lens through which the Bible was read, and liberation from bondage was seen as the Bible's central thrust.[20]

By identifying themselves with the children of Israel, "African slaves declared themselves as insiders in the scriptural drama. The Hebrew model of interpretation placed the slaves squarely in the center of the salvation narrative. While slaveholders focused on ancient Israel as a slaveholding society, the African slaves saw ancient Israel first as a nation descended from slaves. In this sense, slave interpreters were able to reverse the patriarchal paradigm of the slaveholders."[21] The suffering slaves certainly resembled Jesus, the suffering servant, more than their unsympathetic masters did.

As with their image of God, their image of themselves as God's chosen children journeying to Canaan was omnipresent. John Boston, a runaway slave from Maryland, took refuge with a New York regiment during the Civil War. Writing to his wife on January 12, 1862, from Upton Hill, Virginia, he weaves into his letter his "exodus identity." "My Dear Wife, It is with grate joy I take this time to let you know whare I am. I am now in safety in the 14th Regiment of Brooklyn. This day I can adress you thank God as a free man. I had a little truble in giting away but as the Lord led the Children of Isrel to the land of Canon so he led me to a land whare freedom will rain in spite of earth and hell."[22]

The *personal* exodus identity related not only to freedom from the sin of slavery but also to freedom from the slavery of sin. In fact, many African American laypeople, preachers, and writers interpreted God's plan in terms of the "fortunate fall." That is, though American slavery was horribly evil, God turned evil into good by exposing enslaved Africans to the truth of salvation in Christ.

Phillis Wheatley offers a prime example. Born in Senegal, West Africa, in 1753, she was kidnapped at age seven, put aboard a slave ship, and sold to a prosperous Boston family, John and Susannah Wheatley. She began writing poetry at age fourteen and became something of a sensation in Boston in the 1760s.

In her poem "On Being Brought from Africa to America," she shares her poetic vision of God palliating the human evil of slavery.

> 'Twas mercy brought me from my *Pagan* land,
> Taught my benighted soul to understand
> That there's a God, that there's a *Saviour* too:
> Once I redemption neither sought nor knew.[23]

In human free will, Europeans perpetrated the vicious evil of enslaving Africans. In God's sovereign prerogative, he worked beneath, in, through, and around human evil to free individuals like Wheatley from sin's captivity.

God calls us to apply these narrative principles in our ministries today. Edward Wimberly recounts that in past and current African American ministry, pastors have used storytelling in preaching and counseling to deconstruct and reconstruct shame-filled African American stories of being unlovable. He further explains that people bring *secular scriptures* to church—well-formed personal narratives fashioned by the world, the flesh, and the devil.[24]

These worldly narratives of life become idols around which people organize their lives and interpret reality. Changing them requires divine and human intervention. In the language of the apostle Paul, people need to put off the old, secular, idolatrous, lying scriptures and put on the new, worshipful, truth-telling Scriptures (see Col. 3:1–17).

Following this African American model, we can assist people to explore where they were recruited into the shameful narrative they now own, asking, "Who taught you that lie about yourself? Who told you that you can deal with sin self-sufficiently?" After exposing these satanically inspired life narratives, we can then help people examine and apply biblical narratives about who they truly are in Christ. "What does God's Word say about Christ's view of you? How can you receive Christ's grace to cleanse your disgrace?"

God Comes Down

As we've noted, African Americans have applied the exodus/conquest narrative individually *and* nationally. The national examples would fill hundreds of books rather than one section of one chapter. Reverend Absalom Jones's "Thanksgiving Sermon," introduced in chapter 1, provides an excellent synopsis.

You will recall that Rev. Jones chose as his text Exodus 3:7–8. Jones starts by briefly highlighting God's sustaining care and healing comfort for Israel. He then relates the historical exodus narrative to current African American life.

> The history of the world shows us, that the deliverance of the children of Israel from their bondage, is not the only instance, in which it has pleased God to appear in behalf of oppressed and distressed nations, as the deliverer of the innocent, and of those who call upon his name. He is as unchangeable in his nature and character, as he is in his wisdom and power. The great and blessed event, which we have this day met to celebrate, is a striking proof, that the God of heaven and earth is *the same, yesterday, and to-day, and for ever.*[25]

The basis of this comparison is *God's unchanging nature.*

He Has Seen: Paying Attention to the Earthly Story of Suffering

In classic sustaining style, Jones next shows that God has been watching every event of their earthly story. "He has seen the affliction of our countrymen, with an eye of pity."[26] To emphasize how important it is to pay attention to the earthly story, Jones presents an outline of African American history hauntingly similar to the one we have presented in *Beyond the Suffering*: capture; middle passage; auction block sale; enslavement; separation from family;

work from sunup to sundown; deprivation of food, clothing, and shelter; torture of the body; and withholding of religion from the soul.

Jones prefaces each point with the repeated phrase concerning God, *"He has seen."* Thirteen times. Can you hear it? Feel it? Imagine it? Place yourself in the congregation.

"He has seen." "Oh, yeah!" *"He has seen."* "Preach it!" *"He has seen."* "Come on!" *"He has seen."* "Glory!" *"He has seen."* "Yes, he has!" *"He has seen."* Clapping. *"He has seen."* Standing. *"He has seen."* Swaying. *"He has seen."* Hands raised. *"He has seen."* Shouting. *"He has seen."* "Amen!" *"He has seen."* Tears streaming. *"He has seen."* Kneeling.

He has not only seen; he has also heard. Jones preaches, "Inhuman wretches! though You have been deaf to their cries and shrieks, they have been heard in Heaven. The ears of Jehovah have been constantly open to them. He has heard the prayers that have ascended from the hearts of his people; and he has, as in the case of his ancient and chosen people the Jews, *come down to deliver* our suffering countrymen from the hands of the oppressors."[27] The suffering Jews and the suffering African Americans are one people of God.

Four times Pastor Jones repeats the phrase "He came down." This is a healing hope. God sustains *and* he saves. He climbs in the casket *and* he rolls the stone away, leaving an empty tomb. He sees *and* he comes down.

What worship response is appropriate? Celebrate the empty tomb! "O! let us *give thanks unto the Lord*: let us *call upon his name*, and *make known his deeds among the people. Let us sing psalms unto him and talk of all his wondrous works*."[28]

What ministry response is appropriate? Work to extend justice and freedom. "Let us unite, with our thanksgiving, prayer to Almighty God, for the completion of his begun goodness to our brethren in Africa."[29] True to the African American soul care and spiritual direction tradition, our sustaining, healing, reconciling, and guiding are *societal* as well as individual. Liberation starts with spiritual freedom from sin through Christ. It continues with personal freedom from slavery. However, it is never finished until there is universal freedom from the slavery of sin and the sin of slavery.

Deep River: Guiding God's Children into Rest

Homer Ashby suggests that the exodus metaphor alone is insufficient to represent the comprehensive African American national narrative. The exodus narrative involves Moses leading God's people as they flee slavery in Egypt, find emancipation as they cross the Red Sea, and then survive in the wilderness for a generation. Though accepting this archetype as authentic for African Americans, Ashby additionally emphasizes the conquest narrative of Joshua guiding God's people as they journey toward Canaan, find empowerment as they cross the Jordan River, and then thrive in the Promised Land.[30]

As our language in this chapter suggests, we believe the African American national narrative is both-and, not either-or. The historical sermons and songs certainly embrace *both* exodus *and* conquest. For instance, in simple but dramatic language the spiritual "Go Down Moses" adapts the exodus narrative to the African American national experience.

> Oh go down, Moses,
> Way down into Egypt's land,
> Tell old Pharaoh,
> Let my people go.
>
> Oh Pharaoh said he would go cross,
> Let my people go,
> And don't get lost in de wilderness.
> Let my people go.[31]

227

Similarly, Albert concludes her book of slave interviews by uniting the end of American slavery with the end of Israel's slavery in Egypt.

> Sound the loud timbrel o'er Egypt's dark sea;
> Jehovah has triumphed, his people are free!
> Sing, for the pride of this tyrant is broken,
> His chariots, his horsemen, all splendid and brave—
> How void was their boast, for the Lord hath but
>   spoken
> And chariot and horsemen are sunk in the wave.
> Sound the loud timbrel o'er Egypt's dark sea;
> Jehovah has triumphed, his people are free!
>
> Praise to the Conqueror, praise to the Lord!
> His word was our arrow, his breath was our sword.
> Who shall return to tell Egypt the story
> Of those she sent forth in the hour of her pride?
> For the Lord hath looked out from his pillar of
>   glory,
> And all the brave thousands are dashed in the tide.
> Sound the loud timbrel o'er Egypt's dark sea;
> Jehovah has triumphed, his people are free![32]

Yet other spirituals focus equally on crossing the Jordan. At times it is difficult to distinguish whether the Jordan represents earthly freedom from slavery in this life or heavenly freedom from all sin in the next life. (Often the slaves had to code their songs *as if* they were only talking about heaven, lest their masters punish them for singing about freedom from earthly enslavement.) Likely their songs often mingled both messages. "Deep River" is a case in point.

> Deep river,
> My home is over Jordan,
> Deep river,
> Lord, I want to cross over into campground.

Oh, chillun,
Oh, don't you want to go,
To that gospel feast,
That promised land,
Where all is peace?

Walk into heaven,
And take my seat,
And cast my crown at Jesus' feet,
Lord, I want to cross over into campground.[33]

The imagery is indicative of the dual meaning of this spiritual. African American believers clearly understood salvation by grace without human effort. So although the song has implications for our final rest in our heavenly home, it speaks also of the longing for an earthly home of rest and peace.

African Americans have a dream, a vision. But in all honesty, they must cross a deep river to get to that dream. Thus the deep river is symbolic of the struggle, determination, and courage required for African Americans to enter into their rest in the Promised Land in America.[34]

They may be emancipated, but they are not yet empowered. What is their power source? *Who* is their power source?

Even in earthly struggles, African Americans emphasized the spiritual battle and remained consciously aware of their constant need for God's empowerment. They understood that life's battles could be fought and won only on their knees.[35] The following traditional black folk spiritual highlights such dependent trust.

Down here, Lord, waiting on you.
Can't do nothing till you come.
Down here, Lord,
Wid my Bible in ma hand—
Can't do nothing till you come.
Oh, you may be on your knees,

Oh, you ought to ask the Holy Ghost in your
  room.
I'm down here, Lord, waiting on you.
Can't do nothing till you come.[36]

There's power and there's Super-power. Life's strife did
not end for African Americans in 1863, or 1865, or 1964.
Nor is it over today. In order to guide one another, African
Americans have modeled the truth that *it's supernatural to
mature.* To live a Christ-honoring life in a confusing, unfair,
and often still prejudicial world, every believer of every race
must cling to and tap into Christ's resurrection power—
God's ultimate conquest narrative.

Following the North Star

We follow the North Star guidance of African American
faith narratives by remembering that life is the story of God's
conquest of evil in our lives and on our planet. God is the
hero of our biblical faith story. He is not, however, a selfish
hero or a dictatorial one. Our heroic Savior has sovereignly
chosen to work with us, in us, and through us.

The ultimate evil adversary in our story is Satan. He inspires all sin, including the sin of slavery.

Emancipation from sin is God's grace-work. He saves us
by grace, then calls us individually and corporately to work
out our salvation with fear and trembling—in childlike dependence on him.

Faith is childlike, yet it is manly and womanly. It is adult
and mature. Faith requires courage, which is inspired by
hope, which motivates us to love one another for God's
glory. Such daring adult faith refuses to deny the realities of
suffering and sin. Instead, it faces life head-on.

It faces life with the faith of Elisha and the Shunammite
woman. You may have recognized that earlier we ended our
telling of her tale before the end of her story. When we last

left her, she was on the ground in despair, clutching Elisha's feet, agonizing over her hope lost.

Elisha, through his faith in God's resurrection power, raises her son from the dead. His simple words to the Shunammite mother: "Embrace your son" (2 Kings 4:36). That is, "Embrace life, again."

She bows to the ground, then takes her son and leaves. Given that her life was a normal human life, she had many more casket experiences to endure until the casket finally closed on her. Until then, she could live longing for heaven based on her faith in God's resurrection power. She could face life knowing the One who is the resurrection and the life (see John 11:25).

Such faith faces life with the faith of James Weldon Johnson. He is the author of "Lift Every Voice," which has been called "the African American national anthem."

> Lift every voice and sing, till earth and heaven ring,
> Ring with the harmonies of liberty;
> Let our rejoicing rise, high as the listening skies,
> Let it resound loud as the rolling sea.
> Sing a song full of the faith that the dark past has
>   taught us,
> Sing a song full of the hope that the present has
>   brought us;
> Facing the rising sun of our new day begun,
> Let us march on till victory is won.
>
> Stony the road we trod, bitter the chastening rod,
> Felt in the days when hope unborn had died;
> Yet with a steady beat, have not our weary feet,
> Come to the place for which our fathers sighed?
> We have come over a way that with tears has been
>   watered,
> We have come, treading our path through the blood
>   of the slaughtered;
> Out from the gloomy past, till now we stand at last
> Where the white gleam of our bright star is cast.

231

God of our weary years, God of our silent tears,
Thou who hast brought us thus far on the way;
Thou who hast by Thy might, led us into the light,
Keep us forever in the path, we pray.
Lest our feet stray from the places, our God, where
    we met Thee.
Lest our hearts, drunk with the wine of the world,
    we forget Thee.
Shadowed beneath Thy hand, may we forever
    stand,
True to our God, true to our native land.[37]

We've come this far by faith. The journey has been dark, but it's taught us great faith lessons leading us toward the light. The journey isn't over yet. Our path remains strewn with obstacles, but the goal is in sight. God calls us on our voyage to live an emancipated *spiritual* life. Whatever bondage the world, the flesh, and the devil hurl at us, through Christ's power at work within us, we can stand, *as one*, true to God and true to our native land.

Learning Together from Our Great Cloud of Witnesses

1. Reflect on times when life has moved you from hope deferred, to hope, then to hope lost again. How has God moved you in those times from "Why me?" to "Why us?" to "Why God?" and to "Which God?"—finally to trusting in the God who sets the captives free?
2. Concerning the competing national narratives held by European and African Americans:
   a. How surprised are you that there have been such diametrically opposed views of the American experience?
   b. How can your understanding of these dissonant viewpoints equip you to minister more effectively cross-culturally?

232

3. What biblical images of God control your mind and your outlook on life? Is your God the "time-God"? The God of the oppressed? The never-changing, always-comforting God? The in-the-moment real God? The divine love and wisdom God? The Great I AM God?
4. What biblical narratives organize your view of yourself? Are you *God's chosen child*? Is your life story *worth telling and God-glorifying*? Are you *liberated from slavery to sin*?
5. How can you use the concept of narrative images of God and of self in your ministry? How can you help people put off their *secular scripture* and put on God's *sacred Scripture*?
6. Concerning Rev. Jones's repeated phrase *"He has seen"*:
    a. What misery in your life has God seen? What difference does it make knowing that he sees and cares?
    b. How can you help your spiritual friends to know that *God* sees their misery?
    c. How can you communicate that *you* see the misery of your spiritual friends?
7. This side of heaven, life is a deep river.
    a. How can you courageously face the deep river of life like the singers of the African American spirituals, like Elisha, like the Shunammite woman, and like James Weldon Johnson?
    b. How can you help others to honestly face the ups and downs of life by living with faith, hope, and love?
    c. What can *we all* do to cross the deep river *together*?
8. Reflecting on everything that you've read in *Beyond the Suffering*, what one, two, or three thoughts stand out to you? Why? What will you do with these concepts?

Notes

Introduction: So Great a Cloud of Witnesses

1. Botkin, *Lay My Burden Down*, 71.
2. Raboteau, "The Legacy of a Suffering Church," in Altschul, *An Unbroken Circle*, 74.
3. Hopkins, *Cut Loose Your Stammering Tongue*, xv–xvi.
4. Mitchell, *Black Church Beginnings*, ix.
5. Chesterton, *Orthodoxy*, 3 (emphasis added).

Chapter 1: An Unbroken Circle

1. Albert, *The House of Bondage*, 27.
2. Holmes, *Joy Unspeakable*, 46.
3. Pedersen, *A Handbook for Developing Multicultural Awareness*, 43.
4. Altschul, *An Unbroken Circle*, xiii.
5. Oden, *Whatever Happened to History?*, 7.
6. Oates, *Protestant Pastoral Counseling*, 11.
7. Clebsch and Jaekle, *Pastoral Care in Historical Perspective*, xii.
8. Jersild in Johnson, *"Ain't Gonna Lay My 'Ligion Down,"* 139.
9. Johnson, *God Struck Me Dead*, 16–17.
10. Yetman, *Voices from Slavery*, 1.
11. Hopkins, *Cut Loose Your Stammering Tongue*, 33.
12. Katz, *Five Slave Narratives*, iii.
13. Nichols, *Many Thousand Gone*, ix.
14. Starobin, *Blacks in Bondage*, xiii.
15. Katz, iv.
16. McClain, *Songs of Zion*, ix.
17. Lane, *Christian Spirituality*, 1–2.
18. Wimberly, *Pastoral Care in the Black Church*, 17.

19. McNeil, *A History of the Cure of Souls*, 85.
20. Lake, *Clinical Theology*, 21.
21. Kellemen, *Soul Physicians*, 22.
22. Clebsch and Jaekle, 4.
23. Leech, *Soul Friend*, 98.
24. Oden, *Care of Souls in the Classic Tradition*, 10.
25. Kellemen, *Spiritual Friends*, 47.
26. Albert, 15.
27. Ibid., 28–29.
28. Foner, *Lift Every Voice*, 75.
29. Ibid.
30. Johnson, *God Struck Me Dead*, 90.
31. Ibid., 68.
32. Ibid., 73.
33. Randolph, *From Slave Cabin to Pulpit*, 48.
34. Ibid., 49.
35. Osofsky, *Puttin' On Ole Massa*, 205.
36. Johnson, *God Struck Me Dead*, 15.

Chapter 2: Out of Africa

1. Hughes, "Minstrel Man," in Rampersad, *The Collected Poems of Langston Hughes*, 61.
2. Raboteau, "The Legacy of a Suffering Church," in Altschul, *An Unbroken Circle*, 75.
3. Rawick, *From Sundown to Sunup*, 6–8.
4. Ibid., 125.
5. Blassingame, *Slave Testimony*, 687 (emphasis added).
6. Falconbridge, *An Account of the Slave Trade*, 2, 32.
7. Ibid., 17–18.
8. Ibid., 19.
9. Equiano, *The Interesting Narrative*, 4.
10. Ibid., 24.
11. Ibid., 25.
12. Ibid.
13. Ibid., 28.
14. Ibid., 29.
15. Ibid.
16. Ibid., 30.
17. Ibid.
18. Ibid., 32.
19. Cugoano, *Thoughts and Sentiments*, 13.
20. Ibid., 14.
21. Ibid., 15.
22. Blassingame, *The Slave Community*, 12–13.
23. Cugoano, 15.
24. Ibid., 16.

25. Holmes, *Joy Unspeakable*, 69–70.
26. Pinn, *Terror and Triumph*, 28–35.
27. Berlin, *Many Thousands Gone*, 83.
28. Equiano, 35.
29. Ibid., 38.
30. Falconbridge, 20.
31. Ibid., 24, 28.
32. Ibid., 23.
33. Thomas, *The Slave Trade*, 412.
34. Ibid., 412–13.
35. Falconbridge, 31.
36. Kolchin, *American Slavery*, 21.
37. Holmes, 72–74.
38. Noel, "Call and Response," 72.
39. Richardson, *Maria W. Stewart*, 75.
40. Berlin, 2–6.
41. Holmes, 75.
42. Cugoano, 17.
43. Cooper-Lewter, *Soul Theology*, 14–15.
44. Equiano, 254.
45. Thurman, *Deep River*, 39.

Chapter 3: Watered with Our Tears

1. Jacobs, *Incidents in the Life*, 11.
2. Randolph, *From Slave Cabin to Pulpit*, 1.
3. Hopkins, *Down, Up, and Over*, 13–17.
4. Thomas, *The Slave Trade*, 804–805.
5. Bibb, *Narrative of the Life*, 65.
6. Falconbridge, *An Account of the Slave Trade*, 34.
7. Ibid., 35.
8. Equiano, *The Interesting Narrative*, 41.
9. Ibid.
10. Ibid., 41–42.
11. Albert, *The House of Bondage*, 105.
12. Ibid.
13. Randolph, 102.
14. Ibid.
15. Jacobs, 17.
16. Randolph, 102.
17. Ibid.
18. Ibid., 117.
19. Osofsky, *Puttin' On Ole Massa*, 248.
20. Ibid., 253.
21. Ibid., 265.
22. Ibid.
23. Ibid.

24. Randolph, 104.
25. Ibid.
26. Osofsky, 262.
27. Holmes, *Joy Unspeakable*, 79.
28. Randolph, 104.
29. Stroyer, "My Life in the South," in Katz, *Five Slave Narratives*, 40–41.
30. Bontemps, *Five Black Lives*, 69.
31. Equiano, 74.
32. Ibid., 103.
33. Ibid.
34. Andrews, *North Carolina Slave Narratives*, 268.
35. Ibid., 212.
36. Ibid., 212.
37. Keckley, *Behind the Scenes*, 17.
38. Genovese, *Roll, Jordan, Roll*, 51.
39. Ibid., 29–30.
40. Bontemps, 107.
41. Stroyer, in Katz, 14.
42. Hopkins, 81.
43. Fisk, *Unwritten History of Slavery*, 37.
44. *Anti-Slavery Advocate*, 176.
45. Jacobs, 40.
46. Ibid., 10.
47. Ibid., 18.
48. Ibid., 13.
49. Ibid., 27–28.
50. Ibid., 62–63.
51. Ibid., 15.
52. Blassingame, *The Slave Community*, 109, 147.
53. Webb, *The History of William Webb*, 5.
54. Yetman, *Voices from Slavery*, 228.

Chapter 4: From Sunup to Sundown

1. Bontemps, *Five Black Lives*, 151.
2. Jacobs, *Incidents in the Life*, 1.
3. Lane, "Narrative of Lunsford Lane," in Katz, *Five Slave Narratives*, 7–8.
4. Rawick, *From Sundown to Sunup*, 54.
5. Genovese, *Roll, Jordan, Roll*, 60.
6. Andrews, *North Carolina Slave Narratives*, 212.
7. Albert, *The House of Bondage*, 64.
8. Douglass, *Narrative of the Life*, 16.
9. Bontemps, 151.
10. Ibid.
11. Stroyer, "My Life in the South," in Katz, *Five Slave Narratives*, 42.
12. Pennington, "The Fugitive Blacksmith," in Katz, *Five Slave Narratives*, 2.
13. Douglass, *My Bondage and My Freedom*, 48.

14. Keckley, *Behind the Scenes*, 23.
15. Ibid., 24.
16. Blassingame, *Slave Testimony*, 593.
17. Andrews, 211.
18. Bontemps, 30.
19. Johnson, *God Struck Me Dead*, 80.
20. Rawick, *The American Slave*, vol. 4, *Texas*, pt. 1, p. 2.
21. Yetman, *Voices from Slavery*, 174.
22. Ibid., 71.
23. Ibid., 227.
24. Henson, *Father Henson's Story*, 10, 14.
25. Yetman, 102.
26. Ibid., 102–103.
27. Smith, *An Autobiography*, 25–26.
28. Ibid., 26.
29. Ibid., 23.
30. Yetman, 11.
31. Osofsky, *Puttin' On Ole Massa*, 180–181.
32. Pennington, in Katz, 7.
33. Ibid.
34. Ibid.
35. Steward, *Twenty-Two Years a Slave*, 97.
36. Stroyer, in Katz, 22.
37. Driver, *Liberating Rites*, 66.
38. Holmes, *Joy Unspeakable*, 86–87.
39. Yetman, 37.
40. Jacobs, 66.
41. Ibid., 26.
42. Ibid., 27.
43. Ibid., 26.
44. Ibid., 27.
45. Ibid., 38.
46. Ibid., 33.
47. Ibid., 38.
48. Ibid., 70.
49. Ibid.
50. Ibid., 159.
51. Ibid.
52. Albert, 23.
53. Ibid., 24.
54. Ibid., 47.
55. Ibid., 50.
56. Bontemps, 215.
57. Ibid.

Chapter 5: Deep Is the Hunger

1. Johnson, *God Struck Me Dead*, 140.
2. Radin, "Foreword to the First Edition," in Johnson, vii.
3. Redkey, *A Grand Army of Black Men*, 134.
4. Ibid.
5. Ibid.
6. Ibid.
7. Ibid., 135.
8. Ibid.
9. Paris, *The Spirituality of African Peoples*, 34–35.
10. Ibid., 27–28.
11. Raboteau, *Slave Religion*, 8.
12. Bosman, *A New and Accurate Description*, 368.
13. Raboteau, 11–12.
14. Perdue, *Weevils in the Wheat*, 1.
15. Payne, "American Slavery Brutalizes Man," in Foner, *Lift Every Voice*, 177.
16. Payne, *Recollections of Seventy Years*, 28.
17. Thurman, *Deep River*, 36.
18. Andrews, *Practical Theology*, 18.
19. Pennington, "The Fugitive Blacksmith," in Katz, *Five Slave Narratives*, 52 (emphasis added).
20. Johnson, 19.
21. Watson, "Negro Primitive Religious Services," in Johnson, 1–2.
22. Randolph, *From Slave Cabin to Pulpit*, 1.
23. Sernett, *African American Religious History*, 45.
24. Ibid.
25. Johnson, 72–73.
26. Ibid., 164.
27. Sernett, 45.
28. Lee, *Religious Experiences*, 2.
29. Ibid., 4.
30. Ibid.
31. Thurman, *For the Inward Journey*, 147.
32. Andrews, *Sisters of the Spirit*, 60.
33. Ibid., 91.
34. Johnson, 149.
35. Andrews, *Sisters of the Spirit*, 15.
36. Johnson, 111.
37. Ibid., 40–41.
38. Ibid., 99.

Chapter 6: The Old Ship of Zion

1. Mellon, *Bullwhip Days*, 194–95.
2. Carter, *The Prayer Tradition of Black People*, 93.
3. Johnson, *God Struck Me Dead*, 73.
4. Ibid., 76.

5. Mitchell, *Black Church Beginnings*, 34.
6. Osofsky, *Puttin' On Old Massa*, 270.
7. Ibid., 274.
8. Ibid., 304.
9. Ibid.
10. Ibid.
11. Ibid.
12. Ibid.
13. Ibid.
14. Bontemps, *Five Black Lives*, 166.
15. Yetman, *Voices from Slavery*, 45–46.
16. Raboteau, *Canaan Land*, 43.
17. Du Bois, *The Negro Church*, 22.
18. Ibid., 25.
19. Kalm, *Travels Into North America*, 503.
20. Perdue, *Weevils in the Wheat*, 124–25.
21. Ibid., 125.
22. Yetman, 12–13.
23. Ibid., 13.
24. Cade, "Out of the Mouth of Ex-Slaves," 329.
25. Perdue, 241–42.
26. Rawick, *From Sundown to Sunup*, 42–43.
27. Perdue, 100.
28. Randolph, *From Slave Cabin to Pulpit*, 112–13.
29. Ibid., 113.
30. Ibid.
31. Carter, 51.
32. Rawick, *The American Slave*, vol. 4, *Texas*, pt. 2, p. 170.
33. Douglass, *The Life and Times*, 90–94.
34. Albert, *The House of Bondage*, 9, 11.
35. Ibid., 11, 13.
36. Ibid., 12.
37. Carawan, *Ain't You Got a Right to the Tree of Life*, 74.
38. Cummings, "The Slave Narratives," in Hopkins, *Cut Loose Your Stammering Tongue*, 47.
39. Rawick, *The American Slave*, vol. 12, *Georgia*, pt. 2, p. 227.
40. Bontemps, 162.
41. Du Bois, *The Souls of Black Folks*, 159–60.
42. Anderson, *From Slavery to Affluence*, 22.
43. Yetman, 75.
44. Johnson, *Ain't Gonna Lay My 'Ligion Down*, 88–94.
45. *Southern Christian Advocate*, November 24, 1887, n.p.
46. Raymond, "The Religious Life of the Negro Slave," 485.
47. Carter, 21.
48. Yetman, 263.
49. Ibid., 37.
50. Ibid.

51. Holmes, *Joy Unspeakable*, 85.
52. Ibid., 84–85.
53. Bontemps, 163.
54. Fulop, *African-American Religion*, 74–75.

Chapter 7: A Sorrowful Joy

1. Du Bois, *The Souls of Black Folks*, 213–214.
2. Raboteau, "The Legacy of a Suffering Church," in Altschul, *An Unbroken Circle*, 79.
3. Berry, "Lost Heritage of African-Americans," in Altschul, 65.
4. Ibid.
5. Raboteau, *Slave Religion*, 243.
6. Cleveland, "A Historical Account of the Negro Spirituals," in McClain, *Songs of Zion*, 73.
7. Walker, *Somebody's Calling My Name*, 31–32.
8. Rawick, *From Sundown to Sunup*, 34 (emphasis added).
9. Holmes, *Joy Unspeakable*, 109.
10. Rawick, *The American Slave*, vol. 4, *Texas*, pt. 2, 6–7.
11. McKim, "Negro Songs," in Katz, *The Social Implications of Early Negro Music*, 2.
12. Goatley, "Godforsakenness in African American Spirituals," in Hopkins, *Cut Loose Your Stammering Tongue*, 132.
13. Raboteau, *Slave Religion*, 246.
14. Ibid., 265.
15. Ibid., 243.
16. Higginson, *Army Life in a Black Regiment*, 154.
17. Ibid.
18. Ibid., 154–55.
19. Merton, *Seeds of Contemplation*, 136.
20. McClain, songs 170–71, compilation.
21. Johnson, *God Struck Me Dead*, 74.
22. Yetman, *Voices from Slavery*, 205.
23. Douglass, *Narrative of the Life*, 18.
24. Raboteau, *Slave Religion*, 259.
25. Allen, *Slave Songs of the United States*, 55.
26. Garrison, "Song of the Port Royal 'Contrabands,'" in Katz, 10.
27. Douglass, 18.
28. McClain, ix.
29. Ibid.
30. Ibid., 73.
31. Ibid.
32. Solomon and Solomon, *"Honey in the Rock,"* 21.
33. Allen, 94.
34. Ibid., 30–31.
35. Ibid., 93.
36. McClain, song 83.

37. Jones, *Wade in the Water*, 19.
38. Raboteau, *Slave Religion*, 259.
39. McClain, song 95.
40. Randolph, *From Slave Cabin to Pulpit*, 113.
41. McClain, song 158.
42. Thurman, *Deep River*, 25.
43. Osofsky, *Puttin' On Ole Massa*, 197.
44. Thurman, 37–38.
45. Holmes, 94.
46. Johnson, *The Books of American Negro Spirituals*, 2:78–79.
47. Paris, *The Spirituality of African Peoples*, 124–25.
48. Allen, 57.
49. McClain, song 94.
50. Ibid., song 106.
51. Ibid., song 93.
52. Allen, 95.
53. Ibid., 12, 55, 108.
54. Higginson, 157, 168.
55. Ibid., x.

Chapter 8: Sons of Thunder

1. Sernett, *African American Religious History*, 52.
2. Wright, *12 Million Black Voices*, 131.
3. Parker, *Teaching Our Men, Reaching Our Fathers*, 1–25.
4. Frazier, *The Negro Church in America*.
5. Becker, "The Black Church," in Fulop, *African-American Religion*, 180.
6. Arnett, *Proceedings of the Quarto-Centennial Conference of the A.M.E Church*, 384.
7. Payne, *A History of the A.M.E. Church*, 9–12.
8. Payne, *Recollections of Seventy Years*, 28.
9. Ibid., 34.
10. Ibid., 39.
11. Ibid., 17.
12. Ibid., 287.
13. Ibid., 288.
14. Ibid., 16.
15. Ibid., 11.
16. Ibid., 17.
17. Smith, *Sermons Delivered by Bishop Daniel A. Payne*, 58, 64.
18. Sernett, 46.
19. Ibid.
20. Ibid., 47.
21. Ibid., 48.
22. Raboteau, *Canaan Land*, 21.
23. Sernett, 52.
24. Ibid., 53.

243

25. Ibid.

26. Ibid., 55.

27. Minutes of the West Central North Carolina Conference of the AMEZ Church, 4.

28. Wideman, *My Soul Has Grown Deep*, 29.

29. Ibid.

30. Ibid., 29.

31. Ibid.

32. Ibid., 30.

33. Ibid.

34. Ibid., 36.

35. Ibid., 58.

36. Ibid.

37. Ibid.

38. Sernett, 53.

39. Ibid., 53, 57.

40. Woodson, *The History of the Negro Church*, 56.

41. Randolph, *From Slave Cabin to Pulpit*, 47.

42. Wimberly, *Pastoral Counseling*, 25–26.

43. Sernett, 232.

44. Ibid., 232–33.

45. Ibid., 233–34.

46. Ibid., 234, 236.

47. Ibid., 234.

48. Ibid., 235.

49. Payne, *Recollections of Seventy Years*, 137.

50. Wesley, *Richard Allen*, 60.

51. Du Bois, *The Philadelphia Negro*, 19.

52. Douglas, *Annals*, 15.

53. Alexander, *Richard Allen*, 26, 74–81.

54. Woodson, 36.

55. Ibid., 67.

Chapter 9: Sisters of the Spirit

1. Andrews, *Sisters of the Spirit*, 51.

2. Morrison, "What the Black Woman Thinks about Women's Lib," 63.

3. Collier-Thomas, *Daughters of Thunder*, 8.

4. Clayton, *Mother Wit*, preface.

5. Smith, *An Autobiography*, 62.

6. Ibid., 29–30.

7. Ibid., 92–94.

8. Andrews, 51.

9. Ibid., 119.

10. Ibid.

11. Ibid., 118.

12. Ibid., 72.

13. Ibid., 72–73.
14. Ibid., 225.
15. Ibid., 197.
16. Ibid., 217.
17. Ibid., 163.
18. Richardson, *Maria W. Stewart*, xiii.
19. Ibid., 29.
20. Ibid., xiii.
21. Ibid., 28–29.
22. Ibid., 28.
23. Ibid., 29.
24. Ibid.
25. Ibid.
26. Ibid., 30.
27. Ibid., 32.
28. Ibid., 38.
29. Ibid.
30. Wimberly, *Pastoral Care in the Black Church*, 74.
31. Richardson, 34–35.
32. Ibid., 35.
33. Ibid.
34. Ibid., 39–40.
35. Lee, *Religious Experiences*, 18.
36. Ibid.
37. Ibid.
38. Bradford, *Harriet Tubman*, 3.
39. Collier-Thomas, 119.

Chapter 10: This Far by Faith

1. Johnson, *God Struck Me Dead*, 170.
2. Hughes, *The Book of Negro Folklore*, 286.
3. Coffin, *The Boys of '61*, 415.
4. Reed, *An American Diary*, 65.
5. McClain, *Songs of Zion*, song 192.
6. Warner, *American Sermons*, 42.
7. Raboteau, "The Legacy of a Suffering Church," in Altschul, *An Unbroken Circle*, 81.
8. Ibid.
9. Albert, *The House of Bondage*, 31.
10. Raboteau in Altshul, 81.
11. Hopkins, *Down, Up, and Over*, 107.
12. Bontemps, *Five Black Lives*, 73–74.
13. Starobin, *Blacks in Bondage*, 75.
14. Bibb, *Narrative of the Life*, 24.
15. Ibid., 69.
16. Wimberly, *African American Pastoral Care*, 18.

17. Ashby, *Our Home Is Over Jordan*, 56.
18. Albert, 129–30.
19. Ibid., 130.
20. Evans, *We Have Been Believers*, 40–41.
21. Ibid., 41.
22. Berlin, *Free at Last*, 29–30.
23. Carretta, *Unchained Voices*, 62.
24. Wimberly, *Moving from Shame to Self-Worth*, 16–27.
25. Warner, 540.
26. Ibid.
27. Ibid., 541.
28. Ibid., 542.
29. Ibid.
30. Ashby, 22–36.
31. Bradford, *Harriet Tubman*, 37.
32. Albert, 161.
33. Johnson, *The Books of American Negro Spirituals*, 1:100–103.
34. Ashby, 128–33.
35. Carter, *The Prayer Tradition of Black People*, 65.
36. Ibid.
37. McClain, song 32.

Bibliography

Albert, Octavia, ed. *The House of Bondage or Charlotte Brooks and Other Slaves*. Reprint edition. New York: Oxford University Press, 1988.

Alexander, Curtis. *Richard Allen: The First Exemplar of African American Education*. New York: ECA Associates, 1985.

Allen, William, Charles Ware, and Lucy Garrison. *Slave Songs of the United States*. Reprint edition. New York: Peter Smith, 1929.

Altschul, Paisius, ed. *An Unbroken Circle: Linking Ancient African Christianity to the African-American Experience*. St. Louis: Brotherhood of St. Moses the Black, 1997.

Anderson, Robert. *From Slavery to Affluence: Memories of Robert Anderson, Ex-Slave*. Hemingford, NB: The Hemingford Ledger, 1927.

Andrews, Dale. *Practical Theology for Black Churches*. Louisville: Westminster, 2002.

Andrews, William, ed. *North Carolina Slave Narratives: The Lives of Moses Roper, Lunsford Lane, Moses Grandy, and Thomas H. Jones*. Chapel Hill: University of North Carolina Press, 2003.

———, ed. *Sisters of the Spirit: Three Black Women's Autobiographies of the Nineteenth Century*. Bloomington: Indiana University Press, 1986.

Anti-Slavery Advocate. London: July, 1854.

Arnett, B., ed. *Proceedings of the Quarto-Centennial Conference of the A.M.E. Church of South Carolina, May 15–17, 1889*. Charleston, SC: 1890.

Ashby, Homer. *Our Home Is Over Jordan: A Black Pastoral Theology*. St. Louis: Chalice Press, 2003.

Bailey, Anne. *African Voices of the Atlantic Slave Trade: Beyond the Silence and the Shame*. Boston: Beacon, 2005.

Bayliss, John, ed. *Black Slave Narratives*. New York: Macmillan, 1970.

Berlin, Ira. *Many Thousands Gone: The First Two Centuries of Slavery in North America*. Cambridge, MA: Belknap, 1998.

Berlin, Ira, Barbara Fields, Steven Miller, Joseph Reidy, and Leslie Rowland, eds. *Free at Last: A Documentary History of Slavery, Freedom, and the Civil War*. New York: The New York Press, 1992.

Bibb, Henry. *Narrative of the Life and Adventures of Henry Bibb: An American Slave*. Introduction by Lucius Matlack. Mineola, NY: Dover, 2005.

Blassingame, John. *The Slave Community: Plantation Life in the Antebellum South*. Rev. and enlarged ed. New York: Oxford University Press, 1979.

———, ed. *Slave Testimony: Two Centuries of Letters, Speeches, Interviews, and Autobiographies*. Baton Rouge: Louisiana State University Press, 1977.

———. "Using the Testimony of Ex-Slaves: Approaches and Problems." *Journal of Southern History* 41, no. 4 (November 1975): 473–92.

Boles, John, ed. *Master and Slaves in the House of the Lord: Race and Religion in the American South, 1740–1870*. Lexington: University of Kentucky Press, 1988.

Bontemps, Arna, ed. *Five Black Lives: The Autobiographies of Venture Smith, James Mars, William Grimes, The Rev. G. W. Offley, and James Smith*. Middletown, CT: Wesleyan University Press, 1971.

Bosman, William. *A New and Accurate Description of the Coast of Guinea*. London: Routledge, 1705.

Botkin, B. A., ed. *Lay My Burden Down: A Folk History of Slavery*. New York: Delta Books, 1945.

Bradford, Sarah. *Harriet Tubman: The Moses of Her People*. New York: Corinth Books, 1989.

Cade, John. "Out of the Mouths of Ex-Slaves." *The Journal of Negro History* 20 (1935): 328–331.

Carawan, Guy, and Candie Carawan. *Ain't You Got a Right to the Tree of Life*. Rev. ed. Athens, GA: University of Georgia Press, 1988.

Carretta, Vincent. *Unchained Voices: An Anthology of Black Authors in the English-Speaking World of the Eighteenth Century*. Lexington: University Press of Kentucky, 1996.

Carter, Harold. *The Prayer Tradition of Black People*. Valley Forge, PA: Judson, 1976.

Chesterton, G. K. *Orthodoxy*. Whitefish, MT: Kessinger, 2004.

Clayton, Ronnie. *Mother Wit: The Ex-Slave Narratives of the Louisiana Writers' Project*. New York: Peter Lang, 1990.

Clebsch, William, and Charles Jaekle. *Pastoral Care in Historical Perspective*. New York: Harper & Row, 1964.

Coffin, Charles. *The Boys of '61; or Four Years of Fighting*. Boston: Estes and Lauriat, 1886.

Collier-Thomas, Bettye. *Daughters of Thunder: Black Women Preachers and Their Sermons, 1850–1979*. San Francisco: Jossey-Bass, 1998.

248

Cooper-Lewter, Nicholas, and Henry Mitchell. *Soul Theology: The Heart of American Black Culture.* Nashville: Abingdon, 1986.

Cugoano, Quobna Ottobah. *Thoughts and Sentiments on the Evil of Slavery.* Edited by Vincent Carretta. New York: Penguin Books, 1999.

Curtin, Philip. *Africa Remembered: Narratives by West Africans from the Era of the Slave Trade.* Madison: University of Wisconsin Press, 1967.

Davis, Cyprian. *The History of Black Catholics in the United States.* New York: Crossroads, 1990.

Douglas, William. *Annals of the First African Church in the United States of America, Now Styled the African Episcopal Church of St. Thomas.* Philadelphia, 1862.

Douglass, Frederick. *My Bondage and My Freedom.* New York, 1855.

———. *Narrative of the Life of Frederick Douglass.* Unabridged republication. Cheswold, DE: Prestwick House Literary Touchstone Press, 2004.

———. *The Life and Times of Frederick Douglass.* Rev. ed. London: Collier-MacMillan, 1962.

Driver, Tom. *Liberating Rites: Understanding the Transformative Power of Ritual.* Boulder, CO: Westview, 1991.

Du Bois, W. E. B. *The Negro Church.* Atlanta: The Atlanta University Press, 1903.

———. *The Philadelphia Negro.* Philadelphia: University of Pennsylvania, 1899.

———. *The Souls of Black Folks.* Introduction by Donald B. Gibson. New York: Penguin Books, 1996.

Epstein, Dena. *Sinful Tunes and Spirituals: Black Folk Music to the Civil War.* Urbana, IL: University of Illinois Press, 1977.

Equiano, Olaudah. *The Interesting Narrative of the Life of Olaudah Equiano, or, Gustavus Vassa, the African, Written by Himself.* Edited by Shelly Eversley. Introduction by Robert Reid-Pharr. New York: The Modern Library, 2004.

Evans, James. *We Have Been Believers: An African-American Systematic Theology.* Minneapolis: Fortress, 1992.

Falconbridge, Alexander. *An Account of the Slave Trade on the Coast of Africa.* London: J. Phillips, 1788.

Fisk University Social Science Institute. *Unwritten History of Slavery.* Nashville: Fisk University Social Science Institute, 1945.

Foner, Philip, and Robert Branham, eds. *Lift Every Voice: African American Oratory, 1787–1900.* Tuscaloosa, AL: University of Alabama Press, 1998.

Fox-Genovese, Elizabeth. *Within the Plantation Household: Black and White Women of the Old South.* Chapel Hill: University of North Carolina Press, 1988.

249

Frazier, Franklin. *The Negro Church in America*. New York: Schocken Books, 1964.

———. *The Negro in the United States*. Rev. ed. New York: Macmillan, 1957.

Fulop, Timothy, and Albert Raboteau. *African-American Religion: Interpretive Essays in History and Culture*. New York: Routledge, 1997.

Genovese, Eugene. *Roll, Jordan, Roll: The World the Slaves Made*. New York: Vintage Books, 1972.

Gilkes, Cheryl. "The Black Church as a Therapeutic Community: Suggested Areas for Research into the Black Religious Experience." *Journal of the Interdenominational Theological Center* 8 (Fall 1980): 29–44.

Gronniosaw, James. *A Narrative of the Most Remarkable Particulars in the Life of James Albert Ukawsaw Gronniosaw, an African Prince, As Related by Himself*. Leeds, England, 1814.

Gutman, Herbert. *The Black Family in Slavery and Freedom 1750–1925*. New York: Vintage Books, 1976.

Henson, Josiah. *Father Henson's Story of His Own Life*. Gansevoort, NY: Corner House Publishing, 1979.

Higginson, Thomas. *Army Life in a Black Regiment and Other Writings*. Introduction by R. D. Madison. New York: Penguin Books, 1997.

Hiltner, Seward. *Preface to Pastoral Theology*. Nashville: Abingdon, 1958.

Holmes, Barbara. *Joy Unspeakable: Contemplative Practices of the Black Church*. Minneapolis: Fortress, 2004.

Hopkins, Dwight. *Down, Up, and Over: Slave Religion and Black Theology*. Minneapolis: Fortress, 2000.

———. *Shoes That Fit Our Feet: Sources for a Conservative Black Theology*. Maryknoll, NY: Orbis Books, 1993.

Hopkins, Dwight, and George Cummings, eds. *Cut Loose Your Stammering Tongue: Black Theology in the Slave Narratives*. Louisville: Westminster, 2003.

Hughes, Langston, and Arna Bontemps, eds. *The Book of Negro Folklore*. New York: Dodd and Mead, 1958.

Jacobs, Harriet. *Incidents in the Life of a Slave Girl*. New York: Dover, 2001.

Johnson, Alonzo and Paul Jersild, eds. *"Ain't Gonna Lay My 'Ligion Down": African American Religion in the South*. Columbia, SC: University of South Carolina Press, 1996.

Johnson, Clifton, ed. *God Struck Me Dead: Religious Conversion Experiences and Autobiographies of Ex-Slaves*. Cleveland: Pilgrim, 1993.

Johnson, James Weldon, John Johnson, and Lawrence Brown, eds. *The Books of American Negro Spirituals: Including the Book of American*

Negro Spirituals and the Second Book of Negro Spirituals. New York: Da Capo, 1977.

Jones, Arthur. *Wade in the Water: The Wisdom of the Spirituals*. Maryknoll, NY: Orbis Books, 1993.

Kalm, Peter. *Travels into North America*. 2nd ed. Reprinted in vol. 13 of *A General Collection of the Best and Most Interesting Voyages and Travels*. Edited by John Pinkerton. London: Longman, 1812.

Katz, Bernard, ed. *The Social Implications of Early Negro Music in the United States*. New York: Beaufort Books, 1979.

Katz, William, ed. *Five Slave Narratives*. New York: Arno, 1968.

Keckley, Elizabeth. *Behind the Scenes, or Thirty Years a Slave and Four Years in the White House*. New York: Oxford University Press, 1988.

Kellemen, Robert. *Soul Physicians: A Theology of Soul Care and Spiritual Direction*. Rev. ed. Taneytown, MD: RPM Books, 2005.

———. *Spiritual Friends: A Methodology of Soul Care and Spiritual Direction*. Rev. ed. Taneytown, MD: RPM Books, 2005.

Kolchin, Peter. *American Slavery: 1619–1877*. Rev. ed. New York: Hill and Wang, 2003.

Lake, Frank. *Clinical Theology*. London: Darton, Longman, & Todd, 1966.

Lane, George. *Christian Spirituality: An Historical Sketch*. Chicago: Loyola University Press, 1984.

Lee, Jarena. *Religious Experiences and Journal of Mrs. Jarena Lee: "A Preachin' Woman."* Nashville: Legacy, 1991.

Leech, Kenneth. *Soul Friend: The Practice of Christian Spirituality*. San Francisco: Harper & Row, 1977.

Levine, Lawrence. *Black Culture and Black Consciousness: Afro-American Folk Thought from Slavery to Freedom*. New York: Oxford University Press, 1977.

Lincoln, Eric, and Lawrence Mamiya. *The Black Church in the African American Experience*. Durham, NC: Duke University Press, 1990.

McClain, William, Jefferson Ferguson, and Verolga Nix, eds. *Songs of Zion*. Nashville: Abingdon, 1981.

McNeil, John. *A History of the Cure of Souls*. New York: Harper & Row, 1951.

Mellon, James, ed. *Bullwhip Days: The Slaves Remember, An Oral History*. New York: Weidenfeld and Nicolson, 1988.

Merton, Thomas. *Seeds of Contemplation*. New York: New Directions, 1961.

Miller, Randall, ed. *"Dear Master": Letters of a Slave Family*. Rev. ed. Athens, GA: The University of Georgia Press, 1990.

Mitchell, Henry. *Black Church Beginnings: The Long-Hidden Realities of the First Years*. Grand Rapids: Eerdmans, 2004.

Morrison, Toni. "What the Black Woman Thinks about Women's Lib." *The New York Times Magazine*, August 22, 1971, 14–15, 63–66.

Newkirk, Pamela. *A Love No Less: More Than Two Centuries of African American Love Letters*. New York: Doubleday, 2003.

Newman, Richard, ed. *Black Preacher to White America: The Collected Writings of Lemuel Haynes, 1774–1833*. Brooklyn, NY: Carlson, 1990.

Nichols, Charles. *Many Thousand Gone: The Ex-Slaves' Account of Their Bondage and Freedom*. Leidan, Netherlands: E. J. Brill, 1963.

Noel, James. "Call and Response: The Meaning of the Moan and Significance of the Shout in Black Worship." *Reformed Liturgy & Music* 28/2 (Spring 1994): 72–76.

Oates, Wayne. *Protestant Pastoral Counseling*. Philadelphia: Westminster, 1962.

Oden, Thomas. *Care of Souls in the Classic Tradition*. Philadelphia: Fortress, 1983.

———. "Whatever Happened to History?" *Good News*, January-February 1993, n.p.

Osofsky, Gilbert, ed. *Puttin' On Ole Massa: The Slave Narratives of Henry Bibb, William Wells Brown, and Solomon Northup*. Reprint ed. San Francisco: Harper & Row, 1969.

Paris, Peter. *The Spirituality of African Peoples: The Search for a Common Moral Discourse*. Minneapolis: Fortress, 1994.

Parker, Matthew, *Teaching Our Men, Reaching Our Fathers: African American Churches*. Chicago: Moody, 2002.

Payne, Daniel. *A History of the A.M.E. Church, I, 1816–1856*. Reprint ed. New York: Arno, 1968.

———. *Recollections of Seventy Years*. New York: Arno, 1968.

Pedersen, P. *A Handbook for Developing Multicultural Awareness*. Alexandria, VA: American Association for Counseling and Development, 1988.

Perdue, Charles, Thomas Barden, and Robert Phillips, eds. *Weevils in the Wheat: Interviews with Virginia Ex-Slaves*. Charlottesville, VA: University of Virginia Press, 1976.

Pinn, Anne, and Anthony Pinn. *Fortress Introduction to Black Church History*. Minneapolis: Fortress, 2002.

Pinn, Anthony. *Terror and Triumph: The Nature of Black Religion*. Minneapolis: Fortress, 2003.

Raboteau, Albert. *Canaan Land: A Religious History of African Americans*. New York: Oxford University Press, 2001.

———. *Slave Religion: The "Invisible Institution" in the Antebellum South*. New York: Oxford University Press, 1978.

———. *A Sorrowful Joy: The Spiritual Journey of an African-American Man in Late Twentieth-Century America*. New York: Paulist, 2002.

Rampersad, Arnold and David Roessel, eds. *The Collected Poems of Langston Hughes*. New York: Vintage Books, 1994.

Randolph, Peter. *From Slave Cabin to Pulpit*. Edited by Paul Sporer. Chester, NY: Anza, 2004.

Rawick, George. *From Sundown to Sunup: The Making of the Black Community*. Vol. 1 of *The American Slave: A Composite Autobiography*. Westport, CT: Greenwood, 1972.

————, ed. *The American Slave: A Composite Autobiography*. 19 vols. Westport, CT: Greenwood, 1972–1979.

Raymond, Charles. "The Religious Life of the Negro Slave." *Harper's* 27 (September 1863): 479–485.

Redkey, Edwin, ed. *A Grand Army of Black Men: Letters from African-American Soldiers in the Union Army, 1861–1865*. Cambridge, England: Cambridge University Press, 1992.

Reed, Joseph, ed. *An American Diary, 1857–1858*. London: Routledge and Kegan Paul, 1972.

Richardson, Marilyn, ed. *Maria W. Stewart: America's First Black Woman Political Writer*. Bloomington, IN: Indiana University Press, 1987.

Saillant, John. *Black Puritan, Black Republican: The Life and Thought of Lemuel Haynes, 1753–1833*. New York: Oxford University Press, 2003.

Sancho, Ignatius. *Letters of the Late Ignatius Sancho, An African*. Edited with an introduction and notes by Vincent Carretta. New York: Penguin Books, 1998.

Sernett, Milton, ed. *African American Religious History: A Documentary Witness*. 2nd ed. Durham, NC: Duke University Press, 1999.

Smith, Amanda. *An Autobiography: The Story of the Lord's Dealing with Mrs. Amanda Smith, The Colored Lady Evangelist*. Noblesville, IN: Newby Book Room, 1972.

Smith, Charles, ed. *Sermons Delivered by Bishop Daniel A. Payne Before the General Conference of the A.M.E. Church*. Nashville, 1888.

Sobel, Mechal. *Trabelin' On: The Slave Journey to an Afro-Baptist Faith*. Westport, CT: Greenwood, 1979.

Solomon, Olivia, and Jack Solomon. *"Honey in the Rock": The Ruby Pickens Tartt Collection of Religious Folk Songs from Sumter County, Alabama*. Macon, GA: Mercer University Press, 1991.

Southern Christian Advocate, November 24, 1887.

Stamp, Kenneth. *The Peculiar Institution: Slavery in the Ante-Bellum South*. New York: Vintage Books, 1956.

Starobin, Robert, ed. *Blacks in Bondage: Letters of American Slaves*. New York: Barnes and Noble Books, 1974.

Steward, Austin. *Twenty-Two Years a Slave, and Forty Years a Freeman*. Rochester, 1861.

Stewart, Carlyle, III. *Joy Songs, Trumpet Blasts, and Hallelujah Shouts: Sermons in the African-American Preaching Tradition.* Lima, OH: CSS, 1997.

Thomas, Hugh. *The Slave Trade: The Story of the Atlantic Slave Trade 1440–1870.* New York: Simon & Schuster, 1997.

Thurman, Howard. *Deep River* and *The Negro Spiritual Speaks of Life and Death.* Richmond, IN: Friends United, 1979.

———. *For the Inward Journey: The Writings of Howard Thurman.* Richmond, IN: Friends United, 1984.

Walker, David. *David Walker's Appeal.* Introduction by Sean Wlientz. New York: Hill and Wang, 1995.

Walker, Wyatt. *Somebody's Calling My Name.* Valley Forge, PA: Judson, 1979.

Warner, Michael. *American Sermons: The Pilgrims to Martin Luther King Jr.* New York: Library of America, 1999.

Washington, Booker T. *Up from Slavery.* Edited by Louis Harlan. New York: Penguin, 1986.

Washington, James, ed. *Conversations with God: Two Centuries of Prayers by African Americans.* San Francisco: Harper Perennial, 1994.

Webb, William. *The History of William Webb.* Detroit, 1873.

Webber, Thomas. *Deep Like the River: Education in the Slave Quarter Community, 1831–1865.* New York: Norton, 1978.

Wesley, Charles. *Richard Allen: Apostle of Freedom.* Lawrenceville, NJ: African World, 2002.

West Central North Carolina Conference of the AMEZ Church. Minutes. 1914.

Wideman, John. *My Soul Has Grown Deep: Classics of Early African-American Literature.* Philadelphia: Running Press, 2001.

Wimberly, Edward. *African American Pastoral Care.* Nashville: Abingdon, 1991.

———. *Moving from Shame to Self-Worth: Preaching and Pastoral Care.* Nashville: Abingdon, 1999.

———. *Pastoral Care in the Black Church.* Nashville: Abingdon, 1979.

———. *Pastoral Counseling and Spiritual Values: A Black Point of View.* Nashville: Abingdon, 1982.

Wimbush, Vincent, ed. *African Americans and the Bible: Sacred Texts and Social Textures.* Reprint ed. New York: Continuum International, 2001.

Woodson, Carter. *The History of the Negro Church.* 3rd ed. Washington, DC: Associated Publishers, 1972.

———. *The Mis-Education of the Negro.* Trenton, NJ: Africa World Press, 1990.

Wright, Richard. *12 Million Black Voices*. New York: Viking, 1941.

Yetman, Norman. "Ex-Slave Interviews and the Historiography of Slavery." *American Quarterly* 36 (1984): 181–210.

———. "The Background of the Slave Narrative Collection." *American Quarterly* 19 (1967): 534–553.

———, ed. *Voices from Slavery: 100 Authentic Slave Narratives*. Mineola, NY: Dover, 2000.

Dr. Robert W. Kellemen is chairman of the Master of Arts in Christian Counseling and Discipleship (MACCD) Department at Capital Bible Seminary, in Lanham, Maryland. He lives in Crown Point, Indiana.

Karole A. Edwards is director of the "After 5" ministry, a women's small group ministry at the 10,000-member strong McLean Bible Church in McLean, Virginia. Ms. Edwards facilitates the spiritual leadership and management of the ministry, which disciples, shepherds, and cares for over 250 women in small group settings throughout the Washington, D.C., area. She lives in Germantown, Maryland.